PRAISE FOR AND

FODOR'S GAY GUIDE TO THE USA

"A witty, irreverent, and highly informational resource."
—NEWSDAY

"Fodor's, America's travel experts, has published the most comprehensive guide for gay and lesbian travelers—written for us, about us, and by one of us. Quite simply, if it's out there, it's in here."
—HARRY TAYLOR, PUBLISHER, OUT MAGAZINE

"Collins...quickly taps into the pulse of each destination."
—CHICAGO TRIBUNE

"Heavy with detail and description and well written."
—OUT & ABOUT

"Fodor's recognizes that gay travelers are not a homogenous bunch, so to speak...but take an interest in sights beyond gay ghettos." —SAN FRANCISCO CHRONICLE

"Collins is a graceful and knowing writer, his facts are correct, and he won't steer you wrong." —GENRE

"Excellently written...every gay traveler should have a copy."
—XY MAGAZINE

"Don't leave home without it."—BAY AREA REPORTER

LOOK FOR THESE OTHER TITLES IN THE
FODOR'S GAY GUIDE SERIES

Fodor's Gay Guide to Los Angeles and Southern California

Fodor's Gay Guide to New York City

Fodor's Gay Guide to the Pacific Northwest

Fodor's Gay Guide to San Francisco and the Bay Area

Fodor's Gay Guide to South Florida

Fodor's Gay Guide to the USA

Fodor's
GAY GUIDE TO AMSTERDAM

BY ANDREW COLLINS

FODOR'S TRAVEL PUBLICATIONS, INC.
NEW YORK • TORONTO • LONDON • SYDNEY • AUCKLAND
WWW.FODORS.COM/

Fodor's Gay Guide to Amsterdam

EDITOR: Matthew Lore

Editorial Contributors: Kaline J. Carter, James Sinclair
Fodor's Gay Guides Project Editor: Daniel Mangin
Maps: David Lindroth Inc., Eureka Cartography, *cartographers*; Robert P. Blake, *map editor*
Editorial Production: Linda K. Schmidt
Design: Fabrizio La Rocca, *creative director*; Tigist Getachew, *cover design*
Production/Manufacturing: Mike Costa
Cover Photograph: PhotoDisk

Copyright © 1998 by Andrew Collins

Maps Copyright © 1998 by Fodor's Travel Publications, Inc.

Fodor's is a registered trademark of Fodor's Travel Publications, Inc.

All rights reserved under International and Pan-American Copyright Conventions. Published in the United States by Fodor's Travel Publications, Inc., a subsidiary of Random House, Inc., New York, and simultaneously in Canada by Random House of Canada Limited, Toronto. Distributed by Random House, Inc., New York.

No maps, illustrations, or other portions of this book may be reproduced in any form without written permission from the publisher.

First Edition

ISBN 0-679-03379-3

Special Sales

Fodor's Travel Publications are available at special discounts for bulk purchases for sales promotions or premiums. Special editions, including personalized covers, excerpts of existing guides, and corporate imprints, can be created in large quantities for special needs. For more information, contact your local bookseller or write to Special Markets, 201 East 50th St., New York, NY 10022. Inquiries from Canada should be directed to your local Canadian bookseller or sent to Random House of Canada, Ltd., Marketing Dept., 1265 Aerowood Dr., Mississauga, Ontario L4W 1B9. Inquiries from the United Kingdom should be sent to Fodor's Travel Publications, 20 Vauxhall Bridge Road, London SW1V 2SA, England.

PRINTED IN THE UNITED STATES OF AMERICA

10 9 8 7 6 5 4 3 2 1

CONTENTS

Author's Note — vii

Eats Price Charts *viii*
Sleeps Price Charts *ix*

Dutch Gay Culture—An Overview — xii

1 *Out in* Amsterdam — 1

Eats *35*
Scenes *48*
Sleeps *68*

2 *Out in* the Netherlands — 81

Out in Haarlem and Zandvoort *83*
Out in Leiden *86*
Out in Den Haag *90*
Out in Rotterdam *96*
Out in Utrecht *101*
Out in Maastricht *105*

3 *Out in* Belgium — 112

Out in Antwerpen *115*
Out in Gent and Brugge *122*
Out in Brussel *129*

Dutch Vocabulary — 141

Index — 144

Maps

The Netherlands and Northern Belgium *xx–xxi*
Greater Amsterdam *xxii–xxiii*
Central Amsterdam *6–7*
Rembrandtplein, Leidseplein, and Frederiksplein *16–17*
The Jordaan *19*
Rembrandtplein, Leidseplein, and Frederiksplein *50–51*
The Randstad *82*
Leiden *87*
Den Haag *91*
Rotterdam *97*
Utrecht *102*
Maastricht *106*
Antwerpen *116*
Gent *124*
Brugge *126*
Brussel *130–131*

AUTHOR'S NOTE

BEING GAY OR LESBIAN influences our choice of accommodations, nightlife, dining, shopping, and perhaps even sightseeing. This book will enable you to plan your trip confidently and with authority. On the following pages I've tried to provide ideas for every segment of our community, giving you the skinny on everything from bars and clubs to gay beaches, from where to find the gayest Indonesian restaurant in Amsterdam to the best hand-dipped chocolates in Brussel. You'll also find a wide selection of accommodations, from exclusively gay guest houses to mainstream hotels.

About Me

I'm a gay male in my late twenties. I grew up in Connecticut, graduated from Wesleyan University, have lived briefly in London and Atlanta, and currently split my time between a small house in New Hampshire's Monadnock mountains and an apartment in New York City's East Village.

How I Researched this Book

I spent about five weeks in Amsterdam, making numerous side trips to neighboring Dutch and Belgian cities, during a particularly cold and damp autumn. Throughout my travels, I interviewed local gays and lesbians—newspaper editors, activists, innkeepers, barflies, and people on the street. I also grilled friends and associates back in the United States, asking them for their favorite spots in and around Amsterdam.

This is an opinionated book. I don't hesitate to say what I think—my intention is always to relate what I've observed and what I've heard locals say. For the most part I traveled without announcing myself—the majority of the businesses in this book had no idea I was writing about them when I visited. In the end *Fodor's Gay Guide to Amsterdam* is a service not to hotels and guest houses, nor to gay bars and restaurants, nor to anybody in the travel industry. It is a resource for you, the traveler.

Language and Voice

I've written this book in a casual, personal voice, using terms such as "faggy," "dyke," and "queer" the way my friends and I do in general conversation. I know that for some people these words are painful reminders of more repressive times—be assured that no offense is intended. Also, unless the context suggests otherwise, when I use the terms "gay" or "homosexual," I'm referring to gay men and lesbians. I specify gender only as needed for clarity.

When referring to cities and neighborhoods or giving street addresses, I've consistently used the Dutch (Flemish or French in the case of Belgium) names instead of the English ones. What we know as the Hague, for example, I call Den Haag throughout the book. This is not an attempt at pretentiousness (I'm actually not much of a linguist) but a way of familiarizing you with the names as you'll most often hear them and see them written during your travels. Most locals I encountered on my trip spoke English with me fluently, but they usually referred to geographic names and features using their native tongue. Also, since signs at train stations and airports, local timetables, and the like refer to places in this manner, I hope the use of Dutch names here eases your travel throughout the region.

Content

The Amsterdam chapter has several sections, each covering a different aspect of life in the city, from exploring to dining out. The chapters detailing excursions from Amsterdam to different Dutch and Belgian cities are structured similarly. Here's a quick rundown:

The Lay of the Land

If you're looking for a quick summation of each destination's geography, its neighborhoods and major attractions, and its shopping, you'll want to read this carefully.

Getting Around

This is a very brief synopsis of how to get to each destination, to and from the airport, and then how best to maneuver about the city.

Eats

The places I investigated were suggested by gay and lesbian locals, advertise in gay publications, or were reviewed positively in local newspapers and magazines. I stopped by almost every restaurant (and ate at as many as I could).

I've tried to include choices for every budget. Many recommendations are in or near gay-oriented neighborhoods. A few establishments get a nod less for the food than the overtly festive atmosphere. Conversely, some places are listed simply because they represent some of the destination's finest or most unusual dining. The omission of your personal favorite may be more because it was similar to a place I did include than because I think it's not up to snuff. Unless otherwise noted, any restaurant in this book is at least somewhat popular with the community.

The following charts explain the price categories for restaurants throughout this guide:

CHART A

CATEGORY	COST*
$$$$	over Fl. 36
$$$	Fl. 28–36
$$	Fl. 19–28
$	under Fl. 19

*cost of dinner entrée

Author's Note

CHART B CATEGORY	COST*
$$$$	over BF 620
$$$	BF 470–620
$$	BF 300–470
$	under BF 300

cost of dinner entrée

Scenes

I checked out just about every bar in Amsterdam, and dozens of them in cities throughout the Netherlands and Belgium. If a place opened after my visit, I telephoned an employee and also got a report from a knowledgeable local resource to ensure an accurate review.

The most popular spots are listed under the heading "Prime Suspects." I've also written short reviews about neighborhood bars, roving parties, music clubs, bathhouses, brothels, and hash bars—plus a few straight bars with queer-friendly reputations. In the Amsterdam chapter, I've located the most popular gay bars and nightlife venues with bullets on the maps.

Male-oriented places outnumber those that cater mostly to women by about 10 to 1. This is not a reflection of my preferences but of European gay-bar culture—it's overwhelmingly young and male, as it is in the U.S., as well. Still, don't assume that a bar described as 80% male or mostly young doesn't welcome lesbians or older guys. Descriptions of each bar's crowd and its "cruise factor" are based on my own observations and interviews and are provided simply to give you a profile of what's typical.

Sleeps

I've included any gay-specific establishments that I felt confident recommending. If an establishment is straight-owned and I had no knowledge of its gay-friendliness, I checked with the owners to verify their interest in being covered in a gay publication. My descriptions of the clientele, compiled without the owners' input, are there to give you a general sense of the place.

When I discuss larger hotels, particularly those in cities, don't assume that they are gay-friendly (or otherwise) unless the reviews specifically state so. Obviously the degree of tolerance you encounter at a large property with many employees will depend largely on who happens to assist you. I've favored mainstream properties that are in and near gay neighborhoods and those that have a strong reputation with the community.

The following charts explain the price categories used for lodging establishments throughout this guide:

CHART A CATEGORY	COST*
$$$$	over Fl. 330
$$$	Fl. 240–330
$$	Fl. 160–240
$	under Fl. 160

cost of double-occupancy room in high season

CHART B CATEGORY	COST*
$$$$	over BF 5,600
$$$	BF 4,000–5,600
$$	BF 2,800–4,000
$	under BF 2,800

cost of double-occupancy room in high season

The Little Black Book

This resource guide contains tips and information about climate, currency, language, opening and closing times, passports and visas, and telephones. If some establishments have closed by the time you read about them—bars and restaurants often have unpredictable life spans—try the contacts in this section to get the latest scoop. Local tourist boards can be helpful, and lesbigay bookstores and community centers are tremendous resources. I've included some gay-popular gyms, and the phone numbers of resources for persons who are HIV-positive or who have AIDS.

Disclaimer

This is where I'm to remind you that time brings changes, and that neither I nor the publisher can accept responsibility for errors. An incredible amount of time and effort has been spent ensuring the accuracy of this book's information, but businesses move and/or close and restaurants and bars change. Always call an establishment before you go to make sure that it will be open when you get there.

The mention of any business, attraction, or person in this book is in no way an indication of sexual orientation or attitudes about sexual orientation. Unless specifically stated, no business in this book is implied or assumed to be gay-owned or operated.

Send Letters

Whatever your reaction to this book—delight, excitement, unbridled rage—your feedback is greatly appreciated. I'd love to hear about your experiences, both good and bad, and about establishments you'd like me to include or exclude in future editions. Send your letters to me c/o Fodor's Travel Publications, 201 East 50th Street, New York, New York 10022, or e-mail me at gayfodors@aol.com.

In the meantime, I hope you'll have as much fun using this guide as I had writing it.

Andrew Collins

Andrew Collins
November 1997

Acknowledgments

I am grateful to Matthew Lore, associate editor at Fodor's, and Daniel Mangin, a senior editor at Fodor's who is project editor for

Author's Note

the Gay Guide series. Also many thanks to Tony Clark, a frequent visitor to the Netherlands, who read the manuscript at several stages and offered many helpful suggestions.

Many locals shared their insights and opinions with me. My trusty sidekick, Kaline J. Carter, helped me research portions of the guide. As always he contributed constant companionship—for this I will always be grateful.

On this side of the Atlantic, Conrad van Tiggelen, Annemijn de Lavieter, Brigitta Kroon-Fiorita, and Saskia Brandt of the Netherlands Board of Tourism in New York City provided invaluable assistance with arranging my trip, proofreading the manuscript, and making connections abroad. Janice Holden and Marcia Guignet, of Martinair (which has long had a great track record with the lesbian and gay community), provided me round-trip airfare to Amsterdam. And Cece Drummond at Rail Europe arranged for me to travel with a rail pass among Dutch and Belgian cities.

Peter Könighausen, who with the charming Avi Ben-Moshe, runs the Hotel Orfeo, rented me a great little apartment steps from the Leidseplein, met with me on several occasions to show me around Amsterdam and offered his considerable wisdom about the local scene. Transplanted Malaysian Alvin Toh took me bar-hopping, shared several fun moments, and told me where to find authentic Chinese food. Transplanted American Denise Martinez, who is behind the terrific queer section at the American Book Center in Amsterdam, provided valuable insights, as did her colleague Graham Huner. Transplanted Scot Pip Farquharson, creator of the wonderfully informative magazines *Trout* and *Queer Agenda,* gave me the latest dish on Amsterdam's ever-evolving lesbian and alternative scenes. Transplanted Australian Richard Keldoulis offered an amazing number of pointers on where to eat, party, and explore. Marc, whose warm smile greets patrons of the Camp Cafe, helped acquaint me with nightlife. Siep de Haan, at the Amsterdam Gay Business Guild, put me in touch with several excellent contacts and offered countless ideas for improving the manuscript. Harry Visser also provided several tips.

In Leiden, Colin van Gestel showed me around his home city and also Den Haag; thanks also to his friend Katherijne for tips on the dyke scene. Gino Van Dooren in Antwerpen offered advice on the bar scene. Others who offered suggestions and friendship include Anneke Reijnders at Boekhandel Vrolijk, Marga who volunteers at the Lesbian Archive, and Marco "Max" Hermers for his knowledge of the city's hotel scene.

DUTCH GAY CULTURE—
AN OVERVIEW

What Outsiders Notice First

The Dutch are an adamantly inclusive society; this mind-set dates back several centuries to a time when the Calvinist majority allowed the nation's many Roman Catholics to practice (albeit privately) in small chapels typically constructed within the walls of private homes. Although Nederlanders are fiercely proud of many regional and national traditions, their homeland has been the object of countless occupations, annexations, and exploitations throughout history. Regardless of your race, ethnicity, religion, or outlook, the Dutch will accept and welcome you, at least on the most basic level.

But the struggle of outsiders for meaningful inclusion, for a true sense of belonging, is a difficult one in the Netherlands. The Dutch themselves seem almost unaware of the subtle way in which they regard cultural outsiders differently from the way they do each other. But anybody who has ever migrated to the Netherlands is keenly aware that no matter how long you live here, whether you have a Dutch passport and vote in Dutch elections, it's difficult to assimilate fully into Dutch life. One man who moved here from Southeast Asia shares this insight: "When I arrived in Amsterdam, I was accepted almost instantly and welcomed warmly. The Dutch were friendly and outgoing, and never cast me out for coming from a different culture. I've lived here now for six years, and that initial level of tolerance has not changed. However, I am no more Dutch and no less an immigrant than I was the day I arrived. When you come to this country, you instantly attain a fundamental sense of belonging. What's interesting is that this level never really increases in time."

Dutch Tolerance of Gays and Lesbians

Since at least the end of the 19th century, Dutch homosexuals have lobbied for respect, acceptance, and fundamental rights. Gays and lesbians in the Netherlands may still be a step or two from absolute acceptance and equal treatment within mainstream society, but they've come about as close as gays and lesbians have in any country.

By the middle of the 1960s queer Nederlanders had truly *arrived* in their own country, thanks to high visibility, a cohesive agenda, the positive attention of the majority of the country's politicians, and their nation's intensely egalitarian values. Twenty years later, comprehensive laws in the Netherlands had been passed to ensure equal rights for gays and lesbians, and as the 20th century comes to a close, public opinion polls consistently reveal that only a tiny percentage of the country's residents view homosexuality in a negative light.

Gays in the Netherlands are considered a vital part of the national fabric. They are warmly welcomed by people in most social and political circles, and most gays are not discriminated against in the workplace or by landlords or the police. Furthermore, it's totally unacceptable to bad-mouth gays and lesbians in the Netherlands, whether in a public forum or in a conversation among two neighbors. But gays and lesbians do still admit to feeling some sense of exclusion: They may have formed an identity within their own subculture, but somehow fall just outside of the grand notion of what it means to be Dutch.

Attitudes About Sex

Probably one of the most surprising aspects of Dutch culture to outsiders is the open way in which sex is discussed and treated among teens, gay and straight. Once a young man or woman reaches a level of sexual maturity, he or she is typically assumed to be sexually active. The age of consent is 16 in the Netherlands. Gay pornography commonly features young men in their late teens, and male prostitutes are very often under 20. Furthermore, the vast majority of instructional sex guides intended for young people discuss homosexuality in a favorable— or at the least, tolerant light.

The Dutch would suggest that this forward and casual outlook toward sexuality among teenagers has helped encourage healthy attitudes about the topic. In fact, the war against the spread of AIDS and other sexually transmitted diseases has been more successful here, particularly among the younger population, than in societies where frank discussions of sexuality aren't as socially acceptable. Furthermore, because of the open manner in which homosexuality has long been discussed and accepted in the Netherlands, gays were not scapegoated and blamed for the AIDS crisis when it first unfolded in the early '80s. Rather, both political and health officials worked with the community to educate the public on slowing the spread of the disease.

Amsterdam is often perceived as being the most sex-driven city in Europe, if not the world. Visitors can get carried away with the availability of sex and drugs, and with the extremely permissive attitudes of Amsterdammers. In fact, most residents are far from obsessed with getting high or laid. The very fact that they encourage almost any pleasurable activity accounts in part for the reason they're so mellow about such activities. The novelty of these so-called vices is lost on locals, many of whom see frequenting a sex club as no bigger a deal than the residents of neighboring nations see heading to the local pub and enjoying a pint of beer.

The Dutch Gay Struggle Prior to the 20th Century

A glance at the modern history of the gay and lesbian movement in the Netherlands sheds at least some light on the current state of Dutch queer culture. But, as in most societies, there are few records or documents detailing the lives of homosexuals in the country prior to 1800. It is known that authorities throughout the 17th and 18th centuries, particularly in Amsterdam, actively sought to catch and punish "sodomites," a term that generally connoted men leading straight lives but fond of engaging in illicit encounters in public restrooms, alleyways, and other dark and discreet places. Rumors persist to this day that William of Orange slept with several of the men in his army, and other lesser-known figures of the past are routinely held up today as having likely been closeted homosexuals.

During the French occupation of the Netherlands at the beginning of the 19th century, sodomy was decriminalized under the Napoleonic Code. It's worth noting that although the abolition of these laws amounted to the legalization of same-sex relations, the spirit of these moves was in the name of the separation of church and state, not in the name of encouraging or even tolerating homosexual liaisons. At this point in history, while homosexual sex had clearly been acknowledged by the government, meaningful same-sex relationships of the sort we would now consider "gay" or "lesbian" had not.

This secular state of affairs no doubt subtly paved the way for the permissive and tolerant climate that characterizes the nation today. The decriminalization of sodomy in 1811 ultimately reduced the success of far-right, antigay religious movements in the Netherlands.

Pillarization: Agreeing to Disagree

A century after the establishment of the Napoleonic Code, the government's distinction between religious and political rule came to an abrupt end. In 1911 a coalition of Christian bodies, dominated by the Calvinist and Roman Catholic churches, took political control of the country and created a form of government in which individual religious or political factions would rule themselves under the aegis of the state. This system, whereby each of the country's four major sects (Calvinist, Roman Catholic, Socialist, and Liberal) formed its own government-subsidized schools, hospitals, welfare offices, and other social programs and institutions, came to be known metaphorically as pillarization. A collective of four strong and productive subcultures (i.e., pillars) ultimately created a unified and even stronger national foundation. The fact that the pillars disagreed with one another on most major issues was resolved by the autonomy accorded to each of them. Of course, the political majority still had the power to pass general legislation affecting the entire nation, and the conservative religious climate of the time resulted in the recriminalization of same-sex relations.

By the first decade of the 1900s, however, a nascent underground queer scene had formed in the Netherlands. And in reaction to the nation's newly gay-unfriendly political and legal climate, a small band of progressive thinkers formed the NWHK (Nederlandsch Wetenschappelijk Humanitair Komitee, which means Dutch Scientific Humanitarian Committee) to advance the rights of homosexuals. The goal of this group, which was strongly condemned by the Calvinists and Catholics and only grudgingly tolerated by the Socialists and the Liberals, was to educate the public from a gay point of view. In particular, the NWHK approached important political and judicial figures in hopes of swaying them to a point of sympathy for gays. Queer activism of this time consisted primarily of attempting to alter prevailing mainstream attitudes toward homosexuality, rather than attempting to organize gays and lesbians into a distinct subculture.

Between 1911 and World War II, the NWHK attained what may seem like only moderate success: Although the country's collective conscience remained staunchly opposed to and critical of gays, authorities spent far less time and energy in the Netherlands persecuting those having same-sex relations than their counterparts in most nations. If being openly gay was not tolerated or respected, living a discreet and underground queer existence was overlooked by the police and by government officials. The Nazi occupation of World War II spelled an end to above-ground gay activism, but, interestingly, the Germans had limited success in the Netherlands detaining gays and lesbians. The Dutch government did little to abet the Nazis in this regard, partly because the gay movement here was more underground than in Germany (where countless homosexuals were not only detained but sent to perish in concentration camps) and partly because the Dutch legal structure had not, despite the legislation of 1911, made a concerted effort to identify and persecute gays since the early 1800s. There was simply no mechanism in place to assist the Nazis.

Major Strides: The Postwar Gay Rights Movement

Just prior to the war, a group of gay activists had created a publication,

Levensrecht (*Right to Live*), which they immediately shut down upon the Nazi invasion in 1940. Following the war, these same activists resumed their mission and formed the C.O.C. (Cultuur-en Ontspannings Centrum), which in English means the Cultural and Recreational Center. The new organization took on the job of carrying forth the goals of the now defunct NWHK (which, like *Levensrecht,* had also folded when the war began)—particularly of educating the public. Just as importantly, the C.O.C. acted as a key hub of social interaction and networking among gays, and to a lesser but growing extent, lesbians. The first center opened in Amsterdam, and others opened over the next few decades in every major town in the country.

Despite ruthless attacks by the Catholic Church, the Dutch government not only allowed the C.O.C. to form but actually encouraged it—what better way to keep tabs on this potentially troublesome but apparently benign subculture? In this way, Dutch gays and lesbians formed their very own pillar—a largely autonomous social and political group. As movers and shakers within the C.O.C. met throughout the late 1940s and into the 1950s with heads of mainstream Dutch pillars, including the four major ones, homosexuality began gradually to earn acceptance—if not by the general public, at least by an influential core of educators and lawmakers.

For lesbians and gay men, the 1960s marked a new turn in the movement. Up until this time, the C.O.C.'s major goal had been assimilation within mainstream Dutch culture—for gay men and lesbians to earn the respect of society by living and behaving within the mores of mainstream culture. In the Netherlands, as in North America, Australia, and other parts of Europe, the strategy shifted sharply during the late '60s, a time of intense counterrevolutions and confrontational protests. Gays and lesbians abandoned assimilation in favor of creating a separate but equal subculture.

It took some time, but the movement's new direction paid off considerably during the early 1970s, the first decade during which Dutch society openly and unequivocally began to accept homosexuals on their own terms. According to public opinion polls, in 1968 about 75% of all Nederlanders disapproved of homosexuals, and about 60% associated gays and lesbians with dirtiness, deviance, and abnormality. In 1981, those numbers had dropped to about 20% and 10% respectively. The military (of which one year of service had been compulsory for young men until the law was abolished in 1995) began allowing openly gay men to serve during the early '70s, and in 1971 the legislature once again formally decriminalized gay sex, dropping the age of consent between homosexuals from 21 to 16, which was already the age of consent for heterosexual sex. The government finally granted the C.O.C. legal recognition in 1973, thus subsidizing a significant chunk of the center's budget.

The clearest signal that gays and lesbians in the Netherlands would never again be treated as second-class citizens came in 1983 when Parliament completely revised the Dutch Constitution. The document's opening words were rewritten to read: "All persons in the Netherlands shall be treated equally in equal circumstances. Discrimination on the grounds of religion, belief, political opinion, race, or sex, or on any grounds whatsoever shall not be permitted." If this preamble stopped short of mentioning sexual orientation by name, it unquestionably protected residents from discrimination on such grounds.

Lesbians in the Dutch Gay-Rights Movement

As in most cultures with a visible gay movement, lesbians remained initially rather distant from the general homophile organizations and causes of the pre-1960s Netherlands. During the early years of the C.O.C., lesbians were encouraged to join the movement. Few were in a position to do so, however, and those who did were typically relegated to back-seat positions. In 1961 female members of the C.O.C. began organizing an annual women's day and simultaneously established specific women's events at the various C.O.C.'s throughout the country.

In the late '60s, as Amsterdam developed into a center of intense protest and direct political action, feminism emerged as a major force. Lesbians increasingly found themselves in a challenging predicament, inspired by the drive and energy of both the queer and women's movements, but still accorded second-class status by many leaders of the mostly male gay-rights organizations and the mostly straight feminist ones. Over the next few years, many lesbians split partially or entirely from the general C.O.C.-led gay and lesbian movement. Forming their own agendas and social networks, they congregated in squats, cafés, and meeting places of their own. By 1970, still only about 15% of the C.O.C.'s membership was female.

Dutch lesbians today clearly have their own subculture—one that remains distinct from either the gay male or the women's scenes, and yet dykes also now enjoy considerable prominence within each movement. Gay men and women work closely together at the C.O.C., and the well-attended parties at the centers throughout the Netherlands are among the best-attended mixed-gender events you'll find anywhere. Still, there are quite a few lesbians, to use the Amsterdam scene as an example, who prefer socializing at Saarien, a women-only bar, than at Café Françoise or Vive-La-Vie, two dyke-oriented hangouts in which men are quite welcome. Lines between straight and lesbian feminists seem much softer in Amsterdam today, but now there seems to be a great gap between generations. Much of the so-called hard-core lesbian or women's movement is now carried out by a decidedly youthful and collegiate crowd, and there are lesbians in the community who complain that socializing and activism now fall sharply along generational lines rather than ideological ones.

Can Full Gay Marriage Rights Be Far Behind?

Although the 1983 revision of the constitution accorded gays and lesbians basic equal rights, marriage has remained a sticky topic in the Netherlands for some time. For years, organizations such as the C.O.C. expressed little desire to pass a comprehensive marriage law, so the pressure on the Dutch government to accord such rights has been minimal. More recently, however, the issue has become a highly visible—and controversial—one.

One remaining obstacle is swaying public opinion in favor of gay marriage rights. Probably the strangest thing about this country known for its highly progressive social policies is that the Dutch themselves are fairly reserved and traditional when it comes to issues of family and church. Compared with other Western nations, relatively few Dutch women work outside the home. Heroic qualities in a Nederlander are not bravado or daring but calm and foresight. And although everybody's groovy about the gay neighbors down the street, Dutch families are somewhat less comfortable upon learning that a son, daughter, brother, or sister is queer. It's hardly insignificant that the number-one reason the government is reluctant to grant homosexuals full marriage rights is that such a legislation would give gay and lesbian couples the right to adopt children.

Yet polls and studies have shown that already about 20,000 homosexual couples are bringing up children in the Netherlands. And some observers suggest that the government is actually more concerned that full gay marriage rights will upset the nation's European neighbors than they will Dutch citizens themselves. In April 1996, Parliament not only passed legislation to legalize gay marriages (by a vote of 81 to 60), they voted to grant adoption rights, too (by a slightly stronger margin of 83 to 58). But in the Netherlands, the Parliament may vote to pass a particular legislation, but such enactments are not enforceable or binding until approved by the Dutch cabinet, which is not obligated to concur.

The cabinet, whose wishes have been articulated by Justice Minister Elizabeth Schmitz, rejected the outcome of the parliamentary vote. Schmitz is convinced that neighboring European countries will censure the Netherlands for extending gay marriage rights. French politicians already delight in denouncing the Netherlands's progressive—they would say radical—stances on such social hot potatoes as soft drugs, prostitution, euthanasia, and abortion.

Although the Netherlands wouldn't be the first country to extend same-sex marriage rights, it could become the first to legalize adoption by gay couples. Denmark (since 1989), Norway (since 1993), and Sweden (since 1995) allow same-sex couples to register their partnerships with the government; this move immediately entitles the couples the same rights as heterosexual couples in the areas of property ownership, inheritance and divorce, taxes, social benefits, and pensions. The one exemption in each of the Scandinavian countries has been the exclusion of adoption rights. As it currently stands, homosexual couples in the Netherlands may register with their local city hall, but such a gesture is more symbolic than legal. Employers and insurance companies are under no obligation to recognize such unions.

Clearly flying in the face of the majority of her own government's lawmakers, Schmitz essentially shelved the issue in June 1996 by appointing a committee of so-called experts (i.e., political spin doctors) to assess the domestic and worldwide effects of legally granting queers both the rights to marry and to adopt. The committee should have reported back by the time you read this, but most Dutch citizens—no matter what their views on the topic—regard same-sex marriage and adoption rights as an inevitability.

As queers in other nations around the world continue to struggle for legal concessions and civil rights that homosexuals in the Netherlands were granted decades ago, gay culture here offers a glimpse into what may lie ahead in other countries. There are myriad concerns, ranging from the issue of same-sex marriage to fears that a new breed of conservative politicians will once again take aim at the status of gays and lesbians. Although membership of the C.O.C. is now split nearly half and half between women and men, the nation's gay movement appears increasingly divided along generational lines. What's more, a significant chunk of queer activists seems almost to rue the day homosexuals were absorbed into mainstream society, complaining not only of complacency within the community, but also of a loss of cultural characteristics that were once unique to gays and lesbians. Such concerns are often met incredulously by visitors from less tolerant parts of the world—men and women who would gladly trade their intense and aggressive movements at home for even a handful of the rights enjoyed in the Netherlands.

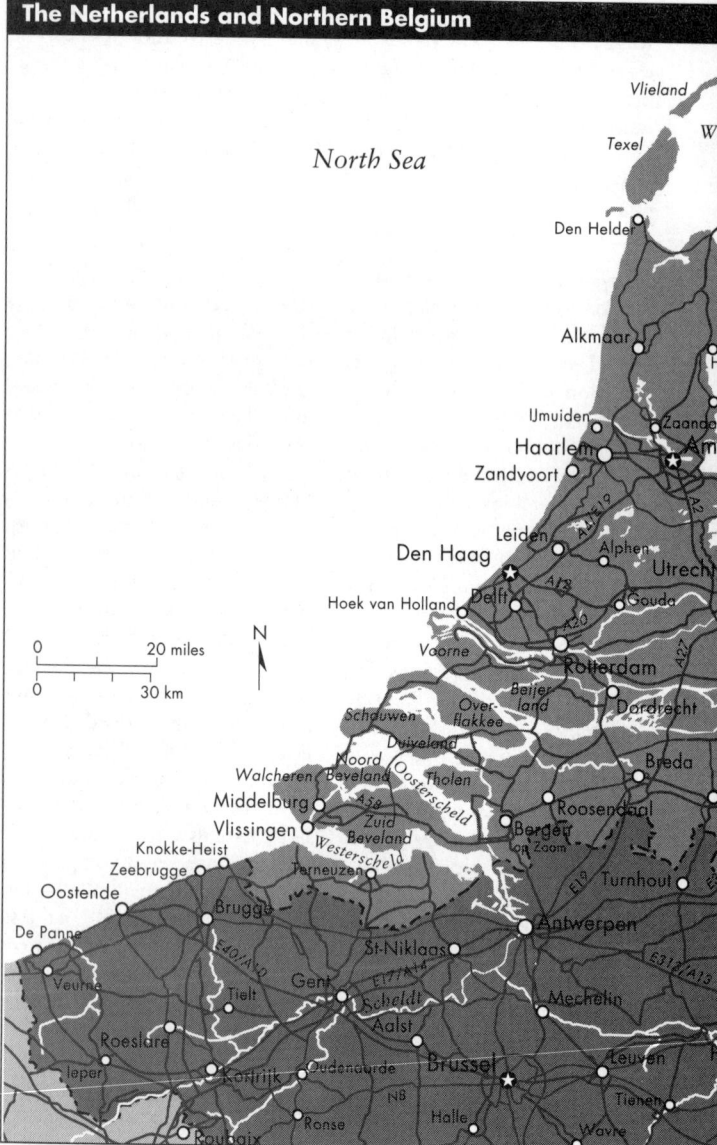

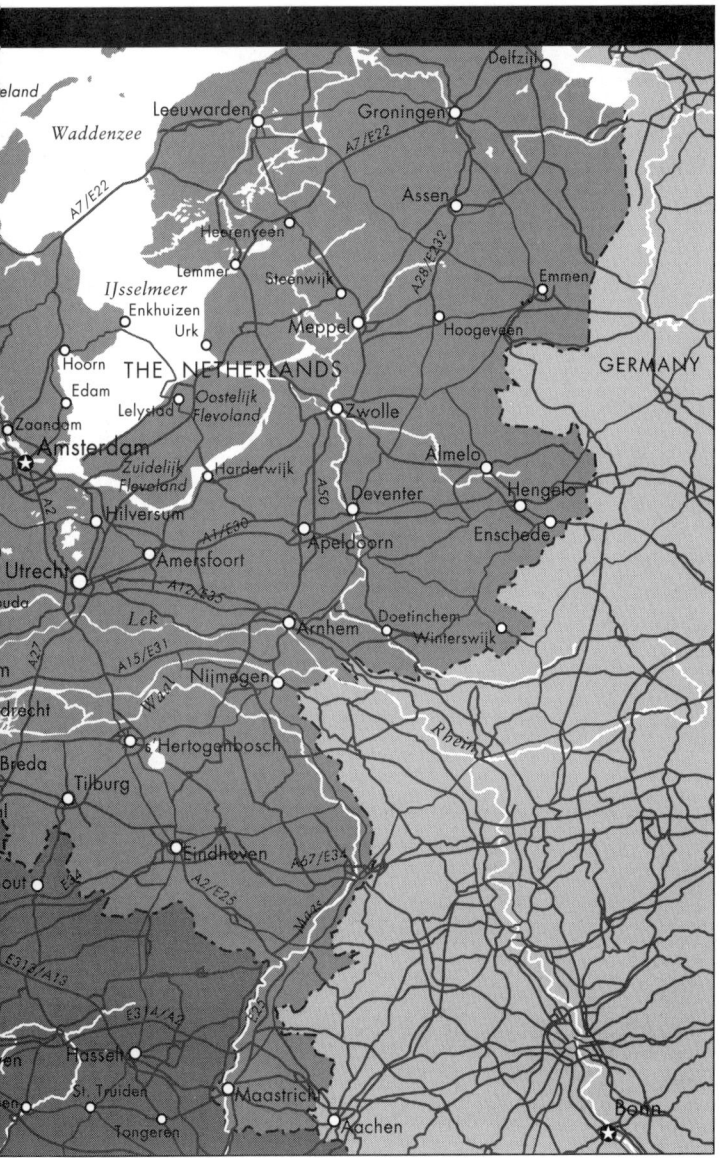

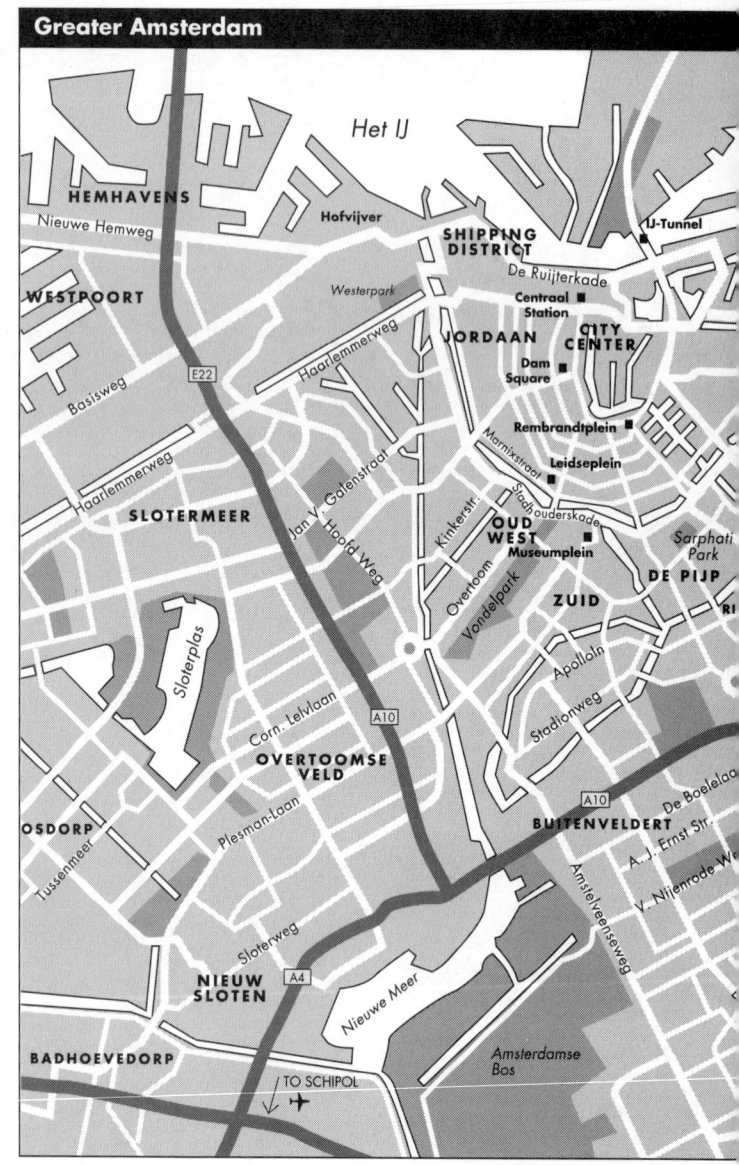

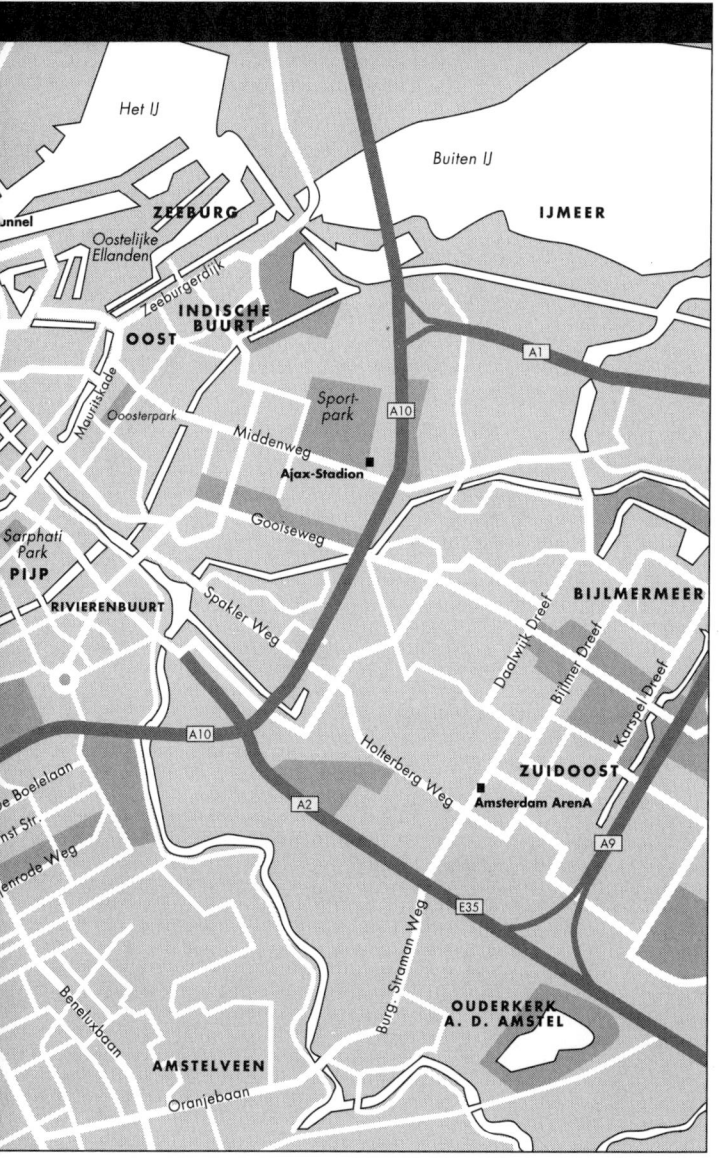

1 *Out in Amsterdam*

COUNTLESS QUEER VISITORS will first experience the Netherlands and its vivacious cultural capital, Amsterdam, when the fifth-ever Gay Games unfold here during the summer of 1998. Locals hope this justifiably mega-hyped event will affirm the city's status as one of the world's preeminent gay destinations. The Gay Games are a fabulous opportunity to show off the nation's considerable attributes, of which the Dutch are unabashedly proud. From their vast museum holdings and distinctive medieval architecture to their tremendously rich history and the vital role they have played for centuries in the world economy, the Dutch have plenty to brag about. But what's remarkable is how sincerely they wish to share their riches and successes with visitors. As one gay local explained his relationship to his lifelong home city, "In a lot of places locals get very possessive about their homelands; that kind of thinking is rare in the Netherlands. I love Amsterdam, but it's not *my* city—it's here for the world to enjoy."

This outlook manifests itself in both positive and problematic ways. Among the nation's most cherished values are justice, tolerance, and inclusion. And largely for this reason the legal, political, and civil rights of lesbians and gays have been attained here as quickly and as comprehensively as anywhere. The Dutch may not openly display their appreciation of outsiders (they're among the world's less expressive souls), but they never appear to grow even the least bit tired of the year-round rush of tourists trampling down their narrow cobbled lanes and crowding onto their trains, trams, and buses.

Unfortunately, the nation's open-door policy continues to tax its resources. The Netherlands is a nation not quite half the size of the state of Maine that's attempting to feed, house, and socially subsidize some 15 million residents. The country scoops up immigrants from former colonial interests (Indonesia, Surinam) and current human-rights debacles (Turkey, Northern Africa) at an astounding pace. It may appear to outsiders that the Dutch would sooner allow their infrastructure to crumble before curtailing their sense of hospitality. But this is a nation of survivors. They created a significant chunk of their country by cheating the forces of nature—literally by stealing acre after acre of arable soil from the sea through an ingenious centuries-old system of dikes, canals, and dams.

Regardless of the practical concerns that lie ahead of them, Nederlanders want you—gay or straight—to visit. The bulk of the nation's gay scene is concentrated in Amsterdam, where visitors from more close-minded countries almost immediately encounter a previously unheard of sense of comfort and freedom. First-timers are also struck by the city's playful, if at times reckless, disposition. Generally speaking, if a significant number of human beings enjoy a particular form of gratification, that act is tolerated and prevalent in Amsterdam (but to a much lesser extent elsewhere in the Netherlands).

Gay Amsterdam Today

Cultural sophistication, progressive attitudes, seemingly limitless potential for the pursuit of hedonism: If these aren't enough to guarantee Amsterdam's place on the shortlist of the world's most desirable destinations (queer and otherwise), there are plenty of others. Amsterdam's intimate scale, for one, makes it easy for visitors to quickly feel at home here: Whether highbrow (i.e., the Rijksmuseum) or puerile (i.e., the Sex Museum), just about every attraction is within a 20- to 30-minute walk of any other. The romance of strolling beside tree-shaded canals and in the shadows of ornately restored 16th-century canal houses is enough to revert any two kindred souls into a state of adolescent heart-thumping bliss. And, guilder for guilder, the cost of lodging, dining out, bar-crawling, and museum-hopping is comparable to or lower than equally popular European cities. Although the Gay Games are certain to be a watershed event in Amsterdam's lesbian and gay history, the city's place as an international queer mecca—alongside Sydney, San Francisco, New York, and London—is virtually assured for many decades to come.

Making the Most of Your Time

What follows are a few general suggestions and strategies that should help you, whether you're coming for the Gay Games or at any other time, to best utilize your time in Amsterdam. All of the attractions mentioned below are fully described elsewhere in this chapter, and all the side-trip destinations mentioned are detailed in the chapters on Dutch (*see* Chapter 2) and Belgian (*see* Chapter 3) excursions.

FEWER THAN 4 DAYS

If you're only going to visit Amsterdam for a few days, choose an accommodation in the City Center (i.e., inside the Singelgracht canal) to be as close as possible to the major attractions. The city's must-see sites include the Anne Frankhuis (during this visit you can catch a glimpse of the nearby Homomonument), the Rijksmuseum, Vondelpark, and the Museum het Rembrandthuis. Neighborhoods no gay visitor should miss are the Jordaan, the canals just west of the City Center, and the Leidseplein and Rembrandtplein entertainment districts. As for nightlife, if you're a single guy on the make you'll want to focus primarily on April, Exit, Havana, de Spijker, and the Cockring; and if you're seeking out the best women's spots, try Vive-la-Vie and Café Françoise. Any queer guy with a penchant for leather and sleaze should wander along Warmoesstraat. No matter what floats your particular boat, try to make it to at least one party at the C.O.C. (the gay and lesbian center) and de Trut (where parties are held only on Sunday nights).

With so little time, you should plan on, at the most, a brief side-trip. In summer, take the train to Zandvoort, Amsterdam's premier gay beach resort. Because they're compact and less than a half hour by train from Amsterdam's Centraal Station, Leiden and Haarlem are two other quick getaways.

FROM 4 TO 7 DAYS

With a few additional days, you'll have no trouble fitting in some of Amsterdam's less obvious but no less engaging sites. Take a full afternoon to explore Dam Square and its notable architecture. Near the Rijksmuseum, both the Vincent van Gogh and the Stedelijk (contemporary art) museums merit exploration. Try to visit one of the city's historic canal-house museums—the Willet-Holthuysen Museum is among the best. Consider a jaunt east of the City Center to see the zoo, the Hortus Botanicus (Botanical Garden), and the Jewish

Quarter. And even if the Red-Light District holds no immediate appeal to you, at least venture through to visit the Museum Amstelkring. With more time for a serious bar-crawl, hit the myriad holes-in-the-wall lining Amstel and the streets in and around Rembrandtplein.

Because a trip to Belgium requires at least an overnight stay, it's not terribly practical to head there if your visit to Amsterdam will be a week or less; however, larger Dutch cities such as Den Haag, Rotterdam, and Utrecht are ideal for day-long visits. Of the three, bustling and modern Rotterdam has the hottest nightlife, Utrecht the most romantic cafés and highest quaint-factor, and Den Haag the best shopping and the greatest appeal for fans of Dutch government and royalty.

MORE THAN A WEEK

With more than seven days in Amsterdam, you can catch your breath and immerse yourself in some of the city's less touristy neighborhoods, such as de Pijp (an artsy countercultural district but with, alas, limited aesthetic appeal) and Utrechtsestraat (an extremely gay-friendly stretch of hip cafés and shops). The kitschy museums in the Red-Light District, as well as some other attractions of limited appeal throughout the city may warrant a visit at this point (the Torture Museum is the best of the oddball attractions).

If you're here for this long, you're likely to have covered much of Amsterdam within the first week, so try to sample at least two or three of the Dutch cities mentioned above. Better yet, plan an overnight excursion to the enchanting medieval city of Maastricht, about two and a half hours away by train, nearly at the Belgium border. You should have enough time to spend upwards of two or three days touring Belgium's most desirable cities: Brussel, Antwerpen, Brugge, and Gent—perhaps combining this journey with a trip to Maastricht.

THE LAY OF THE LAND

Most visitors to Amsterdam explore only the relatively tiny **City Center,** enclosed by the Singelgracht—the outermost of the six canals that ring the city, and not to be confused with the Singel, the innermost of the concentric canals. Within Amsterdam's center are several small neighborhoods; each is easy to explore in a half day or so, depending on how much time you allow for each site. Most of the major attractions, hotels, restaurants, and other diversions are within the City Center. Gays and lesbians will learn quickly that although certain streets and squares contain community-oriented businesses, the entire City Center is gay-friendly.

Centraal Station and Dam Square

Many visitors to Amsterdam arrive by way of the grand neo-Renaissance **Centraal Station,** which was designed by P. J. Cuypers (1827–1921) and opened in the 1880s. The grandiose building flies directly in the face of the Netherlands's spare and utilitarian Calvinist tradition, and looks more than a little like Cuypers's most famous creation, the Rijksmuseum (*see below*). The station opens onto a busy, if at times chaotic, public square—**Stationsplein**—which is filled with trams waiting to whisk passengers around the city. You can while away a few minutes enjoying the exploits of the street performers.

From Centraal Station it's a 10-minute walk down dreary **Damrak** to reach the medieval heart of the metropolis, Dam Square. The Damrak was originally the village harbor but, except for a small stretch nearest the station, was filled in during the 19th century. Along this street you'll pass by unmemorable tourist hotels, some porn parlors and forgettable restaurants, and a few lame attractions, including the **Sex Museum** (⊠ Damrak 18, ☏ 020/622–8376), which, despite its titillating name, impersonates an ordinary porn shop where the goods aren't for sale. The museum was spruced up recently and now has a few mildly entertaining exhibits of vintage erotica, but there's little here of specific interest to lesbians and gays. On the other hand, even non-S/M types may get a rise out of the **Torture Museum** (⊠ Damrak 20–22, ☏ 020/639–2027) next door, which is filled with both familiar and esoteric implements of terror.

A more impressive site along Damrak is the **Beurs van Berlage** (⊠ Buersplein 1, off Damrak, ☏ 020/530–4141), the former Amsterdam stock exchange built at the turn of the century by one of Holland's most celebrated architects, Hendrik Petrus Berlage (1856–1934). The enormous building's flat redbrick walls and restrained ornamentation earned Berlage the sobriquet the "Father of Modern Dutch Architecture." Tours (☏ 020/620–8112) of the interior are available, and as in many of Amsterdam's historic structures, special exhibits are staged here regularly.

Eats ●

Caprese Ristorante Italiano, **8**
Christophe, **2**
De Keuken van 1870, **10**
D'Vijff Vlieghien, **9**
Getto, **14**
Hemelse Modder, **15**
Kam Yin, **11**
Koh-I-Noor, **3**
La Strada, **7**
Lana Thai, **12**
New York Pizza, **13**
Pancake Bakery, **1**
Sisters, **16**
't Sluisje, **6**
Tout Court, **5**
Zomers, **4**

Scenes ○

Argos, **9**
Casa Maria, **5**
Club Jaecques, **7**
Cockring, **10**
Cuckoo's Nest, **3**
Dirty Dicks, **6**
Doll's Place, **1**
Eagle Amsterdam, **8**
Het Wonder, **11**
Stablemaster, **4**
The Web, **2**

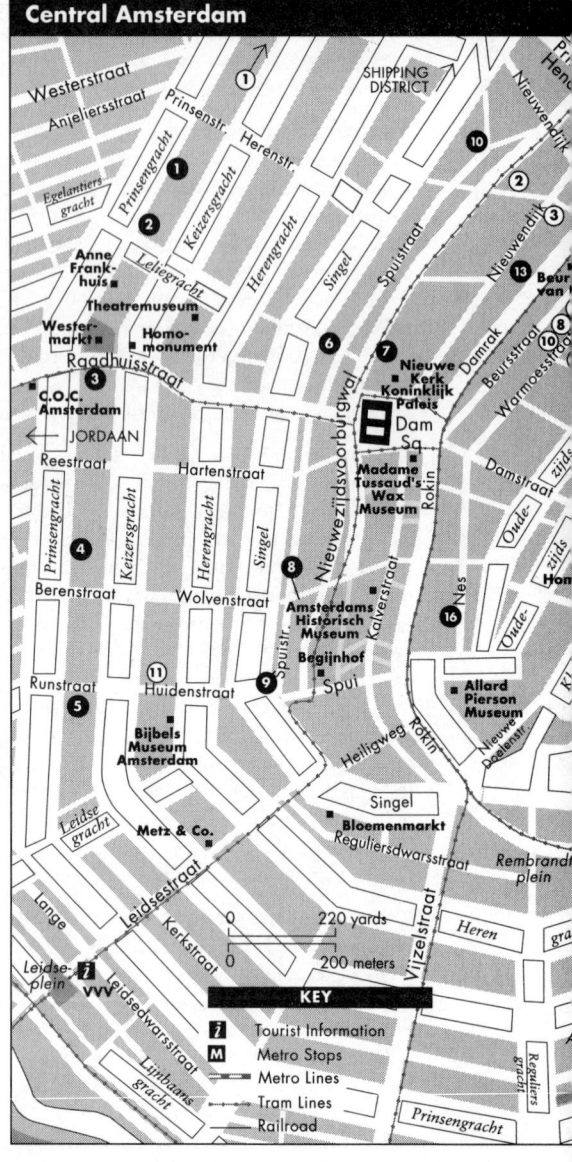

Central Amsterdam

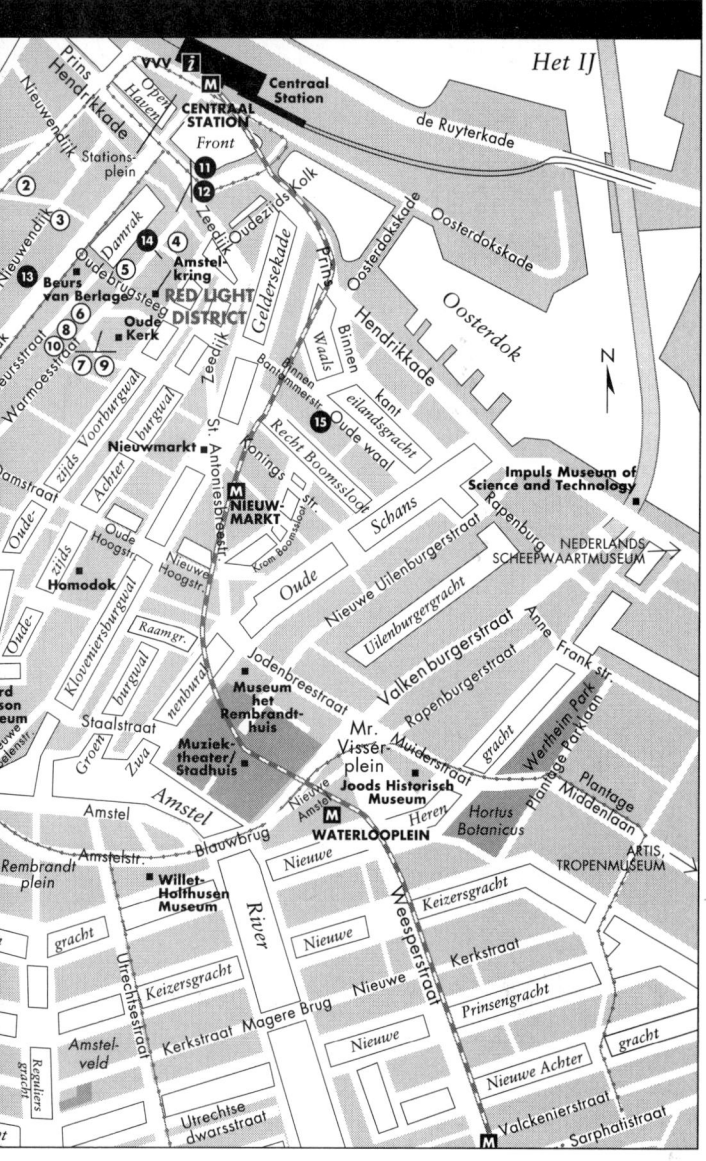

Dam Square has been the center of activity since the 12th century, when the city's earliest inhabitants built a dam here along the Amstel River. For many centuries ships sailed right up the now-filled-in Damrak to the square's weigh house (which was demolished in 1808 by King Louis Napoleon, who complained that it spoiled the view from his bedroom window in the palace across the way). There's nothing particularly quaint about this cobbled square—it's trampled upon all day long by aggressive pigeons, as well as the hordes of fascinated tourists who keep the birds content with bags of bread crumbs. Anchoring the scene is a 1956 monument commemorating the nation's liberation from Nazi occupation following World War II.

Much of Amsterdam's high-end shopping is within steps of Dam Square, including the local department stores, **De Bijenkorf** (✉ Dam 1, ☎ 020/621–8080) and **Peek & Cloppenburg** (✉ Dam 20, ☎ 020/622–8837). Running north from the square back toward Centraal Station (just west of Damrak), pedestrian-only **Nieuwedijk** pulses mostly with discount clothiers, music shops, and fast-food eateries. South of the square, **Kalverstraat** is a slightly more upscale pedestrian lane; the **Marks & Spencer** (✉ Kalverstraat 66–72, ☎ 020/620–0006) department store is particularly popular. Also running south of Dam Square, **Rokin** is lined with high-end fashion and antiques boutiques.

In addition to the hundreds of shops in this section of the city, you'll find some notable examples of historic architecture, including the opulent **Koninklijk Paleis** (Royal Palace; ☎ 020/624–8698), which was built as the city's town hall in 1648, during the height of the Netherlands's Gilded Age. In 1808, Louis Napoleon assumed the nation's throne and decided the city hall was one of the few buildings in Amsterdam fit for a king; he converted the structure into his royal digs. While contemplating its immensity, consider that its foundation rests atop nearly 14,000 wooden pilings sunk deep into the former riverbed of the now-diverted Amstel. Look just north of the palace, across the street, to see the spectacular late-Gothic **Nieuwe Kerk** (New Church; ☎ 020/626–8168), parts of which date from the 14th century. Special exhibitions are frequently held inside the church, in which you can also see two beautiful organs dating from the 16th and 17th centuries.

On the south side of Dam Square, between Kalverstraat and Rokin, fans of wax statuary—of which there seem to be an alarming number in Amsterdam—crowd the Dutch outpost of the famed **Madame Tussaud's wax museum** (✉ P&C Building, Dam 20, ☏ 020/622–9949).

Follow Kalverstraat south of Dam Square to reach two highlights of the City Center. The **Amsterdams Historisch Museum** (Amsterdam Historical Museum; ✉ Kalverstraat 92, ☏ 020/523–1822), set inside the old city orphanage, is regarded as much for its artifacts and exhibits tracing the city's history over the past several centuries, as for its impressive collections of art, including works by Rembrandt and several enormous portraits, dating from the 16th to 18th centuries, of the Amsterdam Civic Guards. The museum's southern face opens onto a serene courtyard, the **Begijnhof** (Beguine Court; ✉ Begijnhof 29, ☏ 020/623–3565), the 14th-century conventlike hall in which unmarried lay women once resided. The square onto which the court opens is also home to the city's oldest extant house (No. 34), which dates from the late 15th century, as well as the tiny 15th-century **Engelse Kerk** (English Church); the square is a delightful place to take five from the bustling shopping lanes surrounding it. From here you're at the edge of another small square, **Spui,** which has a few trendy cafés and shops appealing largely to students and staff of the University of Amsterdam, many of whose buildings are close by. These include the university's **Allard Pierson Museum** (✉ Oude Turfmarkt 127, ☏ 020/525–2556), which contains objects from ancient Egypt, the Near East, Cyprus, and the Greek and Roman empires. Just east of Spui, back on Kalverstraat, are the city's two best sources for English-language books, **Waterstone's** and the **American Book Center** (*see* Bookstores *in* The Little Black Book, *below*).

The Red-Light District and Nieuwmarkt

Amsterdam's raucous Red-Light District, as well as the gay leather-bar strip, couldn't be more centrally located. **Warmoesstraat** (a.k.a. "rue de Vaseline") runs from the northeastern corner of Dam Square and is lined with leather bars (*see* Scenes, *below*), sex shops, and low-budget hotels. Lately a few hip shops and eateries have opened along here, giving this otherwise gritty thoroughfare a slight sheen. Although Warmoesstraat is one of Amsterdam's oldest streets, the city's oldest profession is based a block farther east.

The much-hyped **Red-Light District** is not only seedy but also rather dull. Most of the brothels line **Oudezijds Voorburgwal** and the narrow lanes off of it. Tourists love to stand around and ogle the women posed depressingly in their red-lighted windows; if this interests you, go for it, but don't snap a picture or you'll most likely have your film and possibly your camera destroyed. Prostitutes do not appreciate being photographed or being treated like they're attractions at a carnival. Prostitution, after all, is a multimillion-guilder industry, and sex employees maintain their own trade union, pay taxes, and receive regular medical counseling. You won't see much of it in this neighborhood, but there is plenty of gay prostitution in Amsterdam (*see* Scenes, *below*); most of the rent-boy parlors are just northwest of Dam Square, along Spuistraat and Nieuwezijds Voorburgwal.

On the eastern edge of the Red-Light District, along one of the city's narrowest canals, you'll find **Homodok** (⊠ Oudezijds Achterburgwal 185, ☎ 020/525–2601, e-mail homodok@sara.nl), which is one of the most comprehensive lesbian and gay historical archives in the world. Interestingly, the building once housed a police station in which countless queers were processed after being arrested during raids of gay bars during less-friendly times. Inside is an exhaustive collection of books, periodicals, brochures, papers, and other materials documenting the history of queer culture, both local and international. Homodok was opened in 1978 after lesbian and gay students and faculty at many Dutch universities succeeded in rallying for the introduction of research and educational programs to the nation's university curricula. Another result of this movement was the formation of the recently defunct Dutch gay-and-lesbian-studies journal, *Homologie*. The Homodok is a research library; visitors should write at least a month ahead to request use of the facility. At press time (winter 1997), because of financial difficulties, Homodok's future is uncertain.

Three of the city's quirkiest museums sit on the same canal as Homodok. The cheesiest is probably the **Erotic Museum** (⊠ Oudezijds Achterburgwal 54, ☎ 020/624–7303), which is bigger than the sex museum over on Damrak and even straighter in its focus; there's virtually no mention of the love that dare not speak its name. Moderately more interesting is the **Hash Marijuana Hemp Museum** (⌧ Oudezijds Achterburgwal 148, ☏ 020/623–5961). The museum is as much a place to learn about the drugs (as well as hemp, which has considerable environmental and medical virtues) as it is a center of advocacy for them. A fairly recent addition to this irreverent museum row, the **Tattoo Museum** (⌧ Oudezijds Achterburgwal 130, ☏ 020/625–1565), is run by Henk Sciffmacher, the owner of Hanky Panky, a famous tattoo parlor, and contains some interesting, and artistic, exhibits.

Even if you lack the desire to saunter past a bunch of brothels, do consider a jaunt through the Red-Light District to see **Amstelkring** (⌧ Oudezijds Voorburgwal 40, ☏ 020/624–6604). The roots of Amsterdam's permissive, turn-a-blind-eye attitude extend back long before issues of homosexuality, prostitution, and drug use began making international headlines. In the 16th and 17th centuries, the city's many Catholics were not permitted to worship openly. In essence, the city's powers-that-be agreed not to interfere with or punish the Catholics if they agreed to practice their religion discreetly. To this end, many clandestine chapels were created inside private homes. One of the most elaborate and ingenious such places of worship, the Amstelkring (a.k.a. "Our Lord in the Attic"), was built inside the attic of a wealthy merchant's home in the 1660s. Today the chapel is a beautifully preserved museum.

Rising high above the neighborhood's seediness—in more ways than one—is the ancient **Oude Kerk** (Old Church; ⌧ Oudekerkplein 23, ☏ 020/625–8284), Amsterdam's oldest church, parts of which date from the 1320s, though it was largely built between the 1330s and 1570. It's received plenty of facelifts since then, including a major restoration between 1955 and 1979. Not surprisingly, its architecture represents an amalgam of Gothic and Renaissance styles. Rembrandt's wife Saskia died in 1642 and was buried here.

The eastern edge of the neighborhood is anchored by **Nieuwmarkt,** a somewhat seedy square around which you'll find many excellent ethnic restaurants. The 15th-century **De Waag** (Weigh House) stands in the middle of Nieuwmarkt. This area has a morbid history to suit its currently unattractive appearance; at one time it was Amsterdam's public execution square, and during the Nazi occupation it was where Jews were gathered for deportation. Extending northwest from the square, **Zeedijk** was until recently Amsterdam's combat zone, plagued by drug trafficking and petty and serious crime. During the city's early years as one of Europe's busiest ports, licentious visiting sailors turned the neighborhood into a den of sin, and it hadn't changed much until authorities began aggressively working to drive away the drug scene and encourage entrepreneurs to take over the many historic buildings. Some galleries have begun to open here, but it's still a rather ratty place for a stroll. Before World War II flushed out the city's gay scene, several queer bars and cafés operated along Zeedijk. One of them, Cafe Maandje, was one of Europe's roughest dyke bars before closing a few years ago.

The Canals West and South of Dam Square

The western edge of the City Center, between the Singel and Prinsengracht canals, was constructed mostly during Amsterdam's Gilded Age, during the first half of the 17th century. The grand canal houses along here are beautifully preserved, and you can easily spend half a day exploring and admiring the architecture. Just north of the neighborhood is a more pedestrian section of the city, the **Shipping District**, the main drag of which, **Haarlemmerstraat,** is lined with an increasingly bohemian mix of hash shops, vintage clothiers, and shops with various bric-a-brac and discount items. It's by no means a gay neighborhood, but it does have considerable appeal among younger funky types and latter-day hippies.

Just south of the Shipping District, beginning at the picturesque Brouwersgracht Canal, are the city's three most prestigious canals, in order of age and prominence: **Herengracht** (Gentleman's Canal), **Keizersgracht** (Emperor's Canal), and **Prinsengracht** (Prince's Canal). It's a reflection of the high regard with which the Netherlands views both humility and civility that it's a greater honor to reside on the Gentleman's Canal than on either of the two with grander names. Amsterdam flourished during the 16th century, as it had been only a village (albeit a productive shipping village) up to that point. By 1600 the city's population had grown to 50,000, and for the next century Amsterdam grew into an economic superpower. During this period of extraordinary prosperity, referred to as the "Gilded Age," these concentric canals were constructed, along with the grand homes of the city's wealthiest merchants.

The Lay of the Land 13

For a sense of contrast, before you wander among these courtly residences, take a quick walk along **Singel** (the city's western boundary prior to the 17th century) and take note of the **smallest house** (No. 7) in all of Amsterdam; don't knock on the door, however: It's a private residence, as are most of the houses along these canals. The public can tour a handful of them; a favorite is the stunning **Willet-Holthuysen Museum** (✉ Herengracht 605, ☎ 020/523–1822), a 17th-century canal house furnished with precious 18th- and 19th-century antiques.

Also along Herengracht, the **Bijbels Museum Amsterdam** (Amsterdam Biblical Museum; ✉ Herengracht 366, ☎ 020/624–2436) is filled with ancient documents and artifacts, including religious finds from Jewish and Christian tradition. It's set inside two adjoining 1662 canal houses. The elegant **Theatremuseum** (✉ Herengracht 166–174, ☎ 020/623–5104), which recently underwent a complete restoration, holds a vast collection of costumes, posters, photos, and other memorabilia relating to Dutch theater.

Raadhuisstraat slices through this neighborhood, from Dam Square until it becomes Rozengracht once it crosses the Prinsengracht Canal. This is a picturesque but curious part of Amsterdam, with a mix of divey squats, funky restaurants, and budget hotels, the latter located inside the Art Nouveau **Utrecht Building** (between Herengracht and Keizersgracht).

Where the street crosses the Keizersgracht Canal, right beside the 17th-century **Westerkerk** (West Church), you'll see one of the world's only tributes to the gay rights movement, the **Homomonument.** Sitting directly on the canal, the pink granite–stepped monument was designed by Karin Daan in 1987. On it an inscription reads: "Commemorates all women and men ever oppressed and persecuted because of their homosexuality. Supports the international lesbian and gay movement in their struggle against contempt, discrimination, and oppression. Demonstrates that we are not alone. Calls for permanent vigilance. Past, present, and future are represented by the three triangles on this square." Even on the coldest winter day the steps are decked with flowers, typically to commemorate the passing of fallen friends and loved ones. It's also one of the few visible acknowledgments that gay men and lesbians were persecuted, and in many cases executed, by the Nazis during World War II. Major commemorative events are held here April 30 (Queen's Day), May 5 (to remember those victimized during World War II), and September 5 (the day on which the monument was unveiled in 1987). At press time (winter 1997), plans are under way to establish a gay information booth. Homomonument is right by Westermarkt, where at No. 6 philosopher René Descartes once lived.

Appropriately, the Homomonument is just steps from the **Anne Frankhuis** (✉ Prinsengracht 263, ☎ 020/556–7100), one of the city's must-see attractions. Few experiences are more moving than walking through the makeshift home in which Frank and her family and four friends lived for two years during the war. The Nazis confiscated the original furnishings after discovering the family and sending them to their deaths. When Anne's father Otto (the only one of the group to survive the concentration camps) was asked if the museum should re-create the rooms as they had existed while they were lived in, he requested instead that they be left bare to better illustrate the inhumanity of the ordeal. The museum is currently expanding, and in 1998 a huge addition will include a replica of the house, complete with the re-created furnishings.

As you walk south from Raadhuisstraat along any of the canals, you'll enter the **Gouden Bocht** (Golden Bend), the city's most costly stretch of real estate. This begins around Leidsestraat and continues to Nieuwe Spiegelstraat, leading into an antiques district, the **Spiegel Quarter.** All the canals in the area have plenty of fancy shops along them, but the area's main thoroughfare, **Nieuwe Spiegelstraat** and its continuation, **Spiegelgracht,** have the densest concentration of antiques stores, extending five blocks from the Gouden Bocht of the Herengracht nearly to the Rijksmuseum. Several dealers operate under one roof in the **Amsterdam Antiques Gallery** (✉ Nieuwe Spiegelstraat 34, ☎ 020/550–2200). The Spiegel Quarter also has its share of contemporary and classic art galleries, particularly along the 500s stretch of **Keizersgracht.**

Leidseplein and Rembrandtplein

Because of its historical significance and central location, Dam Square is most often cited as the true hub of the city. You must head a bit south, however, to find Amsterdam's most action-packed squares. **Leidseplein** is on the southern edge of the City Center by the Singelgracht. **Rembrandtplein** is

The Lay of the Land

southeast of Dam Square, just beyond the Amstel River. Each square possesses certain elements of London's Piccadilly Circus and New York City's Times Square: pulsing neon signs, theaters and music clubs, mega shops, theme restaurants, and a parade of curious characters. The Leidseplein was something of a gay entertainment hub in the 1950s and early '60s; eventually, most of the bars as well as the lesbian and gay community center moved on to other parts of the city. Rembrandtplein, however, has maintained a strong base of gay-popular businesses. Many gay bars are just off the square, along the south bank of the Amstel River. Today's most popular gay entertainment districts, **Kerkstraat** and **Reguliersdwarsstraat,** are between the Leidseplein and the Rembrandtplein. This entire area is the hub of mainstream tourism, arts, dining and nightlife, and also the gay hub.

Lange Leidsedwarsstraat and **Korte Leidsedwarsstraat,** the streets just south of the Leidseplein, have the highest concentration of restaurants anywhere in the city. If you need to find foreign newspapers, exchange money, buy a phone card or tram tickets, or learn about local attractions, the Leidseplein is your place. There's a tourism office and bureau de change just off the square (*see* The Little Black Book, *below*), and nearby numerous shops sell sundries and newspapers. Avoid the wares hawked at most of the souvenir shops, which are mostly ordinary and overpriced. Many of the city's first-run movie theaters are around the square. Finally, if you need to place a phone call and it's cold or rainy outside, try the pay phone in the lobby of the American hotel (*see* Sleeps, *below*), which is at the north end of the square; it's very handy in a pinch (as are the public restrooms). The Leidseplein is also a great spot for people-watching; it's even a bit cruisy when the weather's nice.

Pedestrian-and-tram-only **Leidsestraat** extends north from the Leidseplein and was once lined with some of the fanciest boutiques and department stores in the city. By the 1970s, many of these places had moved on, but its cachet seems to be returning. Visiting Americans may wish to drop by **Eichholtz Delicatessen** (✉ Leidsestraat 48, ☏ 020/622–0305), which carries many imported goods you won't find elsewhere in the city. It's great when that yearning for marshmallows, Kraft salad dressing, or Kellogg's Pop Tarts kicks in.

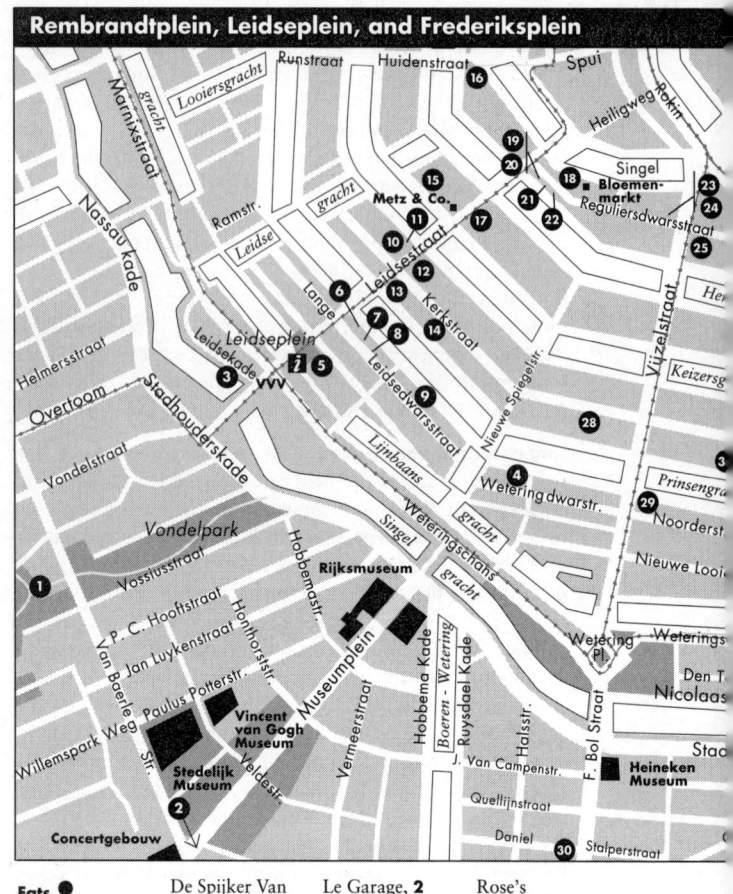

Rembrandtplein, Leidseplein, and Frederiksplein

Eats

Aphrodite, **9**
Backstage, **34**
Bojo, **8**
Café Françoise, **28**
Cafe Morlang, **15**
Camp Cafe, **12**
Casa di David, **16**
Coffee Co., **11**
De Kroon, **27**
De Spijker Van Der Mei, **30**
De Ysbreker, **36**
Downtown, **18**
Dynasty, **20**
Gary's Muffins, **6, 23**
Het Tuynhuis, **19**
Huyschkaemer, **35**
Izmir, **14**
Kort, **32**
Kriterion, **37**
Le Garage, **2**
Le Monde, **26**
Le Pêcheur, **21**
Le Zinc, **31**
Malvesijn, **4**
New York Pizza, **17**
Panini, **29**
Pizzeria Calzone, **24**
Portugália, **10**
Rama Thai, **7**
Rose's Cantina, **22**
Shiva, **25**
Sluizer, **33**
Smoeshaan Cafe and Theatre, **3**
't Balkje, **13**
't Schwarte Schaep, **5**
Vertigo, **1**

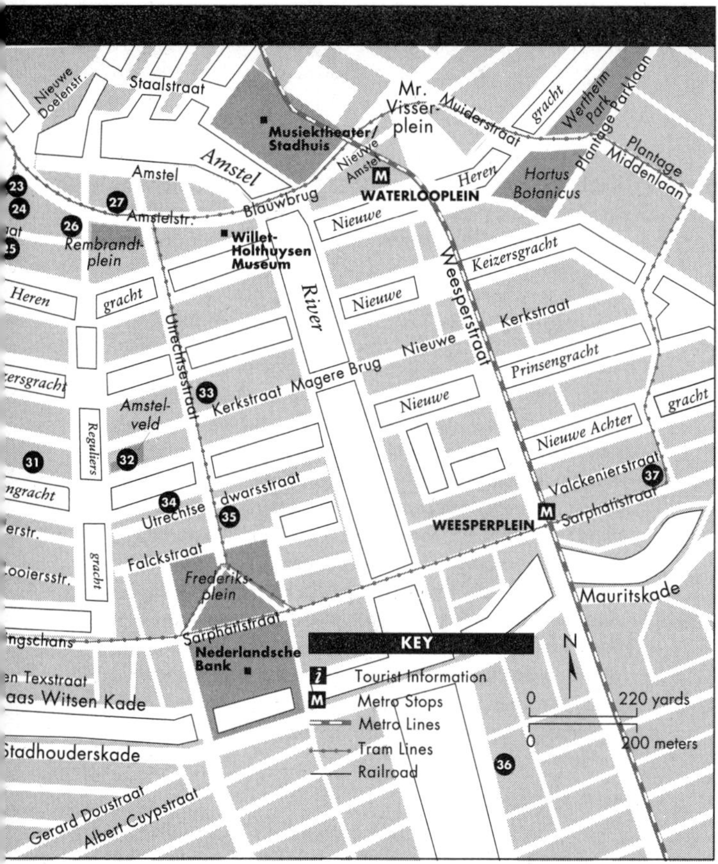
Nieuwe Doelenstr.
Staalstraat
Musiektheater/ Stadhuis
Mr. Visser-plein
Muiderstraat
gracht
Wertheim Park
Plantage Parklaan
Plantage Middenlaan
Amstel
Amstel
Nieuwe Amstel
WATERLOOPLEIN
Heren
Hortus Botanicus
Amstelstr.
Blauwbrug
Nieuwe
Rembrandt-plein
Willet-Holthuysen Museum
Keizersgracht
Weesperstraat
Heren
gracht
River
Nieuwe
Kerkstraat
Utrechtsestraat
Nieuwe
Prinsengracht
Magere Brug
Kerkstraat
Amstel-veld
Nieuwe
gracht
Reguliers
Nieuwe Achter
Valckenierstraat
dwarsstraat
Utrechtse
WEESPERPLEIN
Sarphatistraat
Falckstraat
gracht
Frederiks-plein
Mauritskade
Sarphatistraat
Nederlandsche Bank
KEY
Tourist Information
Metro Stops
Metro Lines
Tram Lines
Railroad
N
0
220 yards
0
200 meters
Stadhouderskade
Gerard Doustraat
Albert Cuypstraat
23
24
25
26
27
31
32
33
34
35
36
37

Leidsestraat crosses **Kerkstraat** at the latter's queerest stretch, chock-full of gay hotels, some bars and restaurants, and a few shops, such as **ZX** (✉ Kerkstraat 113, ☎ 020/620–8567), a purveyor of trendy club gear. A bit farther up Leidsestraat, at the intersection with Keizersgracht, the fancy department store **Metz & Co.** (✉ Keizersgracht 455, ☎ 020/624–8810) has been serving the city since 1740. For terrific views of central Amsterdam, take the elevator to the top (sixth) floor, where tall windows surround the informal café and tearoom, which, with its tasty food, makes a good spot for a break.

Farther north, just before reaching the Singel, Leidsestraat crosses **Reguliersdwarsstraat,** the heart of the city's trendy and youthful gay scene, as well as a row of sophisticated first-rate restaurants. Fashion plates should check out **Stringslip** (✉ Reguliersdwarsstraat 59, ☎ 020/638–1143), a gay-popular shop with scanty clothing, mostly for guys. Reguliersdwarsstraat is a block from the city's famously fragrant **Bloemenmarkt** (Flower Market), which extends along the Singel from Koningsplein to Muntplein. The market is open daily. Reguliersdwarsstraat leads east to the Rembrandtplein, where the rate of excessively commercial development has skyrocketed recently. A massive electric Planet Hollywood sign now looms shamelessly above the square's historic roofline. Extending south of the square, **Utrechtsestraat** is lined with hip boutiques and some of the best queer-friendly restaurants in the city; it's very much a see-and-be-seen thoroughfare, but without the conservative haughtiness of Rokin.

The Jordaan

West of the City Center, to the immediate west of the Prinsengracht, Amsterdam's Jordaan (pronounced Yoahr-**dahn**) exudes charm and is a favorite neighborhood for exploring, café-hopping, and window-shopping. The Jordaan earned its name during the early-19th-century occupation by the French, who developed it into a plot of vegetable gardens and called it *Le Jardin* (The Garden). During the latter half of the century, the gardens were razed to make way for residential construction—at this period in its history, Amsterdam's population was rising dramatically, and housing had grown scarce. For the next 100 years the Jordaan existed as a modest working-class neighborhood and industrial swath of tanneries and breweries. Enamored of its quaint homes and narrow lanes, many of which retrace the vegetable gardens' original

Eats ●
Barney's Breakfast Bar, **2**
Bolhoed, **10**
Caramba, **8**
Gary's Muffins, **1**
Moeders Pot, **6**
Reibach, **5**
't Schooiertje, **11**
Toscana, **3**
Toscanini, **7**
Vandenberg, **4**
Vliegende Schotel, **9**

Scenes ○
C.O.C., **3**
De Trut, **1**
De Twee Zwaantjes, **2**
Saarein, **4**

The Jordaan

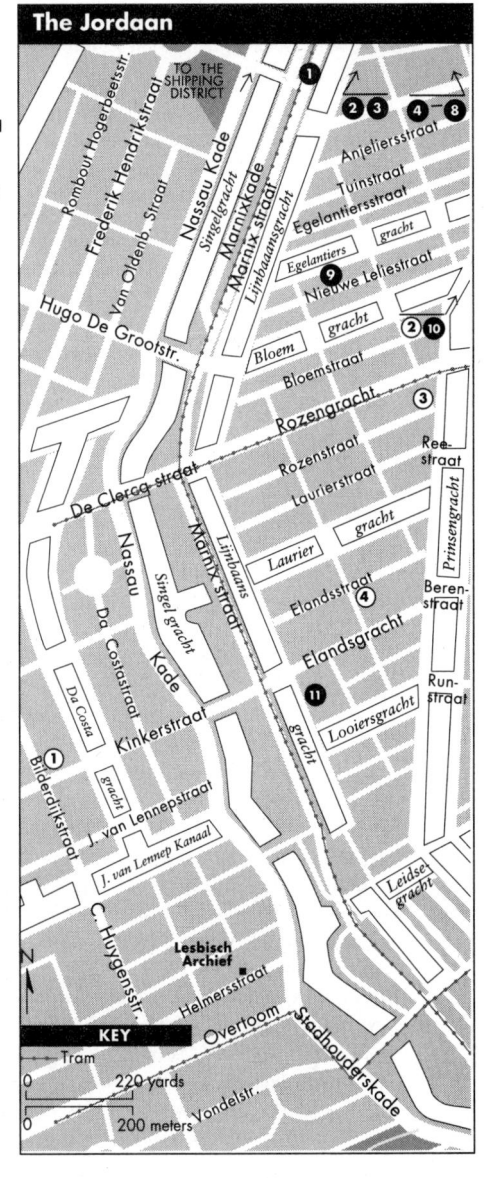

irrigation ditches, Amsterdammers began gentrifying the neighborhood during the latter half of this century.

Although there are very few gay bars in the Jordaan, it is the home of the C.O.C. (the gay and lesbian community center), and most of the businesses here are popular with family. Weekends and weekday evenings are the best time for strolling.

The **C.O.C. Amsterdam** (Cultuur-en Ontspanning Centrum [Cultural and Recreational Center], pronounced say-oh-say; ✉ Rozenstraat 14, ☎ 020/623–4079, Web site www.xs4all.nl˜cocasd) celebrated its 50th anniversary in 1996 and continues to be one of the world's best utilized lesbian and gay community centers. The huge old building, which is set inside a former school, crackles with character and feels busy every day of the week. Inside are various gathering areas, from cafés and bars to meeting rooms to offices occupied by different queer organizations. You needn't be a resident of the city to take advantage of the C.O.C.'s many resources and offerings. Visitors can come for gay newspapers, information and suggestions on where to go and what to see, advice on health issues, or simply to meet fellow gays and lesbians. You can also pick up information on upcoming events and gatherings, or come on weekend evenings to the disco, which is mostly gay male on Fridays, lesbian on Saturdays, and mixed on Sundays (*see* Scenes, *below*). The C.O.C. Netherlands, the national headquarters, is also in Amsterdam but near Dam Square, along Nieuwezijds Voorburgwal (*see* The Little Black Book, *below*).

In addition to the dyke dances held weekly at the C.O.C., the Jordaan has several other attractions popular with women. It's home to the feminist bookstore, **Xantippe Unlimited** (*see* Bookstores *in* The Little Black Book, *below*); a women's bar, **Saarein** (*see* Scenes, *below*); and the extensive **Lesbisch Archief** (Lesbian Archive; ✉ Eerste Helmersstraat 17, 1st floor, ☎ 020/618–5879), whose collection of tapes, books, articles, magazines, and photos detailing the city's (and Europe's) lesbian history is open by appointment. On certain days (often the first Sunday of each month), the archive usually sponsors an open house, along with events such as a presentation or a tour of the city's lesbian historical sights.

Although it's not specifically lesbian, **Het Vrouwenhuis** (The Women's House; ✉ Nieuwe Herengracht 95, ☎ 020/625-2066) is another excellent resource with a library, feminist books and magazines, and a wealth of resources and information for women.

There are hundreds of cool shops in the Jordaan, but antiquers and junkaholics should be absolutely sure to visit **de Rommelmarkt** (✉ Looiersgracht 38), a vast flea market with about 200 stalls; and **de Looier** (✉ Elandsgracht 109, ☎ 020/624-9038), which is right around the corner. Both are terrific places to while away rainy days.

East of the City Center

The section due east of the City Center, beginning around Nieuwmarkt, is a patchwork of low-income housing, ancient and contemporary architecture, and engaging attractions. A good place to begin your explorations of the area is southeast of the Nieuwmarkt, at **Waterlooplein.** Here on the north bank of the Amstel River sits one of the most controversial buildings in the Netherlands, the **Muziektheater/Stadhuis** (Music Theater/Town Hall; ✉ Waterlooplein 22, ☎ 020/625-5455, known locally as the Stopera (as in *St*adhuis and *opera*). This vast contemporary complex has drawn fire for several reasons. In the first place, parts of the historic blocks around the Stopera were torn up to make way for its construction. Amsterdam's more left-leaning activists were particularly appalled that during the housing crunch of the past two decades the government decided to convert one of the City Center's poorest neighborhoods into something so grand as an opera house. At some point during the battle over how best to proceed, it was decided that this complex would accommodate not only the opera but also the city's municipal buildings, thereby providing a space that would be utilized by every element of Dutch society, from welfare applicants to Wagner aficionados. Plenty of Amsterdammers also disparage the Stopera on aesthetic grounds—its postmodern design conflicts strongly with the city's conservative architectural tradition. The Stopera has considerable queer significance—and not only because of the opera. All Dutch marriages are performed at the town hall (church-performed weddings are optional, carrying symbolic but no legal significance), including gay ceremonies. Same-sex marriages are recognized by the government, but same-sex couples are still not yet accorded the same rights and privileges as heterosexual ones. Tours of the Stopera are given Wednesday and Saturday at 4 PM.

On the north side of Waterlooplein, a popular outdoor **flea market** is held daily; it's an ideal spot for picking up funky second-hand clothing and household goods but offers little in the way of antiques or pricier items. Architecture buffs should check out the **ARCAM Galerie** (✉ Waterlooplein 213, ☎ 020/620–4878), which serves to educate visitors about the city's architecture; about eight different exhibits run annually. Northwest of Waterlooplein is **de Zuiderkerk** (South Church; ✉ Zuiderkerkhof 72), an impressive 17th-century cathedral, which today is where the city planning department has its offices.

Waterlooplein is at the southern edge of Amsterdam's once-thriving **Jewish Quarter.** At the start of World War II, about one of every 10 Amsterdammers was Jewish; nearly 75% of the city's Jews were killed during the Nazi occupation. Decimated during the war, and further wrecked by a road-widening project that brought down many streets of buildings, the neighborhood has yet to really bounce back. It is, however, the site of one of the city's most remarkable restorations, the **Joods Historisch Museum** (Jewish Historical Museum; ✉ Jonas Daniël Meijerplein 2–4, ☎ 020/626–9945), which comprises four former 17th- and 18th-century synagogues enclosed by an ingeniously designed and executed glass-and-steel exterior. The museum has frequent changing exhibitions and a fine permanent collection of objects that relate to Dutch Jewish history.

The Quarter is also home to one of the most-visited sites in the Netherlands, the **Museum het Rembrandthuis** (Rembrandt House Museum; ✉ Jodenbreestraat 4–6, ☎ 020/624–9486), which is inside the house into which Rembrandt and his young wife, Saskia, moved in 1639. He was at the pinnacle of his fame and fortune during this period and created many of his most important works here. The death of Rembrandt's wife three years later precipitated his fall in popularity, and the painter subsequently lost the house to bankruptcy. It was restored in the early part of this century and now contains the majority of his etchings, as well as considerable information on his life.

The Lay of the Land

East of the Jewish Quarter, Plantage Middenlaan leads to the **Artis** (Zoo complex; ✉ Plantage Kerklaan 38–40, ☏ 020/523–3400), a 19th-century park with not only a respected zoo but also a planetarium, zoological museum, and geological museum. Here you can also stroll through the **Hortus Botanicus** (Botanic Gardens; ✉ Plantage Middenlaan 2A, ☏ 020/625–8411), which dates from 1683 and is one of the oldest such parks in existence. The three-climate greenhouse and 300-year-old collection of palm trees are particularly noteworthy. A good time to visit these attractions is on Sunday afternoon, when you can also see a movie at the nearby **Desmet** (✉ Plantage Middenlaan 4, ☏ 020/627–3434), a restored art deco cinema with queer-theme films on Sundays at 4 PM (and also on Saturdays at midnight).

Still farther east, far enough from the City Center to be overlooked by many visitors, the **Tropenmuseum** (Tropical Museum; ✉ Linnaeusstraat 2, ☏ 020/568–8215) definitely merits a visit. Built to exalt the Netherlands's colonial links to Indonesia and the West Indies, the museum is now more generally dedicated to the cultures of the tropics and subtropics. Exhibits such as a painstakingly reproduced street of an overpopulated Third World city are presented with great imagination and intelligence.

North and northeast of the Jewish Quarter is Amsterdam's downcast **Old Town,** a port neighborhood from which the Dutch East India Company conducted much of its international shipping trade and colonization. You can verse yourself in this history with a visit to the **Nederlands Scheepvaartmuseum** (Netherlands Maritime Museum; ✉ Kattenburgerplein 1, ☏ 020/523–2222), which comprises a 17th-century maritime warehouse filled with exhibits; it also has a re-created 1749 Dutch East India Company ship, the *Amsterdam*. Looming over Old Town is the **Schreierstoren** (Weeper's Tower; at the northern end of Geldersekade), now a shop with nautical books and maps; during the 16th century women gazed out across the harbor from atop the tower in hopes of seeing their husbands' ships returning home from fishing trips at sea.

Not far from here, the **Impuls Museum of Science and Technology** (✉ Oosterdok 2, Prins Hendrikkade, ☏ 020/531–3233) opened in summer 1997 and has already established itself as a city landmark. Designed by Renzo Piano, the architect of Paris's Pompidou Center, it resembles the prow of a mammoth futuristic ship as it rises up into the skyline right above the entrance to the **River IJ Tunnel.** Inside, state-of-the-art explore-by-touch exhibits cover historic, present-day, and futuristic technology.

Vondelpark and Museumplein

The one section of Amsterdam outside the City Center that virtually every visitor to the city makes a point of visiting is the **Oud Zuid** (Old South), an upscale neighborhood that was settled and constructed mostly throughout the 19th century during the same population boom that precipitated the residential development of the Jordaan. The neighborhood is anchored by splendid Vondelpark, as well as the city's top art museums, which are set around the mostly grassy Museumplein.

Should the City Center's narrow traffic-laden streets begin to work your nerves, plan a jaunt to 120-acre **Vondelpark,** named upon its 1865 creation for the so-called Dutch Shakespeare, playwright Joost van den Vondel. To reach the park, walk due south from the Leidseplein, crossing the Singelgracht then walking a block east along busy Stadhouderskade. To the right, you'll come upon the gates to what is at this point a narrow landscaped preamble to the park itself. Wander all the way through the park (a.k.a. "Amsterdam's Green Lung") to watch the battery of street performers, musicians, and tarot card readers assembled, usually around the outdoor theater. Or stroll through the formal Rose Garden, blade or jog among dozens of trails, or laze in the sun—typically among quite a few dykes and fags. A park highlight, particularly among queers, is the **Nederlands Filmmuseum and Library** (✉ Vondelstraat 69–71, ☎ 020/589–1400), which stands at the northwestern edge of the park overlooking a 19th-century pavilion. Rotating exhibits are mounted at the museum, which always presents daily art films in its two cinemas. On summer Saturdays there are free outdoor screenings on the terrace. The scenically set café, **Vertigo** (*see* Eats, *below*), usually brims with interesting people and is a good spot to relax over a light snack.

Continue along Stadhouderskade, a couple of blocks beyond the park gates, to reach the art museums, detouring briefly perhaps for a stroll up and down ritzy **P.C. Hooftstraat** (a.k.a. the PC, pronounced *pay*-say). This fashionable street is home to many of the city's fanciest men's and women's clothiers. The conservative style of threads you're likely to

The Lay of the Land   25

find along this drag won't work well at too many queer venues—although there is a Scottish clothier, **McGregor and Clan** (✉ P.C. Hooftstraat 113, ☎ 020/662-7425), where you can pick up an authentic Scottish tartan kilt to wear at your next gay pride parade.

The first museum you will encounter, **Rijksmuseum** (State Museum; ✉ Stadhouderskade 42, ☎ 020/673-2121), is without question one of the most striking architectural works of 19th-century Europe. Like Centraal Station, it was built in the 1880s by P. J. Cuypers, who clearly loved to push beyond the austere limits of the nation's Calvinist sensibilities. The Netherlands's largest, the museum contains a vast, dazzling collection of fine and decorative arts dating from the Middle Ages through the 18th century. Inside countless galleries are hung with 20 works by Rembrandt (including the famed, if overhyped, *Night Watch,* which has recently been cleaned and has its own accompanying exhibit) and hundreds of paintings by such Gilded Age masters as Vermeer (including *The Kitchen Maid* and *Woman Reading a Letter*), Jan Steen, Jacob van Ruisdael, and Frans Hals. Beyond the imposing main building, the recently restored and reopened South Wing contains an exhaustive collection of 18th- and 19th-century paintings, costumes, textiles, and statuary. To appreciate the entire collection you'll need to make several visits.

The rear of the Rijksmuseum opens onto the Museumplein, which leads to the **Vincent van Gogh Museum** (✉ Paulus Potterstraat 7, ☎ 020/570-5200). This museum's reputation ranges from subpar to superb, depending on whom you ask. Some refer sneeringly to it as "the best of the rest," alluding to the fact that many of Vincent van Gogh's most desirable works hang in major museums and private collections elsewhere around the world. Although the collection does include an astonishing number of works (about 200 paintings, 500 drawings, and 700 letters), relatively few of them are displayed at any given time and virtually all of his letters are kept out of the public eye (because the fragile paper on which they were written must be kept out of the light). The museum does exhibit a small but germane selection of works by van Gogh's contemporaries, including Toulouse-Lautrec and Gauguin. The building itself, designed after plans by the De Stijl architect and furniture designer Gerrit Rietveld (1888–1964), opened in 1973; it too receives mixed reviews.

Although the galleries are well lighted and easy to navigate, there is precious little biographical material accompanying van Gogh's works. This is still clearly one of the nation's most important museums, but it does leave a bit to be desired. Renovations and the construction of a new wing will close the museum from fall 1998 through spring 1999, but these improvements may remedy some of its shortcomings.

Earning considerably more praise for both the quality of its collection and the presentation of each work, the **Stedelijk Museum** (Municipal Museum; ✉ Paulus Potterstraat 13, ☏ 020/573–2911) is one of Europe's greatest museums of contemporary art, with a collection of works by such late-19th-century and 20th-century luminaries as Chagall, Matisse, Mondrian, de Kooning, Warhol, Picasso, Judd, Baselitz, Nauman, and many more. Other estimable collections include those devoted to American pop art and paintings of the CoBrA (Copenhagen-Brussels-Amsterdam) school. Be sure to phone ahead or check with the office of tourism to find out about upcoming temporary exhibits, which often deal explicitly with the contribution of gay and lesbian artists to the modern art movement. The museum's café has a very queer following.

South of the Museumplein is the city's dramatic **Concertgebouw** (Concert Building; ✉ Concertgebouwplein 2–6, ☏ 020/675–4411), the Netherlands's premier concert hall and longtime home of the Royal Concertgebouw Orchestra, immediately recognizable by the distinctive lyre atop the exterior. The Grote Zaal (Great Hall), the larger of the two halls, hosts the world's top classical musicians, thanks in large measure to its perfect acoustics. The Borodin Quartet is resident in the Kleine Zaal (Small Hall), which attracts leading chamber groups and soloists. There are no tours of the building, so you'll need to attend a concert or, if you visit on a Wednesday before 12:30 September–June, you can attend a free lunchtime concert.

De Pijp and Outside the City Center

With its contemporary architecture, high-rises, and broad avenues, much of greater Amsterdam, once you get beyond the Singelgracht, looks and feels like any other modern Dutch city. Although you won't find many attractions out here, the

The Lay of the Land

once-shabby neighborhood just southeast of the City Center, **de Pijp,** has become one of the funkiest parts of town. Racially and economically diverse, de Pijp is a mix of genXers, alternateens, queers, students, and mostly working-class immigrants, including quite a few first- and second-generation Surinamese and Turkish transplants. You'll find some inexpensive restaurants, an impressive market, and a fair number of offbeat shops, mostly along the main drags of **Ferdinand Bolstraat** and **Albert Cuypstraat.** The latter thoroughfare is the main spine of the bustling **Albert Cuypmarkt,** which is loaded with food, housewares, clothing, and various goods.

At the edge of the neighborhood, the **Heineken Brewery** (✉ Stadhouderskade 78, ☎ 020/523–9239) halted beer production here in 1988, but its sign is still visible from many parts of the city. The brewery is open for tours, where you can learn a thing or two about the company's history and how beer is brewed, before enjoying a tasting at the end.

One attraction that's worth a jaunt beyond de Pijp in southeast Amsterdam is the **Verzetsmuseum** (Museum of the Dutch Resistance; ✉ Lekstraat 63, ☎ 020/644–9797). The perceived or interpreted role of the Dutch in World War II is controversial, to say the least. But there's no question that many brave and valiant Nederlanders risked their lives to shelter Jews and attempt to confound the Nazi forces who occupied the country from 1940 to 1945. This museum traces the struggle with moving photographs, documents, and a replica of a printing press used to publish illegal resistance literature. It's a thoroughly engaging museum. To reach Verzetsmuseum, follow Van Woustraat from the east end of Albert Cuypstraat south, past the Amstel Canal, until it becomes Rijnstraat; Lekstraat is your first left upon passing Vrijheidslaan; it's about a 15-minute walk from Albert Cuypmarkt.

If the Vondelpark (*see above*) merely whets your appetite for more greenery, consider a trip just south of the city, nearly to Schiphol Airport, to enjoy the lush greenery of **Amsterdamse Bos** (Amsterdam Woods; reached via Buses 170, 171, and 172). The prettiest section—and also the cruisiest (*see* Action, *below*)—is around **Nieuwemeer,** a lake near the entrance. Although it's easy to reach the park by bus, consider cycling here for a little exercise and a chance to see the southern half of the city; it's about a 10-km (6-mile) ride.

GETTING AROUND

Getting to Amsterdam

From North America

From North America, **KLM Royal Dutch Airlines** (☎ 800/374–7747) is the Netherlands's national carrier, but **Martinair Holland** (☎ 800/627–8462), which has contibuted to gay causes, has reduced-rate flights from about a dozen major North American cities. U.S. airlines with regular service to Amsterdam include **Delta** (☎ 800/241–4141), **Northwest** (☎ 800/225–2525), **TWA** (☎ 800/221–2000), and **United** (☎ 800/538–2929).

From the United Kingdom

From the United Kingdom, consider the **KLM City Hopper** (☎ 0990/750–900), **British Airways** (☎ 0345/222–111), and **Aer Lingus** (☎ 0181/899–4747), all of which have regular service to Amsterdam. With the completion a few years ago of the Channel Tunnel, you can also drive to Amsterdam from London. Rail options from London include **British Rail International** (☎ 0990/848–848), which runs three times daily from London to Amsterdam. Or you can take the high-speed **Eurostar** (☎ 0171/922–4486 in the U.K., 800/942–4866 in the U.S.) to Brussels, from which numerous connections to Amsterdam are available. Less expensive but slower options from Britain include a combination bus/ferry trip on **Euro-City Tours** (☎ 0171/828–8361), or ferry service between Harwich and Hook on **Sealink/Stena** (☎ 0990/707–070), or between Hull and Rotterdam on **North Sea Ferries** (☎ 01482/795–141).

Getting to and from the Airport

Amsterdam Schiphol Airport (☎ 06/350–34050) is about 9 km (15 miles) southeast of the city, and is very easy to reach by train or by bus. A **taxi** will set you back from Fl 50 to Fl 60, but is obviously the most direct and pleasant way to reach your Amsterdam hostelry. **Rail service** (Schiphol Rail Line, ☎ 06/9292) between the airport and Amsterdam's Centraal Station costs just Fl 6 for the 15-minute ride, but then you may need a cab (from Fl 7 to Fl 20 to get from Centraal Station to your hotel). Trains run around the clock. **Bus service** runs between the airport and the Leidseplein (the ride takes 20 minutes), which is within walking distance or a short cab ride of many City Center hotels; the cost is Fl 4.75 and service is hourly. More expensive but farther reaching is the **KLM Hotel Bus Shuttle** (☎ 020/653–4975), which runs from the airport to a series of downtown hotels, essentially hitting every major tourist section of the city. The ride costs Fl 17.50 per person one-way (Fl 30 round-trip); buses run regularly from 6:30 AM until 10 PM daily. You do not need to be a KLM passenger of guest at any of the hotels along the route to use this shuttle. For specific information on rail and bus service into Amsterdam, stop first at the ground transportation desk directly outside the baggage claim.

Getting Around the City

Although locals rely heavily on trams and bicycles, most visitors find that walking is an easy and interesting way to get to most of the city's important attractions, hotels, restaurants, and bars.

Automobiles

Do not drive in the City Center; it's traffic-ridden and a nuisance, and it's very dangerous. Parking is scarce and expensive, especially inside the Singelgracht. It's hardly necessary to have a car while in Holland, even to explore the outlying cities. If you do rent a car, keep it secured in a car park outside of the immediate City Center, and use it only to get in and out of the city.

CAR RENTALS

Avis (✉ Nassaukade 380, ☎ 020/683–6061). **Hertz** (✉ Overtoom 333, ☎ 020/612–2441). **Budget** (✉ Overtoom 121, ☎ 020/612–6066).

Bicycles

If you're here for more than three or four days, or you simply want a quick way to get around the city, consider renting a bicycle. You can buy a cheap used one with two warped wheels and a rusted fender from several sources. Visitors spending more than a week in the city may save money this way. One major disadvantage of renting or buying a bicycle is the possibility of its being stolen—an enormous problem in Amsterdam. Always be sure to follow the rental shop's advice and lock your bike in the 6 trillion ways in which you're instructed. If someone rides up to you and offers his wheels at a bargain rate the bike is probably hot.

Good bike-for-hire outfits include **Bike City** (⌂ Bloemgracht 68, ☎ 020/626–3721) and **MacBike** (⌂ Marnixstraat 220, ☎ 020/626–6964). Rates are Fl 12.50 to 22.50 per day (Fl 50–100 per week), plus a substantial deposit (at least Fl 50) and the presentation of a passport. You will also find inexpensive bikes for sale outside **de Rommelmarkt** (⌂ Looiersgracht 38), set around a tree overlooking the canal. This is always a decent spot to find cheap wheels, or to sell back your bike when you're finished with it. A note about locks: If you do rent a bike, a lock (and often more than one, so you can lock different parts of the bike) is included. If, on the other hand, you plan to buy a bike and you own a lightweight bike lock, you may want to bring it with you.

Public Transportation

Trams and **buses** whiz around the city with great speed and efficiency, and travel most routes more speedily than automobiles (many streets are open only to pedestrians, bicycles, and trams). The city also has a three-line **subway system,** which is practical for commuting from the suburbs but is of little use to visitors sticking around the City Center. Pick up a transit map from **GVB** (⌂ Prins Hendrikkade 108–114, ☎ 020/551–4911), the **GVB ticket office** at the Centraal Station, or the **VVV Amsterdam Tourist Offices** (*see* The Little Black Book, *below*).

One reason you may wish to walk or bicycle rather than deal with trams and buses, especially if you're only in Amsterdam for a few days, is the city's confusing and archaic ticketing system. You can buy a single-ride ticket, but most visitors invest in a *strippenkaart,* which has from two to 45 strips that you punch according to the distance you're traveling. You punch your ticket in a machine in the rear or center of the vehicle, and you're on your honor to punch your ticket correctly (young plain-clothed monitors frequently board the trams and check to see that you've punched the right number of strips; the fine is Fl 60 if you haven't).

Taxis

Taxis are pricey, but in a pinch they can come in quite handy. Consider a cab if returning home from the bars late at night, for although violent crime in Amsterdam is virtually unheard of, pickpockets are fairly commonplace. You can phone for a cab at **Taxicentrale** (☎ 020/677–7777) or catch one at Centraal Station, Dam Square, the Leidseplein, the Rembrandtplein, most major hotels, and other key points around the city. Taxis are metered, and it's rare that a ride anywhere within the City Center will cost less than Fl 10 or more than Fl 20.

Excursions from Amsterdam

Two chapters in this book, one on other major Dutch cities and the other on major Belgian destinations, give the ins and outs on exploring within three or four hours of Amsterdam. All of these cities are easy to reach by train.

Rail Passes
If you're planning to spend more than a couple of days outside the city, investigate the many rail passes available. The **Benelux Tourrail** is good for five days of travel within any one month throughout Belgium, Luxembourg, and Holland. The **Holland Rail Pass** comes with several options, allowing from three to 10 days of travel within a one-month period. Also look into **Dagkaarts** (good for a day of unlimited travel within Holland) and **Holland Rail Pass Transport Links** (which allow free travel on local public transportation for an additional fee). For details on these and the other rail passes, contact **Rail Europe** (☎ 800/848–7245; Web site www.raileurope.com).

WHEN TO GO

Amsterdam is popular with business and leisure travelers year-round, which means there isn't really a low season when hotels and businesses reduce their rates. For information on the several queer-popular events described below, contact the Gay and Lesbian Switchboard (*see* The Little Black Book, *below*).

Winter
You would think that the city's dreary, wet, and raw winter would be a turnoff to visitors, but tourism still booms at this time, partly because of the many festivities during the month of December. St. Nicholas's Day (December 5) is celebrated in the Netherlands with all the excitement that Christmas generates in North America and much of the rest of Europe. In recent years, however, the Dutch have begun also to celebrate

Christmas with parties and festivals. New Year's has also long been a major time for revelry. If you come during these months, realize that temperatures typically hover at or just above freezing, and rain and sleet are near-daily occurrences.

Spring

Spring is a fantastic time to visit Amsterdam. Although conventioneers favor this sunny temperate season, therefore driving up the demand for hotel rooms, the city is still largely without the seething hordes of vacationers that descend during the summer months. From late March onward, attractions, restaurants, and nightlife are in full swing, but lines remain manageable until about the end of June. Another great reason to visit in the spring is to see Amsterdam when the city's tulips are in bloom. This time of year marks the beginning of the **Cultural Season,** which lasts until early October and is marked by countless festivals and parties, several of which are central to the gay community.

The big spring fete, **Queen's Day,** occurs April 30, the symbolic birthday of Queen Beatrix. In fact, Beatrix was born January 30. But because the weather in Holland is so relentlessly grim at the end of January, Beatrix decided to move the celebrations to lovely April 30, which is actually the day of her mother Juliana's birth. Quite some time ago, the queer community more-or-less co-opted this event as a special time to cut loose and pay tribute not only to the Queen, but to queens everywhere. To this end, celebrations are held at the Homomonument and culminate with a fabulous outdoor dance party. Many gay-popular businesses stage their own shindigs at this time. Shortly after Queen's Day, the community reflects on the lesbian and gay victims of World War II on **Remembrance Day** (May 4), just before the entire nation relives the close of the war on **Liberation Day** (May 5). Later in the month, Amsterdammers observe **AIDS Memorial Day** (the last Saturday of May) with an eloquent musical ceremony at the Beurs van Berlage, followed by a candlelight procession to Dam Square.

Summer

Holland enjoys relatively mild and dry summers, and tourists invade the city at this time. Bars and many attractions typically extend their hours a bit, and restaurants set up tables outside in courtyards and along the canals. There are few better times to enjoy the city.

For many years the gay community has kicked off the summer with **Roze Zaterdag** ("Pink Saturday," held the final Saturday in June), a pride celebration held in a different Dutch city each year. For the past few years, there has been controversy over how best to organize this event, which is more of a political rally than it is a party-oriented festival.

Fueling the Roze Zaterdag disarray was the introduction in the summer of 1996 of **Amsterdam Pride,** a three-day party (eight days in '98) created by the city's gay business association. With the Gay Games slated to occur in Amsterdam in 1998, the owners of bars, restaurants, and other queer-oriented businesses decided this would be an opportune time to throw an annual party. Those who lament the apparent demise of Roze Zaterdag view Amsterdam Pride as a shameless display of commercialism. But the event has been a smashing and highly enjoyable success during each of its first two years, and there's little question that the Amsterdam Pride festivities will be well attended during the Gay Games (*see* Gay Games, *below*). There are typically several important and well-publicized AIDS fundraisers and circuit-style parties also held in July and August; these can change date and venue from year to year.

Although it's not specifically queer, the relatively new **Dance Valley Festival** (☎ 020/627–3900; Web site www.dancevalley.nl) brings together thousands of diverse music fans to hear 75 top European DJs and 15 bands. This open-air "Dutch Woodstock" has quickly become a major event. It's held on a Saturday in August at the Spaarnwoude Recreational Area, which is just outside of the city (there's regular bus service from Amsterdam's Sloterdijk train station).

Fall

The weather continues to be pleasant and fairly dry through early October before giving way rapidly to the wet chill of winter. As with the spring, this is a major time for conventions and business travel, so accommodations continue to be at a premium. Gays and lesbians hold **Galafest** sometime in the middle of September as an end-of-summer finale, with many parties and events. In October, the weeklong **Leather Pride** festivities are among the best attended in Europe, drawing scads of visitors from all over the world for some intense partying, culminating with a three-day-long nonstop fete.

Gay Games Amsterdam 1998

The **Gay Games** were begun in San Francisco in 1982 by the late Dr. Tom Waddell as a forum for gay and lesbian athletes from all over the world to participate in an Olympic-style format. The games, which are held every four years, have subsequently been held again in San Francisco (in '86), Vancouver ('90), and New York City ('94). In 1998 the Gay Games will be held in Amsterdam beginning August 1 and culminating with a closing ceremony on August 8.

The games have a comprehensive **cultural program,** consisting of four elements: **community art,** where individuals may exhibit or perform their art; **exhibitions,** which will be gay-themed and staged at the Stedelijk Museum, the Rijksmuseum, and the Amsterdams Historisch Museum; **festivals,** ranging from choral concerts to women's arts forums to storytelling; and **performing arts,** consisting of dance, theater, and musical productions.

The **sports program** comprises three elements: **official sports competitions, demonstration sports,** and the **finals.** All events will be held in Amsterdam. Expected to attend are roughly 12,000 competitors in 30 sports, including badminton, ballroom dancing, basketball, billiards, body building, bowling, bridge, chess, cycling, figure skating/ice skating, ice hockey, judo, karate, marathon, martial arts, power lifting, rowing, soccer, softball, sport climbing, squash, swimming, table tennis, tennis, track and field, triathalon, volleyball, water polo, windsurfing, wrestling.

The individual sports and cultural events will be bracketed by the grand **opening** and **closing ceremonies,** both of which will be staged in the new **Amsterdam ArenA** (⊠ Haaksbergweg 59, ☎ 020/691–2906), which can hold up to 50,000 people. The opening ceremonies will be marked by the presentation of a flag that has been carried by bike for three months through Europe as part of the Rainbow Tour for the End of AIDS. For the closing ceremonies, more than 50 decorated boats will ride through the city on its canals. And from a stage moored in the Amstel River there will be various entertainment and art presentations nightly for the entire week.

You can obtain specific information on what will surely be one of the most memorable gay and lesbian gatherings of the decade by contacting **Gay Games Amsterdam 1998** (⊠ Box

2837, 1000 CV, ☎ 020/620-1998, ℻ 020/626-1998, e-mail info@gaygames.nl). The gay games also have an extremely helpful **Web site** (www.dds.nl˜gaygames).

EATS

Foodies shouldn't come to Amsterdam—or to any city in the Netherlands—with high expectations, although the city's dining scene has improved vastly over the past decade. Ethnic restaurants—many of them specializing in the cuisine of the former Dutch colony, Indonesia—have long provided an alternative to the fairly bland and conservative old-school Dutch cooking found in most traditional eateries.

But like elsewhere in Europe, Amsterdam's rising culinary elite is quite sophisticated. Many chefs have trained internationally, and quite a few up-and-coming restaurants have begun ushering in the "New Dutch" cuisine, which utilizes the region's vast bounty of local produce and seafood. The more interesting restaurants can be pricey (although most of them gay-popular). If you're on a budget, stick with Asian (especially Indonesian) and Surinamese (more for fast food) spots for the most flavor. Also consistently decent, if unspectacular, are the many Italian, Greek, and Turkish restaurants that you'll find in all the major tourist neighborhoods.

Hearty Dutch breakfasts often include bread, butter, jam, ham, cheese, chocolate, boiled eggs, juice, and steaming coffee or tea. Lunch tends to be a *broodje* (sandwich) from a delicatessen. At later meals, most Dutch home-style menus include *hutspot* (means literally "hodgepodge"), a beige blob of mashed potatoes, overcooked peas and carrots, boiled meats, a generous dousing of gravy, and just a soupçon of salt; many outsiders consider this winter stew inedible, but locals claim to love it. The tradition of hutspot dates from the reclamation of the city of Leiden by William of Orange in 1574; according to local lore, William and his troops discovered a hefty kettle of the indestructible stew simmering over the fire left by the deposed Spanish army. Being a thrifty lot, the Dutch incorporated into the national menu what may very well have been a practical joke on the part of the Spaniards.

Haring (herring) is another local favorite many nonnatives approach with great trepidation. The year's first catch (herring season begins the final Saturday of May) is celebrated with great fanfare. The fish are eaten raw with onions, much in the way goldfish have been consumed by drunken college students on dares for many decades in the United States. Because herring season extends only to September, the fish are pickled and salted so they'll be available until next May, when the fresh version is once again available. Be forewarned: The closer it is to late June, the longer the herring has been preserved (and the more you'll taste the brine).

As you might expect in one of the world's gayest cities, restaurants throughout Amsterdam are consistently gay-friendly, from the divey ethnic restaurants in the Red-Light District to the formal Continental dining rooms in some of the city's top hotels. A few trendy bistros—most notably La Strada, Getto, and Huyschaemer—have an overwhelmingly gay following, as do several informal snack bars near the densest concentrations of gay bars. At virtually any restaurant along Kerkstraat, Warmoesstraat, and Reguliersdwarsstraat, you're sure to see same-sex couples; Utrechtsestraat is also loaded with trendy restaurants, most of which have somewhat queer followings. But at no restaurant near the City Center or at any of the more touristy neighborhoods will you ever have to feel worried about homophobia, at least on the part of restaurant staff.

To sample some of the city's best (and cheapest) ethnic foods, wander along the once-dangerous and now-merely-seedy Zeedijk, which has many bare-bones Asian restaurants (as well as importers, clothiers, and other such shops). Most Chinese restaurants (at least in touristy areas) in Amsterdam serve a mild ersatz combination of Chinese and Indonesian cuisine, which immigrants seeking an authentic experience shun. The eateries along Zeedijk, no matter how modest in appearance, offer the real thing.

Dinner at restaurants in Amsterdam is usually served until 10 PM, but most diners eat between 7 PM and 9 PM. Increasingly, menus are available in several languages, including English. Your bill will include a 17.5% tax and a 15% service charge, but you should still round up a guilder or two for good service.

Eats

For price ranges, *see* dining Chart A at the front of this guide.

City Center, Red-Light District, and Nieuwmarkt

$$$$ ✗ **D'Vijff Vlieghien.** So uncompromisingly traditional it verges on being campy, this formal eatery offers a glimpse into Dutch society as you might have imagined it during the Gilded Age. Two of Rembrandt's original etchings are among the artwork and bric-a-brac in the dining room, which also has exquisite paneled walls and carved wooden chairs. The Continental fare is stellar. Consider grilled turbot on a bed of fresh sauerkraut, capers, and currants, or the poached loin of venison with baked potato slices and spinach. It's worth braving the mostly corporate and straight crowd. ⊠ *Spuistraat 294–302,* ☏ *020/624–8369.*

$$–$$$ ✗ **Caprese Ristorante Italiano.** This corner trattoria on funky-meets-sleazy Spuistraat serves commendable Italian food, including 15 varieties of pasta and many grilled meat and fish entrées, such as salmon with white wine and steak au poivre. The cream-and-pink color scheme and flattering indirect lighting make the warm, unpretentious dining room a nice place to linger. ⊠ *Spuistraat 261,* ☏ *020/620–0059.*

$$ ✗ **Getto.** This relatively new and funky addition to lovably seedy Warmoesstraat suggests a great deal about the direction of the neighborhood. The restaurant is smartly furnished with art on the walls and colorful furnishings; downstairs is a festive pub that attracts artsy, grungy, and hip sorts. The dining room gets a more mixed crowd (although both sections are extremely queer-popular), and serves creative comfort food such as rib-eye steak with a piquant pepper sauce, garbanzo-bean burgers, and a beef-and-Guinness hutspot. Thursday night's Dusty Bingo Balls, a bingo night, is a fun time to come. ⊠ *Warmoesstraat 51,* ☏ *020/421–5151.*

$$ ✗ **Hemelse Modder.** A bit off the beaten tourist track, this French and Italian eatery charms its significantly gay clientele with reasonable prices, a quaint ambience, and internationally influenced grills such as rack of lamb with pesto, as well as numerous vegetarian dishes. The menu changes every three months, to take advantage of local produce and seasonal specialties. ⊠ *Oude Waal 9,* ☏ *020/624–3203.*

$$ ✗ **La Strada.** Gay and lesbian couples favor this handsome bistro around the corner from Dam Square. Mood lighting, soft music, and personable servers provide the backdrop for a romantic dinner. A pâté of guinea fowl, a leafy-green salad with baked mussels, veal casserole, and roast rack of lamb are some of the country French–style dishes you can expect. Up front is a busy cocktail bar. ⊠ *Nieuwezijds Voorburgwal 93,* ☏ *020/625–0276.*

$–$$ ✕ **Lana Thai.** This colorful Thai eatery is a gay fave along the forbidding "rue de Vaseline," where butch bears, potheads, and alternative creatures dine side-by-side on *satays* (grilled skewers of meat, fish, poultry, and vegetables), curries, and noodles. ⊠ *Warmoesstraat 10,* ☏ *020/624–2179.*

$–$$ ✕ **'t Sluisje.** This campy restaurant succeeds on a number of fronts: It's a steak house, a drag cabaret, and a bar, with a diverse menu ranging from hefty grilled meats to bountiful salads, plus some Asian dishes. The *dagschotel* (dish of the day) is always a good bet. ⊠ *Torensteeg 1,* ☏ *020/624–0813.*

$ ✕ **De Keuken van 1870.** This informal restaurant near Centraal Station specializes in mom-style Dutch cooking and ranges from decent to a bit bleak (the only spices apparently known to this kitchen are salt and, sparingly, pepper). The funky crowd comes for the meat stews, potatoes, and convivial atmosphere. ⊠ *Spuistraat 4,* ☏ *020/624–8965. No credit cards.*

$ ✕ **Kam Yin.** It's a dive, but this characterless cafeteria at the northern end of Warmoesstraat has tasty and filling Asian fare, including chop suey, rice with brown beans, and chicken-fried rice. The plates come overflowing with food, so you may have to loosen your harness a notch or two before heading into one of the nearby leather bars. ⊠ *Warmoesstraat 6,* ☏ *020/625–3115.*

$ ✕ **Sisters.** This is an informal and cheerful vegetarian restaurant on a quiet street (on which the philosopher Spinoza once resided) just below Dam Square. It's ideal for anything from a light snack to something more substantial, and the portions are large and the prices low. And, as the name suggests, it has a definite following in the community. ⊠ *Nes 102,* ☏ *020/626–3970.*

The Jordaan and Western City Center

$$$–$$$$ ✕ **Christophe.** Named for Algerian-born chef Christophe Royer, this much-revered nouvelle French restaurant serves some of the most creative fare in the city. An international influence prevails, particularly with regard to seasonings—

Eats

try pigeon cooked with coriander and other sharp spices. Also try terrine of eggplant with cumin or finish with roasted fresh figs with fresh thyme ice cream. The staff is polite, knowledgeable, and gay-friendly. ✉ *Leliegracht 46,* ☎ *020/625–0807.*

$$$–$$$$ ✕ **Tout Court.** Owner-chef John Fagel likes to say he serves "good food without a fuss" at his sophisticated French restaurant on funky Runstraat. His menus (spring lamb, summer fruits, game in autumn and winter), which change monthly, focus on both classic and contemporary fare, including frogs' legs with garlic and herbs, and ravioli with sweetbreads, wild mushrooms, and Madeira sauce. The roast pheasant for two is a signature dish. The mood here is a bit less formal and stuffy than some of Amsterdam's other upscale restaurants. ✉ *Runstraat 13,* ☎ *020/625–8637.*

$$–$$$ ✕ **Koh-I-Noor.** It's a little pricey, but this Indian restaurant across from the Westerkerk has attractive dining rooms decorated with Indian art and designs, and serves first-rate cuisine, including shrimp tandoori, *sag paneer* (spinach with homemade cheese in a mild curry), and many lamb and poultry grills and curries. The interior, from the table linens to the walls, is pink—a tribute to the nearby Homomonument? Probably not, but the management is very gay-friendly just the same. ✉ *Westermarkt 29,* ☎ *020/623–3133.*

$$–$$$ ✕ **Toscanini.** For a true taste of Tuscany, and not another annoying nod to the flavorless quasi-Italian fare found at many of the city's imposters, visit this ultratrendy trattoria along the Lindengracht's restaurant row, at the northern end of the Jordaan. The pastas and risottos are homemade and the grills, such as trout with fresh basil, are prepared to perfection. ✉ *Lindengracht 75,* ☎ *020/623–2813.*

$$–$$$ ✕ **Zomers.** As you're strolling along courtly Prinsengracht, you may be taken aback by this offbeat bistro renowned for its artful window displays—chicken roasting on a spit, or creative arrangements of fowl—and innovative postmodern decor. The menu is no less eye-catching, with such world-beat fare as duck liver–stuffed ravioli with a beurre blanc sauce, grilled sea bream with potatoes and fried lettuce, and cinnamon ice cream with warm blueberries. ✉ *Prinsengracht 411,* ☎ *020/638–3398.*

$$ ✕ **Caramba.** Although this bustling, spacious spot gets less attention (and slightly smaller crowds) than Rose's Cantina (*see below*), it has better and more varied Mexican and U.S.

40   **Out in Amsterdam**   Chapter 1

southwestern and New Orleans–style cooking. Jambalaya with chorizo sausage, chicken enchiladas, and grilled tuna with spices are recommended. Place mats with pictures of parrots adorn the tables, set amid the tropical-color decor. The crowd is mostly young and trendy. ✉ *Lindengracht 342,* ☎ *020/627–1188.*

$$ ✕ **Toscana.** This inexpensive Italian eatery in the Shipping District draws a hip crowd for socializing in the high-ceiling bar and restaurant. There are many pastas and thin-crust pizzas to choose from, and every dish is available in full or half portions. ✉ *Llaarlemmerdijk 176,* ☎ *020/624–8358.*

$–$$ ✕ **Bolhoed.** The boho decorating scheme is postmodern thrift-shop in this tiny healthful hangout overlooking a Prinsengracht canal; the walls are painted lime green and banana yellow, eclectic antiques and bric-a-brac are strewn about, and some of the chairs are upholstered in exotic zebra print. The food is creative, low-cal, and tasty; try the ragout croissant (filled with seaweed, tofu, leeks, and curry), or the mixed seafood in a spicy tomato-saffron broth. There's live music some evenings. ✉ *Prinsengracht 60–62,* ☎ *020/626–1803. No credit cards.*

$ ✕ **Barney's Breakfast Bar.** If you're coming from or going to nearby Centraal Station, and you're looking for a filling but cheap bite, make a quick detour to this trippy diner in the Shipping District. As the name suggests, breakfast is the main event—whatever you wish, from vegan to American to traditional Irish, Barney's offers a tasty rendition. For lunch or dinner, consider a burger, a tuna melt, or any number of sandwiches. The crowd tends toward hippies and grungers (note the psychedelic prints on the walls). ✉ *Haarlemmerstraat 102,* ☎ *020/625–9761.*

$ ✕ **Pancake Bakery.** Tourists cram the city's well-known pancake houses to sample these local specialties; this plain dark basement dining room is one of the most reliable ones, offering about 40 sweet and savory toppings, including bacon and onion, and cherry ice cream with kirsch brandy. Save your visit here for the day you plan on buying wooden shoes and Delft tchotchkes. ✉ *Prinsengracht 191,* ☎ *020/625–1333.*

$ ✕ **Moeders Pot.** If you had grown up in a Dutch household, your mom probably would have cooked the brand of robust (but bland) food doled out in huge servings at this zero-ambience hole-in-the-wall. Students and budget travelers love it, and it has a queer following. ✉ *Vinkenstraat 119,* ☎ *020/623–7643.*

Eats 41

$ ✕ **Reibach.** This comfy lunch room is along the famed Brouwersgracht (Brewers' Canal), one of the prettiest waterways in the city. The broodjes and basic snacks are simple and filling, the crowd very alternative. ✉ *Brouwersgracht 319,* ☏ *020/626-7708. No credit cards.*

$ ✕ **'t Schooiertje.** This cozy queer-popular lunch room is right inside de Looier antiques market—it's also very close to the Thermos Day Sauna in case you meet somebody here you'd like to invite for an afternoon romp. ✉ *Lijnbaansgracht 190,* ☏ *020/638-4035.*

$ ✕ **Vandenberg.** This casual café in the northern end of the Jordaan is the closest the city has to a lesbian restaurant (other than the dykey coffeehouse, Café Françoise), although plenty of guys come here, too. The pub-style food (plus some vegetarian dishes) is tasty but less of a reason to come than to sit on the spacious terrace and ogle the cute crowds. ✉ *Lindengracht 95,* ☏ *020/622-2716.*

$ ✕ **Vliegende Schotel.** Veg-heads, backpackers, squatters, and hipsters love the Vliegende Schotel ("flying saucer"), a simple vegetarian café on a quiet lane in the Jordaan. Greek salads, vegetarian goulash, lasagna, and tagliatelle pasta are among the diverse offerings; the portions are enormous. ✉ *Nieuwe Leliestraat 162,* ☏ *020/625-2041.*

Leidseplein, Rembrandtplein, and Frederiksplein

$$$$ ✕ **Het Tuynhuis.** It's worth a splurge—a big splurge—for a meal inside this formal 19th-century town house with one of the priciest menus in the city. The white-glove service is smooth without being pretentious, and the management extremely welcoming of gay and lesbian patrons. Among the classic French and Continental dishes are *Pommeizarine* (potatoes, sour cream, and lots of Iranian caviar), an appetizer that will set you back Fl 74, and sea bream with herb puree and truffle anchovy vinaigrette. ✉ *Reguliersdwarsstraat 28,* ☏ *020/627-6603.*

$$$$ ✕ **'t Swarte Schaep.** Since the 1930s, this formal traditional Dutch restaurant inside a late-17th-century building has charmed patrons, and for as long as any locals can remember, the management has warmly welcomed gay and lesbian patrons. Copper pots and ancient tools hang from the ceilings of the dining rooms, which are framed in dark wood beams and posts; window tables overlook the bustling Leidseplein. Although the menu focuses on such old-fashioned

standbys as chateaubriand with béarnaise sauce, you'll find some surprisingly current creations here as well. Dinner orders are accepted until 11 PM. ⊠ *Korte Leidsedwarsstraat 24,* ☏ *020/622-3021.*

$$$–
$$$$ ✕ **Le Pêcheur.** This chic contemporary restaurant on busy Reguliersdwarsstraat is one of the city's top purveyors of nouvelle-inspired seafood. Innovative dishes like salmon *en feuilleté* (steamed in parchment paper) with caramelized lobster, and tuna consommé with profiteroles and shiitake mushrooms arouse the taste buds. Not very gay despite the location, but top-notch in every way. ⊠ *Reguliersdwarsstraat 32,* ☏ *020/624-3121.*

$$$ ✕ **De Kroon.** For the perfect view of the Rembrandtplein, great late-night dining, or a fine martini, check out this supper club decked with glittering chandeliers, gilt-frame mirrors, high ceilings, and tall windows overlooking the street action down below. With several TV and radio stations in this building, the restaurant is popular among young movers and shakers in the media industry. The French cuisine is expectedly showy; highlights include a steak of wild boar with mushrooms and elderberry sauce, and corn-fed chicken with Parma ham and an orange Cointreau sauce. ⊠ *Rembrandtplein 17,* ☏ *020/625-2011.*

$$$ ✕ **Dynasty.** With so many affordable ethnic restaurants around the city, people are sometimes put off by this pricey purveyor of haute Asian cuisine, but the innovative fare—which has its roots mostly in China but also Thailand, Malaysia, Vietnam—is memorable and the presentation sublime. Typical dishes are tender sliced rabbit with wild mushrooms, and young chicken and fried duck liver with bamboo shoots. ⊠ *Reguliersdwarsstraat 30,* ☏ *020/626-8400.*

$$$ ✕ **Kort.** New management and a cutting-edge menu have turned this long rectangular restaurant tucked by the magnificent Amstel Kerk into one of Amsterdam's hippest eateries. New Dutch specialties include swordfish and prawns over lime couscous and a chicory tart with a walnut-and-apple salad, and chocolate mousse with caramelized chestnuts. Very stylish interior. ⊠ *Amstelveld 12,* ☏ *020/626-1199.*

$$–$$$ ✕ **Aphrodite.** There are perhaps a dozen Greek restaurants near the Leidseplein; this one gets the least pedestrian traffic, and it's rather far down one of the side streets. Possibly for this reason, it has the most authentic, and romantic, taverna-inspired ambience and the best food. It's also a touch more

expensive than the others. Top dishes include tangy *tzatziki* (a tart cucumber-garlic-lemon yogurt served with bits of toasted pita) and salmon grilled with Greek spices or shrimp with *saganaki* (cheese sautéed in butter and sprinkled with lemon juice). The knowledgeable staff is always willing to explain the ins and outs of the menu's more complicated dishes. ⊠ *Lange Leidsedwarsstraat 91,* ☎ *020/622–7382.*

$$–$$$ ✕ **Casa di David.** It's not all that gay, but few of the city's many Italian restaurants offer a more romantic setting: Prints of Renaissance art and vintage photos of Italian street life line the walls, soft music is heard in the background, and efficient servers whisk about cheerfully. The menu fits plenty of budgets, with the wood-fire pizzas, bruschetta with prosciutto, veal scaloppine, and linguine with shrimp and porcini mushrooms among the many good possibilities. ⊠ *Singel 426,* ☎ *020/624–5093.*

$$–$$$ ✕ **Le Zinc.** On the ground floor of a fascinating old redbrick canal house along Prinsengracht, this rustic eatery's beamed ceiling, chandeliers, and dim lighting impart an authentic country French ambience, matched perfectly by the first-rate hearty French fare, such as grilled salmon with sauerkraut and bacon and a rich house terrine. Nice wine list, too. ⊠ *Prinsengracht 999,* ☎ *020/622–9044.*

$$–$$$ ✕ **Portugália.** Sandwiched between several gay hotels and taverns, this cozy and queer purveyor of authentic Portuguese cooking is decked in nautical paraphernalia and seafaring murals. Appropriately, the emphasis is on seafood, including panfried sea devil, clams, and potatoes in a rich cream sauce, and a hearty mixed grill of swordfish, salmon, sardines, shrimp, and fried clams in olive oil with white wine and garlic. Bring your appetite. ⊠ *Kerkstraat 35,* ☎ *020/625–6490.*

$$–$$$ ✕ **Sluizer.** This restaurant along snazzy Utrechtsestraat has two parts—one specializing in seafood and the other in meat and poultry. The seafood side is most reliable, with such tasty fare as swordfish grilled with soy sauce and sea devil with finely sliced vegetables and a heady lobster sauce. Marble floors and tables, mustard walls, and a beamed ceiling impart a relaxed but tasteful look. ⊠ *Utrechtsestraat 43–45,* ☎ *020/622–6376.*

$$ ✕ **Cafe Morlang.** Yuppies with an artistic bent frequent this snazzy postmodern café inside a handsome old canal house beside the Metz & Co. department store. The menu is international, with dishes ranging from red snapper tandoori to

a tempting mango cream tart for dessert. ⊠ *451 Keizersgracht,* ☎ *020/625–2681.*

$$ × **Huyschkaemer.** New owners have completely transformed this queer-popular haunt—once a fairly modest "living room" café with plain but cozy furnishings—into one of the trendiest bistros along fashionable Utrechtsestraat. Inside you'll find a courtly bar and several tables, beyond which a sleek metal staircase leads up into a second dining loft. The food—seawolf with white wine and baked *uitjes* (baby onions) and pork with a hazelnut crust—is uncommonly delicious yet reasonably priced. A great choice for a date. ⊠ *Utrechtsestraat 137,* ☎ *020/627–0575.*

$$ × **Izmir.** This intimate sumptuously decorated Turkish restaurant is one of the best in the city; it's inside the former gay bar, Route 66 (now called Meia Meia 66 and across the street at No. 63), and still draws a fairly queer crowd. Try the spicy chicken salad with walnut sauce, the stuffed rolls of beef, tomatoes, paprika, cheese, vegetables, and onion, and the grilled minced-lamb meatballs. The Turkish rice pudding is a favorite dessert. ⊠ *Kerkstraat 66,* ☎ *020/627–8239.*

$$ × **Malvesijn.** On a peaceful stretch of Prinsengracht, this dapper queer-popular neighborhood bistro serves a nice, informal selection of Continental dishes, many of them with American influences: baked salmon with Cajun herb butter, pork medallions with oyster sauce, and spicy chicken wings. Locals stop in simply for drinks and light snacks at the bar. Framed prints and show posters line the walls. ⊠ *Prinsengracht 598,* ☎ *020/638–0899.*

$$ × **Rama Thai.** Don't think the touristy location translates to mild food—the cooks here are liberal with their peppers and spices. Their culinary skills make this one of the better eateries along busy Lange Leidsedwarsstraat's restaurant row. Green beef curry, satay with a rich peanut sauce, and chicken with cashews and mushrooms are fine choices; be sure to sample a bottle of imported Singha beer. ⊠ *Lange Leidsedwarsstraat 27,* ☎ *020/625–9835.*

$$ × **Rose's Cantina.** This festive Mexican cantina is usually brimming with wild margarita-logged tourists and locals, content with the mildly spiced, reasonably tasty quesadillas, tacos, and other Tex-Mex specialties. It's not going to make any Texans forget home, but it makes for a fun night on the town. ⊠ *Reguliersdwarsstraat 38,* ☎ *020/625–9797.*

Eats 45

$$ ✗ **Smoeshaan Cafe and Theatre.** Attached to a fringe performance space, this two-part restaurant has a smoke-and-chatter-filled dining room on the lower level and a dressier room upstairs—in warm weather you can also dine on the terrace overlooking the canal. Wherever you dine you'll be given the same menu, which focuses on traditional Dutch and Continental dishes such as tagliatelle pasta with a rich salmon sauce. ✉ *Leidsekade 90,* ☎ *020/627–6966.*

$–$$ ✗ **Bojo.** This fanatically popular Indonesian restaurant near the Leidseplein is a great place for an introduction to this flavorful cuisine—it's prepared here authentically, so you'll need to indicate how spicy you'd like it. If you're in a group, consider the traditional rijstafel, which consists of many small plates of meat and vegetables accompanied by sweet and savory sauces. The intense crowds can be a drag, as can the slow service, but Bojo serves food until well after midnight, so you can pop in for a late-night snack. ✉ *Lange Leidsedwarsstraat 51,* ☎ *020/622–7434.*

$–$$ ✗ **Camp Cafe.** A queer restaurant has stood on this spot for many years; the homey Camp Cafe opened here in 1996 to high praise for its friendly service, cute patrons, and reasonably priced basic Continental cooking. Such hearty fare as salmon with a dill sauce and wild game are typical. Cane chairs and marble tables decorate the dining room, and the unusual ceiling is covered with prints of famous Dutch-master paintings. A small bar is very popular, especially in the early evening on weekdays. ✉ *Kerkstraat 45,* ☎ *020/622–1506.*

$–$$ ✗ **Panini.** This two-tier café with yellow and cream walls and indirect lighting attracts a stylish crowd for desserts, coffee, wine, and excellent but light food, from focaccia sandwiches to pasta salad. It's near several antiques shops, and also in the shadows of the Rijksmuseum. ✉ *Vijzelgracht 3–5,* ☎ *020/626–4939.*

$–$$ ✗ **Pizzeria Calzone.** Of the numerous cheap pizza joints around this neighborhood, this one is a cut above average (also serving many pastas and grills), and it's also a rather impressive two-level space. Expect to see a mix of gay party kids, college students, and other young folk. ✉ *Reguliersdwarsstraat 55,* ☎ *020/627–3833.*

$–$$ ✗ **Shiva.** One of the best bargains in the city, this popular Indian restaurant serves huge portions of outstanding food. Especially good is the chicken *tikka* (marinated chicken in a mildly sweet curry) and fluffy garlic nan bread. If you're in a rush, the efficient service will have you in and out fast. ✉ *Reguliersdwarsstraat 72,* ☎ *020/624–8713.*

$ ✗ **Backstage.** You simply need to walk by this riotously colorful café and lunchroom to earn a warm smile from the beguiling owners, Greg and Gary—twin brothers from Boston who have been a big hit in Amsterdam since they moved here many years ago. The dining area is decked with knit sweaters, hats, and gloves—a line of clothing created by the twins, all for sale. They serve sandwiches, coffees, teas, and other casual but filling dishes. Gary and Greg love to chat, so come willing to mingle. ✉ *Utrechtsedwarsstraat 67,* ☎ *020/622–3638.*

$ ✗ **Café Françoise.** A homey, sedate coffeehouse filled with Oriental carpets, art displays, and lounge furnishings, Françoise is one of the most dyke-popular spaces in the city, although all are welcome. The breakfasts are a strong point, with fresh-baked goods and jams, but lunch is also busy. Many women find that this is a spot more conducive for meeting new friends than most of the bars are; unfortunately, it's not open in the evening. ✉ *Kerkstraat 176,* ☎ *020/624–0145.*

$ ✗ **Coffee Co.** With the opening of this sleek tile-and-glass beanery on Leidsestraat, Amsterdam has its first genuine Seattle-style coffeehouse, complete with sacks of beans in the window and a full range of macchiatos, lattes, cappuccinos, and espressos. There's no food but for the rich brownies (not the hash variety), nor are there seats, but there is a counter to lean on. ✉ *Leidsestraat 60,* ☎ *020/421–6092.*

$ ✗ **Downtown.** Dishy queens yuck it up inside this upbeat two-tier lunchroom that's always packed with a stylish bunch. There's art displayed on the walls, in case the cute crowd and staff aren't enough of a distraction for you, plus magazines for your perusal. The sandwiches and salads are quite good, but the cakes and brownies are the top draw. ✉ *Reguliersdwarsstraat 31,* ☎ *020/622–9958.*

$ ✗ **Gary's Muffins.** A Los Angeles transplant opened this extremely successful minichain selling American-style muffins, sweets, and bagels. From the chocolate chip cookies to the fresh-baked muffins, there's plenty here to keep any U.S. expat or visitor happy. The bagels are offered with an array of delicious toppings, including goat cheese with walnuts and honey. The branch along gay-bar-infested Reguliersdwarsstraat is open late at night (the others close in the early evening). ✉ *Reguliersdwarsstraat 53,* ☎ *020/420–2406; Prinsen-*

gracht 454, ☏ *020/420–1452; Marnixstraat 121,* ☏ *020/ 638–0186. Jodenbreestraat 15,* ☏ *020/421–5930.*

$ ✕ **Le Monde.** Don't let the self-important name fool you: This longtime fixture overlooking the action of the Rembrandtplein is simple and snug, the food a mix of home-style Dutch, German, and French favorites. Turkey fillets with a brandy cream sauce and the traditional hutspot are typical. Breakfast is also a major to-do here. You'll see plenty of family. ✉ *Rembrandtplein 6,* ☏ *020/626–9922.*

$ ✕ **New York Pizza.** Say what you will about the rather depressing Americanization of Dutch culture, these by-the-slice, fast-food-style parlors serve damn good pizza. The trays of sliced pies (prepared with many toppings) in the humongous storefront window, mirrored self-service dining rooms, and a big electric sign with red, green, and white letters will make you think you're in Times Square. Best of all in a city whose eateries close early, it's open late. ✉ *Leidsestraat 23,* ☏ *020/ 622–8689; Damstraat 24,* ☏ *020/622–2123.*

$ ✕ **'t Balkje.** The Dutch equivalent of an American diner, this eatery is a snack bar on one side and more of a sit-down restaurant on the other. Chili con carne, coq au vin, and meatloaf typify the simple home-style fare. 't Balkje is steps from the gay bars along Kerkstraat and very busy late in the evening. ✉ *Kerkstraat 46–48,* ☏ *020/622–0566.*

Elsewhere

$$$$ ✕ **Le Garage.** Chef Joop Braakhekke is a household name among Dutch gourmands; he presides not only over this stark sophisticated dining room near the Concertgebouw but over his own TV cooking show. The see-and-be-seen set piles into this converted auto garage nightly for innovative New Dutch cooking and a sliver of glamour. Typical offerings include seared rare tuna steak in a pepper sauce, and a tender lamb shank served Moroccan-style on a bed of couscous and grilled vegetables. ✉ *Ruysdaelstraat 54,* ☏ *020/ 679–7176.*

$ ✕ **De Spijker Van Der Mei.** Grungiqueers, starving artists and musicians, lefty activists, and other scruffy souls fill this rustic café in de Pijp, right by the Albert Cuypmarkt. There's a decent menu of fresh salads and sandwiches, and good coffees and beers. ✉ *Ferdinand Bolstraat 24,* ☏ *020/671– 2395.*

$ ✕ **De Ysbreker.** With beautiful vaulted ceilings, tall Palladian windows, and a terrace overlooking the Amstel River, this is one of the most charming settings in Amsterdam, especially in warm weather. In the evening you might catch a show inside the small fringe theater behind the dining room. Light and healthful soups, sandwiches, and salads are on the menu; there's also a good selection of beers and coffees. ✉ *Weesperzijde 23,* ☎ *020/668–1805.*

$ ✗ **Kriterion.** Many departments of the University of Amsterdam are across the street from this lively café that's decorated with a mishmash of boho furnishings and attached to a funky cinema (you can always count on a young, intellectual, and chatty crowd). There's light food for both lunch and dinner, and many coffees, beers, cognacs, and whiskeys. ✉ *Roetersstraat 170,* ☎ *020/623–1708.*

$ ✗ **Vertigo.** The dining room and terrace attached to Amsterdam's Nederlands Filmmuseum overlooks Vondelpark and a serene duck pond. On any sunny afternoon you're likely to see plenty of same-sexers sipping beer and munching on light snacks while discussing the latest queer Dutch movie. ✉ *Vondelpark,* ☎ *020/589–1400.*

SCENES

Amsterdam's bar scene is amazingly compact and within a short walk of virtually every central tourist attraction, hotel, and restaurant. Intrepid bar-crawlers have little trouble hitting a dozen bars in one evening. The city has five main queer sections: **Kerkstraat** is the longest-running gay-bar area, with several fairly mellow bars and taverns. Nearby **Reguliersdwarsstraat** draws the trendy queers into a few beautifully decorated bars and discos. **Amstel** is famous for its festive sing-along bars and intimate *bruin cafes* (brown cafés, the Dutch term for an old-fashioned, smoke-stained, cozy pub)—the bars here have a warm neighborhoody feel. **Warmoesstraat** is the center of Amsterdam's leather scene. **The Jordaan** has very little in the way of specific gay nightlife but is a funky, hip neighborhood with many gay-friendly taverns and cafés, as well as the C.O.C. (the city's lesbian and gay community center).

Amsterdam's reputation for after-hours fetes is somewhat overrated. There are always a few on weekends, but the well-known ones charge anywhere from 25 to 50 guilders for a couple of hours of dancing with a drugged-out crowd. This may be fun if you yourself are strung out or desperate to keep the night alive, but most discos stay open till 5 or 6 anyway.

Partying beyond this hour is definitely on the decline. There are usually some sex parties after hours, too. These can be at most any venue. Best bet is to go to the Cockring and ask around as the bar is closing. With persistence you will latch on to a crowd.

Like many large cities, Amsterdam is a tourist haven on weekends. Many locals deplore the Saturday-night crowds and swear by weekday partying, which is less self-conscious, attititudy, and touristy. If you want to meet and know the Dutch, try hitting the clubs during the week. Most bars are open until 2 on weekdays, an hour later in summer, and also an hour later on weekends.

Kerkstraat

PRIME SUSPECTS

Cosmo Bar. When the other Kerkstraat and Reguliersdwarsstraat bars have closed, a diverse—and often aggressively cruisy—bunch piles into this salty cocktail bar open till 3 on weeknights and an hour later on weekends. ⌧ *Kerkstraat 42, ☏ 020/624–8074. Crowd: mostly male, mostly over 35 and local before midnight, all ages and types after that.*

De Spijker. "The Nail" opened in 1983 and was a fairly intense leather-and-Levis bar for many years before recently changing a bit. It now attracts a diverse mix of all ages and styles. It's big with the after-work set, then slows down before picking up steam again at about 10. A narrow, tightly packed bar with an extremely popular pool table is in back; upstairs leads to a tiny and only sporadically busy dark room (what Americans call a back room; *see* Action, *below,* for more about dark rooms), as well as some urinals backed by angled mirrors (which, of course, heightens their cruisiness). Two TV monitors hang side-by-side over the bar; one shows porn and the other typically airs cartoons—a great juxtaposition. A fireplace, extremely sweet and cute bartenders, and cool music (from alternative rock to old camp disco) add to the engaging ambience; also fun are the plaques around the bar labeling the de Spijker's exact distance from various international locales, from Tel Aviv to Marrakesh. Probably this bar's best attribute is its variety of offerings; a horny leather guy can find plenty to do here, and just as easily two dykes visiting from abroad will receive a warm welcome. ⌧ *Kerkstraat 4, ☏ 020/620–5919. Crowd: 80/20 m/f, all ages, guppies, leather men, grungers, regular guys (and gals).*

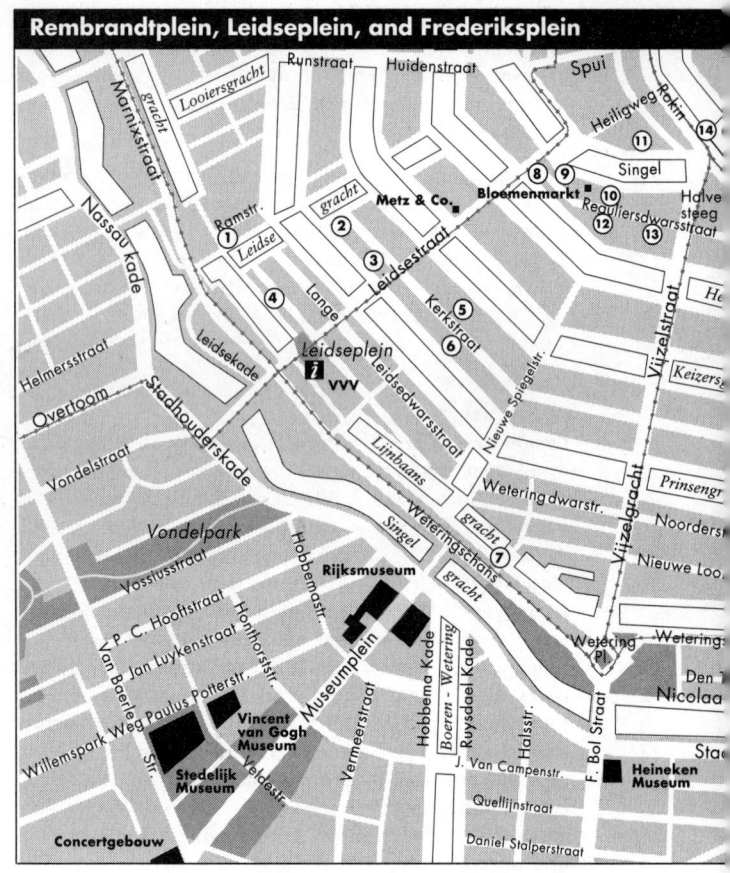

Rembrandtplein, Leidseplein, and Frederiksplein

Scenes ○
Amstel Taveerne, **16**
April, **10**
Boom Chicago, **4**
Cafe Entre Nous, **18**
Cafe Reality, **25**
Club Havana, **12**
Company, **23**
Cosmo Bar, **3**
Cupido, **27**
De Falck, **32**
De Spijker, **2**
De Steeg, **17**
Exit, **13**
Fellow's, **15**
Festival, **27**
Gaiety, **14**
Havana, **9**
iT, **30**
Krokodil, **31**
Le Shako, **20**
Mankind, **7**
Meia Meia, **5**
Milord, **22**
Monopole Taveerne, **21**
Montmartre, **19**
Music Box, **29**
The Otherside, **8**
The Roxy, **11**
Schiller, **24**
Thermos Day Sauna, **1**
Thermos Night Sauna, **6**
Vive-la-Vie, **26**

51

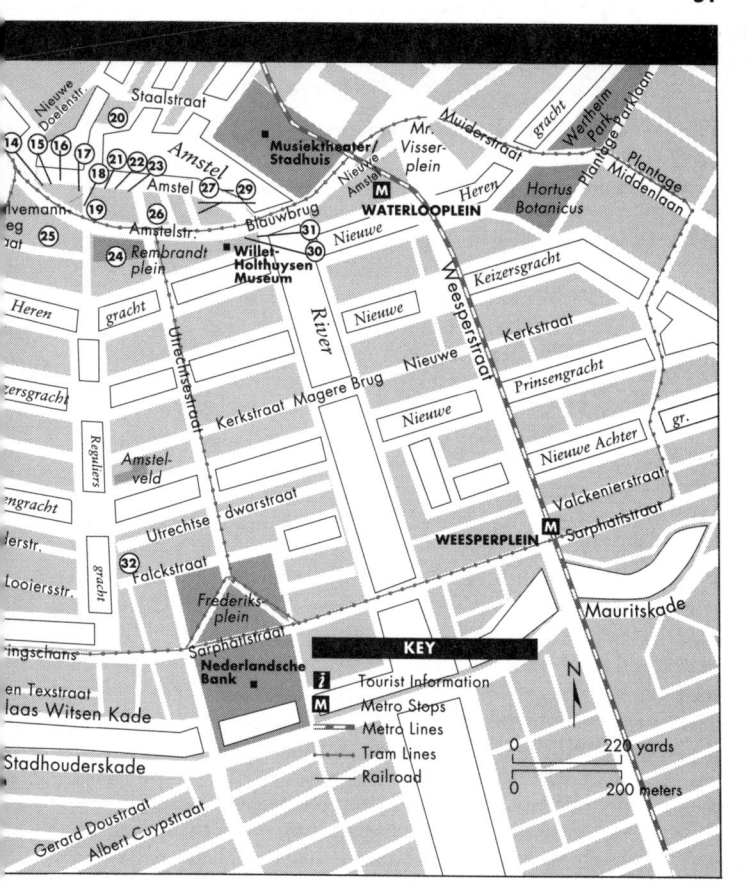

Map Labels

- Nieuwe Doelenstr.
- Staalstraat
- Amstel
- Muiderstraat
- gracht
- Wertheim Park
- Mr. Visserplein
- Plantage Parklaan
- Musiektheater/Stadhuis
- Nieuwe Amstel
- Heren
- Hortus Botanicus
- Plantage Middenlaan
- WATERLOOPLEIN
- Amstelstr.
- Blauwbrug
- Nieuwe
- Amstel
- Rembrandtplein
- Willet-Holthuysen Museum
- Keizersgracht
- Heren gracht
- Nieuwe
- Kerkstraat
- River
- Nieuwe
- Weesperstraat
- Prinsengracht
- zersgracht
- Reguliers
- Kerkstraat Magere Brug
- Nieuwe
- engracht
- Amstelveld
- Nieuwe Achter gr.
- Utrechtsestraat
- erstr.
- Looiersstr.
- dwarstraat
- Valckenierstraat
- WEESPERPLEIN
- Sarphatistraat
- Falckstraat
- gracht
- ingschans
- Frederiksplein
- Mauritskade
- en Texstraat
- Sarphatistraat
- laas Witsen Kade
- Nederlandsche Bank
- Stadhouderskade
- Gerard Doustraat
- Albert Cuypstraat

KEY

- 🛈 Tourist Information
- Ⓜ Metro Stops
- ▬▬ Metro Lines
- ┄┄ Tram Lines
- ─── Railroad

N

0 — 220 yards
0 — 200 meters

NEIGHBORHOOD HAUNTS

Meia Meia Lele (✉ Kerkstraat 63, ☏ 020/623–4129) is a friendly locals' bar, with plenty of nice guys of all ages.

Reguliersdwarsstraat

PRIME SUSPECTS

April. One of the most popular video and cruise bars in the Netherlands, April draws guppies, stylish students, stand-and-model boys, moneyed tourists, and pre-clubbers. The front half of the bar is dominated by a comfy lounge. Farther back is a central bar, beyond which steps lead into a pea soup–like haze of cigarette smoke. This section has a big circular bar that, believe it or not, rotates. Throughout the bar, the decor is postmodern and innovative, particularly the busy bathrooms. ✉ *Reguliersdwarsstraat 37,* ☏ *020/625–9572. Crowd: 85/15 m/f, mostly under 35, cute, slick, well dressed, a tad attitudy, international.*

Club Havana. The trendy Reguliersdwarsstraat bar strip's latest club, which opened its doors in late 1997, favors the postindustrial look of its neighbors. DJs and music styles alternate nightly, but you can always count on the latest Eurodance tunes. ✉ *Reguliersdwarsstraat 38,* ☏ *020/422–9836. Crowd: 80/20 m/f, young, hip.*

Exit. This and the new Club Havana are the most consistently popular gay discos in Amsterdam. The sizable and very slick warehouse-style Exit has a chrome bar in one room and a dance floor in the other; divas gravitate toward the small stage. The bar has plenty of seating and space for mingling, and although the music is typically loud and current, you can still carry on a conversation. Remember that you must tip Fl 1 when you leave the john; if you don't, you'll get a very cold stare, and probably a firm tap on the shoulder. On the plus side, Exit typically charges no cover. In case you're not in the mood for an intense disco scene, check out the comfy and extremely festive sing-along bar downstairs; this area gets a more diverse crowd, including more women. ✉ *Reguliersdwarsstraat 42,* ☏ *020/625–8788. Crowd: 75/25 m/f, mostly 20s and early 30s, mostly a mix of the guys from April and Havana.*

Havana. Amsterdam's other trendy cruise and cocktail bar, Havana is a snazzy place with two main bars filled with vaguely tropical furnishings. Stairs from one bar lead up to a small lounge with comfy rattan chairs, magazine racks, and a pool table. Stairs from the other bar lead up to the bathrooms, which are quite possibly the most artistic you'll find in the city; the urinals are painted with murals of naked men standing in a waterfall (fine inspiration should you need it). Beyond the bathrooms is another bar. ✉ *Reguliersdwarsstraat 17,* ☎ *020/620–6788. Crowd: 80/20 m/f, mostly 20s to early 30s, nicely dressed, guppies, lots of tourists, a touch of attitude.*

ONE-NIGHTERS AND MOVEABLE FETES

The Roxy. This elegant former cinema that's been converted into a chic disco with spacious balconies and a glitzy dance floor is always gay-friendly, and predominantly queer on Wednesday nights. There's also a major dyke party, Pussy-lounge, the third Sunday of every month. ✉ *Singel 465,* ☎ *020/620–0354. Crowd: identical to the crowd at Exit; very trendy, 75/25 m/f on Wed.; mostly straight other times, except for the dyke parties.*

The latest monthly mixed gay/straight event is **Trade,** a dance party imported from London and held at the usually hetero club **Time** (✉ Nieuwezijds Voorburgwal 163–165, ☎ 020/423–3792); it's on the third Sunday of each month.

Amstel

PRIME SUSPECTS

Amstel Taveerne. The quintessential queer bruin cafe, the Amstel Taveerne has been a center of the city's social scene for many decades, and is a must-do for anybody wishing for a candid glimpse into traditional Dutch gay culture. The old-fashioned interior is so infused with Dutch paraphernalia (beer steins, wooden shoes, a portrait of the royal family) to the point of high camp, and the decor of dark-wood beams and benches further imparts a warm and authentic ambience. The after-work set packs the place, and the bar often has sing-alongs. ✉ *Amstel 54,* ☎ *020/623–4254. Crowd: 80/20 m/f, all ages, extremely convivial, lots of rosy cheeks and warm smiles.*

Gaiety. Of the bars along the Amstel, most of which are old-fashioned and quaint, Gaiety is probably the trendiest, and also the most Americanized stylistically: Note the Disney prints, photo montage of New York City, and other fun touches. The decor is black and somewhat contemporary, the music quiet enough for conversation, and the crowd eclectic. In back is a typical selection of video games. ✉ *Amstel 14,* ☎ *020/624–4271. Crowd: mostly male; mix of students and older guys, locals and tourists; outgoing; flirtatious but not intensely cruisy.*

Le Shako. You might begin your bar tour of the Amstel section at this *gezellig* (a popular Dutch word with no direct English equivalent but that suggests equal parts coziness, warmth, and antiquity) bruin cafe with show posters on the walls (check out the smashing one of Marlene Dietrich) and a long bench against the wall that's ideal for lounging and ogling the diverse but mostly local crowd. Early in the evening you'll see some students and younger guys; as the night wears on, a more mature crowd moves in. It's the only one of the neighborhood's gay bars on the north side of the Amstel. ✉ *'s Gravelandseveer 2,* ☎ *020/624–0209. Crowd: mostly male, 20s to 50s, friendly, engaging, cheerful, down-to-earth.*

Monopole Taveerne. Inside the small gay budget hotel of the same name, this handsome bruin cafe on the Amstel River has pretty French doors opening onto the street and zillions of interesting posters and bills pasted to the walls. It's a classic chat bar, complete with outgoing bartenders and down-to-earth regulars. ✉ *Amstel 60,* ☎ *020/624–6451. Crowd: mostly male, mostly 35 and older, mellow, friendly, and unpretentious.*

Montmartre. With danceable Dutch (and other European) pop tunes blaring in the background, this quaint and busy sing-along tavern feels as though it was air-lifted from Paris and dropped onto the edge of the Rembrandtplein. If there's any drawback, it's that most people come here with friends, which makes it a little difficult to meet anyone if you're an outsider. The staff is friendly and helpful, however. A uniquely Dutch (or at least Western European) experience. Also cabaret shows some nights. ✉ *Halvemaansteeg 17,* ☎ *020/624–9216. Crowd: 70/30 m/f, mostly 20s and 30s, mix of locals and French or Belgian expats, energetic and upbeat, not cruisy, zero attitude.*

ONE-NIGHTERS AND MOVEABLE FETES

Once the internationally acclaimed domain of a late queer-club promoter (and megalomaniac) named Manfred Langer, **iT** (✉ Amstelstraat 24, ☎ 020/625–0111), which is gay only on Saturday nights, has devolved into a touristy, snotty, and overrated bastion of Eurotrashiness. Few locals bother with it, and outsiders are often turned away (the door policy is members only, which is enforced according to the mood of the doorman). Two final complaints: outlandishly high cover charges and an alleged anti-lesbian bias, except when there's a specific lesbian event being held here. It's definitely an interesting space, and one of the largest dance venues in Amsterdam—particularly impressive are the light shows. But you're more likely to have fun at the other big discos.

NEIGHBORHOOD HAUNTS

Cafe Entre Nous (✉ Halvemaansteeg 14, ☎ 020/623–1700) is a sing-songy bruin cafe along festive Halvemaansteeg; as with Montmartre, plenty of women and straights hang out here with the guys. Although it's on Reguliersdwarsstraat, **Cafe Reality** (✉ Reguliersdwarsstraat 129, ☎ 020/639–3012), a casual tavern, is close to the Rembrandtplein and Amstel bars. Tom of Finland art and red mining lights lend a lusty mood to **Company** (✉ Amstel 106, ☎ 020/625–3028), the one leather bar (although plenty of nonleather creatures hang here, too) outside of Warmoesstraat. **De Steeg** (✉ Halvemaansteeg 10, ☎ 020/620–0171) is a small but intensely loud, cruisy, and fun locals' hangout with a fabulous spinning strobe light up front and provocative framed photos lining the walls—the crowd is mostly male, but women are quite welcome. **Fellow's** (✉ Amstel 50, ☎ 020/622–5202) is a laid-back lounge with friendly bartenders. Chickens and chicken-hawks tend to frequent the old **Krokodil** (✉ Amstelstraat 34, ☎ 020/626–2243), a pleasantly lascivious tavern on Amstelstraat, midway between Rembrandtplein and Waterlooplein; it's jam-packed for happy hour sing-alongs and drink specials, between 5 and 7. **Milord** (✉ Amstel 102, ☎ 020/622–8335) is a tiny old tavern overlooking the river, with a mature, mixed male-female crowd.

A few steps east of the Rembrandtplein, there are four queer hustler bars in a row along **Paardenstraat,** with one straight one, appropriately named Adam and Eve, interrupting the pink streak. All these bars are loud, raucous, and more or less interchangeable, but **Festival** (✉ Paardenstraat 15, ☎ 020/623–1217) is the most popular. The others are **Cupido** (✉ Paardenstraat 7, ☎ 020/622–1789), and the **Music Box** (✉ Paardenstraat 9, ☎ 020/620–4110).

HANGIN' WITH THE HETS

For a glimpse into the city's thriving literary-café society, drop by **Schiller** (✉ Rembrandtplein 26, ☎ 020/624–9846), a swank slice of erudite gentility overlooking the otherwise touristy Rembrandtplein. By day this place is relatively subdued and filled with arch students and culture vultures; when the sun sets, the music blares and the mood turns more festive. It's not gay per se, but you'll usually spot plenty of family in here. The well-preserved art deco interior makes it a good destination for architectural buffs.

Warmoesstraat

PRIME SUSPECTS

Argos. One of the oldest leather bars in the city, the Argos has helped maintain the sleazy and sexy mood of infamous Warmoesstraat. It's not as popular with younger guys anymore, but no self-respecting leather aficionado should visit Amsterdam without checking this place out. If you're lucky (and reasonably good looking), you'll be asked to one of the club's notorious (invitation-only) sex parties. If not, take heart—there's plenty of action to be had in the dark room, and if you meet somebody interesting, you can whisk him off to one of the cabins, one of which is outfitted with S/M gear. ✉ *Warmoesstraat 95,* ☎ *020/622–6595. Crowd: male, mostly 30s to 50s, butch and lethal looking, leather, uniforms, very hard-core, aggressively cruisy, glaring and staring.*

Casa Maria. This is a good spot to begin your Warmoesstraat bar crawl. The staff is friendly, the crowd easygoing, and the space pleasantly decorated and lined with big windows ideal for watching the nightly parade of leather men rumble by. The popularity of the bars in this neighborhood shifts from season to season, but you can easily pick up some up-to-the-minute advice from the folks here. ✉ *Warmoesstraat 60,* ☎ *020/627–6848. Crowd: mostly male, mostly 30s to 50s, plenty of leather and uniforms but all are welcome.*

Cockring. Amsterdam's quintessential sleaze disco is hot, hazy, and horny. Everybody here is bumped up on something, especially late at night. As you enter, you'll find a small industrial-theme dance floor in the basement, which also has a bar; exposed metal pipes and chain-linking help set the tone. From here, stairs lead up to the main bar, which is brightly lighted and filled with stools and benches, video monitors with porn, and nooks and crannies ideal for making new friends. This room is a major meat market; a small door leads into one of the city's most popular dark rooms (which you can also access via a narrow twisting stairwell that leads conveniently from the bathroom, which is off the rear stairway landing between the bars' two levels). The dark room is tiny, and men are packed in here like sardines on weekend evenings; watch your wallet and pay attention to what (and who) you're doing in here. For a true Amsterdam nightlife experience, this club shouldn't be missed. But bear in mind that it's not a particularly easy place to meet the locals—other than whatever brief encounters you happen upon. The crowd is very intense and somewhat attitudy, although the staff is surprisingly friendly for such a rough place. A note to drag queens: It's not advisable to walk along the Warmoesstraat north of the Cockring. ✉ *Warmoesstraat 96*, ☎ *020/623-9604. Crowd: male, mostly 20s and 30s, more leather early, a wasted blur of club kids, glam queens, horn dogs, and wired revelers later in the evening (and morning); very intense and muscle-centric.*

Stablemaster. It's fairly difficult to see anything in this pitch-black leather club on the ground floor of the rowdy gay hotel of the same name, but fumble your way through the crowds and you'll get a fairly good sense of what it's all about. This is possibly Amsterdam's most tactile bar; it's famous for its jack-off parties held weekend evenings from about midnight till 2. Leather, rubber, and black denim are the expected attire, and they can be strict about this depending on the night and who's working the door. Not a good place to lose your contact lens on the floor. ✉ *Warmoesstraat 23*, ☎ *020/625-0148. Crowd: male, mostly 30s and 40s, beefy, kinky, rough, and ready.*

The Web. This place is incredibly packed some nights and always quite cruisy, when it draws a mix of leather guys and curious onlookers. There are a few levels, including a main bar, a busy upstairs dark room, and without question its greatest attribute, a small roof garden with great views of the City Center. Leather and denim are encouraged, but unless you're wearing something dressy or quite preppy, they'll let you in. ✉ *St. Jacobsstraat 6*, ☎ *020/623-6758. Crowd: male, 20s to 40s, butch, lots of leather, denim, some uniforms, on the make.*

NEIGHBORHOOD HAUNTS

Other leather options in this district include **Club Jaecques** (✉ Warmoesstraat 93, ☎ 020/622-0323), a small and packed bar that's one of the most hard-core along this stretch; **Dirty Dicks** (✉ Warmoesstraat 86, ☎ 020/627-8634), where the name pretty much sizes up the clientele; and the **Eagle Amsterdam** (✉ Warmoesstraat 90, ☎ 020/623-6758), the McDonald's of leather bars.

The Jordaan

PRIME SUSPECTS

C.O.C. The parties and various social activities at Amsterdam's gay and lesbian community center are among the best-attended events in the city, and although they tend to draw more locals than tourists, everyone is welcome. Over the past two years, the main disco at the C.O.C. has been geared more for men on Friday nights and women on Saturdays. The crowd is mixed on Sundays for the "Arabian Disco," which was begun chiefly as a way to provide a safe and comfortable social space for the many young queer immigrants or children of immigrants who often lack acceptance and tolerance in their own ethnic communities. Gay Turks, in particular, have a difficult time finding support among their fellow immigrants. In addition to the main disco, which is on the top floor of this creaky cavernous old building and is typically only open from Friday to Sunday, the C.O.C. has two cozy lounges downstairs. Depending on the night, these two spaces host underage-26 events, queer senior gatherings, games nights, high teas, and other lively events, some geared to specific groups and others open to the general homopublic. On Friday and Saturday nights the disco doesn't really get purring until midnight; on Sundays, the Arabian Disco commences at 8 PM. Many of the folks who attend this event move on to de Trut (*see below*) around 11 PM. ✉ *Rozenstraat 14, ☏ 020/623–4079. Crowd: depends on the event.*

NEIGHBORHOOD HAUNTS

Any day of the week you'll find a spirited crowd of closet cabaret singers crooning at **de Twee Zwaantjes** (✉ Prinsengracht 114, ☏ 020/625–2729), a cozy mixed bar on the edge of the Jordaan; Sundays, however, are gayest (the blaring opera music may have something to do with this).

Elsewhere

PRIME SUSPECTS

Mankind. One of the most attractive and friendly of Amsterdam's many intimate chat bars, Mankind is one of the only queer options near the Rijksmuseum and Vondelpark. The small bar is cozy and colorful; postcards decorate the ceiling, the bar has an elegant copper top, and tables have candles on them. There are plenty of diversions, from staring out at the pretty canal to browsing the magazine rack; you can also order snacks (pizza, sandwiches). ✉ *Weteringstraat 60, ☏ 020/638–*

4755. Crowd: 80/20 m/f, mostly over 35, a few suits after work, laid-back, fairly local.

ONE-NIGHTERS AND MOVEABLE FETES

De Trut. This Sunday-night queer get-together began several years ago in a squat about 15 minutes by foot from the Leidseplein; it's volunteer-run and thus the drinks are cheap and the mood distinctly noncommercial and fun. The music tends toward cutting-edge trance, techno, and such. The space is tiny and absolutely packed, so much so that the door-minders stop allowing people in at around midnight—the doors open at 10 and if you don't arrive by 11:30 you might not get in. At around 2 or 2:30 in the morning, enough patrons will have left to allow new guests inside. For a lot of Amsterdammers, many of them tired of the usual bar scene, this is a must-do. ✉ *Bilderdijkstraat 165, 020/612-3524. Crowd: 65/35 m/f, mostly gay, mostly under 30, spicy, shabby-chic, funky, groovy, alternative, pierced, perverse.*

NEIGHBORHOOD HAUNTS

A cheerful bruin cafe near Frederiksplein with a chandelier and comfy seats and tables, **De Falck** (✉ Falckstraat 3, ☎ 020/624–7532) is a nice spot for a beer before heading over to nearby Utrechtsestraat for dinner or shopping; the crowd is mostly gay. **Doll's Place** (✉ Vinkenstraat 57, ☎ 020/627–0790), north of the Joordan, is a sleepy semi-hustler bar with a very local following.

HANGIN' WITH THE HETS

It's not gay, but **Boom Chicago** (✉ Korte Leidsedwarsstraat 12, ☎ 020/422–1776), a comedy-improv dinner theater whose performers are mostly American expats, is usually a hit among visitors from all over.

Women's Amsterdam

For such a queer city, Amsterdam has nowhere near as many lesbian venues as gay male venues. To make matters worse, only a handful of the guys' bars have a significant women's following. Of those establishments reviewed above, the following draw a visible number of women (although not necessarily dykes): Amstel Taveerne, April, Cafe Entre Nous, the C.O.C. (especially on Saturday nights), Havana, iT, Montmartre, the Roxy (especially the third Sunday of every month), Schiller, de Spijker, de Steeg, de Trut (on Sundays), and de Twee Schwaantjes.

PRIME SUSPECTS

Saarein. Although it's a women's bar and not a lesbian bar per se, most of the crowd is queer at this two-level bruin cafe with a strong following among feminists, activists, squatters, and others with progressive political leanings. Many of the women here know each other, but the staff is knowledgeable about local women's resources. The main level has a bar and seating; downstairs is more of a rec room with games, a pool table, and other diversions. Men are not permitted, even as guests. ✉ *Elandstraat 119,* ☎ *020/623–4901. Crowd: female, mostly lesbian, mostly under 20s to 40s, fairly hardcore politically, not necessarily butch but definitely not lipstick, not cruisy, somewhat cliquey.*

Vive-la-Vie. The city's main lesbian disco is just off the Rembrandtplein, near the gay-bar strip along the Amstel. Spacious and nicely decorated, it's divided into two parts, one for lounging and mingling, the other for dancing and cabaret. The front section is packed almost every night; the entire place fills up on weekends. Owner Mieke Martelhof is also a local club promoter; watch for her parties (they're sometimes held across the street at iT). Men are in the minority but quite welcome. ✉ *Amstelstraat 7,* ☎ *020/624–0114. Crowd: mostly female, all ages, fairly diverse in look and background, very friendly, somewhat cruisy.*

ONE-NIGHTERS AND MOVEABLE FETES

Much of Amsterdam's dyke nightlife centers around roving, often one-time-only events and parties held throughout the city. There's no central number you can call for this information, although the **Gay and Lesbian Switchboard** (*see* The Little Black Book, *below*) can sometimes offer advice. It's best to check for posters or fliers in the gay periodicals—**Queerfish** (*see* Gay Media *in* The Little Black Book, *below*) is the best source of such happenings. Also drop by the **C.O.C.** (*see above*); **Café Françoise** (*see* Eats, *above*), the main lesbian coffeehouse; the lesbigay or women's bookstores (*see* Bookstores *in* The Little Black Book, *below*); or either of the two women's bars reviewed above—you can often find information there. The hip Warmoesstraat restaurant, **Getto** (*see* Eats, *above*) has a women's night on Tuesdays that draws a hot crowd of lipstick lesbos. Cocktails are served from 5 to 7, with food available after that.

EROTICA AND TOYS

Female & Partners (✉ Spuistraat 100, ☎ 020/620-9152) is one of the best women's erotica shops in Europe, with a vast selection of lingerie, vibrators, and sexy stuff, and a helpful staff to show you the ropes (and whips, and chains . . .).

Alternative Culture

Amsterdam's queer scene has its own subculture, one that tends to cross both gender and sexual orientation. To this extent, several mostly straight or mixed alternative clubs have a strong following among young queers.

SQUATS AND ALTERNATIVE CAFÉS

Squats have long played a role in the gay-rights movement of Amsterdam, as they have acted as a symbol of many forms of activism. The movement dates from the early '70s, when the city faced a housing shortage brought on largely by the influx of refugees from Surinam (the last of the Dutch colonies to become independent). City planners in Amsterdam sought to solve this crisis by ripping up historic neighborhoods and building grim low-income housing projects. Greed-driven real estate speculation ran rampant as the government began buying out swaths of the city. Disgusted with the turn Amsterdam had taken, and also provoked by the injustices of capitalism; the war in Vietnam; issues of race, gender, and sexual orientation; and a hornet's nest of other concerns, some activists began illegally taking over buildings that had been dormant for long periods of time. Throughout the '70s and early '80s, this activity grew to the point of chaos, as authorities used increasingly violent and confrontational means to evict the squatters. (The City Center Holiday Inn was built in 1984 on the site of one of the last important squats, Wyers, which was torn down after months of violent fighting.) Although the role of squats has diminished some over the years, it's worth realizing that many of today's clubs, cafés, and gay-friendly businesses originated as squats.

There are dozens of funky hangouts all over the city; many of the best are listed in the magazine **Trout** (*see* Gay Media *in* The Little Black Book, *below*). A few popular options include **Bar Lac** (✉ Haarlemmerstraat 118, ☎ 020/624-4265), a handsome art deco space that's fashioned out of an old bank; **Cafe de Pels** (✉ Huidenstraat 25, ☎ 020/622-9037), a convivial bruin cafe with a trendy following.

MUSIC AND PERFORMANCE

On Sunday afternoons, the devotees of Amsterdam's artistic fringe check out the doings at **Christina's Wet Dream** (⊠ at the Kasbah, Amstelveenseweg 134, ☏ 020/671–7778), a queer café and performance space. Events typically challenge convention in as many ways as possible, and often have a participatory component.

Look especially for events at **Arena** (⊠ 's Gravesandestraat 51, ☏ 020/694–7362), which is part of the budget hotel compound of the same name (*see* Sleeps, *below*) and draws plenty of alternative rockers—the parties are held in a formal sanctuary of a convent; **Escape** (⊠ Rembrandtplein 11, ☏ 020/622–1111), a massive disco on Rembrandtplein that's reasonably gay-friendly; **de Melkweg** (⊠ Milky Way; Lijnbaansgracht 234A, ☏ 020/624–1777), a famed multimedia space with a theater, cinemas, dance spaces, and all sorts of innovative and often gay-popular events (it's inside a former dairy, in case you're wondering about the name); **Paradiso** (⊠ Weteringschans 6–8, ☏ 020/623–7348), which hosts everything from experimental performance art to modern rock; and **Vrankrijk** (⊠ Spuistraat 216, no phone), a long-running squat with live music, politically charged performance art, and other goings-on, often of interest to the queer community. Both de Melkweg (which helped launch the careers of such luminaries as Laurie Anderson and David Bowie) and Paradiso were centers of Amsterdam's hippie movement during the '60s, and they retain an enlightened and society-challenging mission to this day.

COFFEE SHOPS

In Amsterdam, any bar selling pot and hash (and usually not beer or other alcoholic drinks) is given the charmingly euphemistic term "coffee shop." In some cases, you can't even buy coffee at these establishments. The police turn a blind eye to these operations, although contrary to popular belief, the sale of marijuana is not technically legal. Rather, the government focuses its energy on combating hard-core drug use and dealing, and lets these small-time businesses operate as long as they comply with a few local regulations. What you can purchase in these shops are quantities of pot or hash suitable for personal consumption; you're supposed to smoke or eat (in the form of "space cakes" and cookies) whatever you purchase on site. In 1997 the government began allowing these shops to depict marijuana leaves on their windows or logos, but they still must refrain from explicitly calling attention to the fact that they sell drugs. As you walk down the street, you can usually figure out which coffee shops exist to sell pot and hash, and which are legitimately cafés; reggae blasting out the front door and Jamaican flags draped above them are typical "coffee shop" cues.

Few locals spend their time smoking hash in coffee shops, as the novelty is lost on anybody who has lived in Amsterdam for significant chunk of time. Visitors who have never used pot or hash before are often advised by those in the know to consider avoiding the hash-laced brownies and cookies until they feel comfortable with the establishment in question. These innocuous-seeming baked goods are often very potent, and customers have no way of knowing how much hash has been folded into each brownie until they've eaten a few— but by then it may be too late. Prevailing local wisdom is to buy joints and always ask for advice from the staff.

The gay-popular coffee shops in Amsterdam, include **Het Wonder** (✉ Huidenstraat 13, ☏ 020/639–1032) and **The Otherside** (✉ Reguliersdwarsstraat 6, ☏ 020/625–5141).

Action

DARK ROOMS

There is no stigma associated with seeking anonymous sex in Amsterdam. This is not to suggest that the majority of queers in the Netherlands have multiple partners and spend their evenings in dark rooms and sex clubs. In fact, most of the city's sex business is derived from tourists. But it is safe to say that those in the Dutch gay community discuss cruising, dark rooms, pornography, and to a lesser degree prostitution freely and without passing judgment.

Visiting one of the many clubs or bars in Amsterdam with dark rooms is probably the easiest way to become acquainted with the city's seamy side. Clubs go to varying lengths to ensure the safety of dark rooms; all are required to provide safe-sex supplies and enforce safe-sex measures, but not every club seems equally concerned with this practice. It's important to assess the situation yourself before slipping in to one of these rooms; always place your wallet and watch some place secure (leave any valuables back in your hotel room). And if you've been drinking or doing drugs, think very seriously about whether you possess the judgment and control to conduct investigations safely and smartly. Dark rooms can be plenty of fun if you're in the right mood, but they're not without their risks.

All of the major clubs with dark rooms are geared toward men; however, many of the roving dyke parties (*see* Women's Amsterdam, *above*) have begun to introduce dark rooms and cruisy areas, so far with great success.

Popular bars with busy dark rooms include just about all the bars near or on Warmoesstraat, most notably Argos, the Cockring, and the Web. Also, on Kerkstraat, de Spijker has a somewhat busy dark room. Probably the most popular venue in the city is the **Cuckoo's Nest** (✉ Nieuwezijds Kolk 6, ☎ 020/627–1752), which is just off of Nieuwezijds Voorburgwal, across from the Intel Hotel. There are safe-sex-goods dispensers at the bar, and the crowd tends toward leather and Levi's, but all kinds of horny guys frequent this place.

SAUNAS

Some visitors are surprised by the fact that Amsterdam has only two major saunas, and because they're operated by the same owners and each is open when the other is closed, they draw pretty much the same crowd. The **Thermos Night Sauna** (✉ Kerkstraat 58–60, ☎ 020/623–4936) is somewhat busier than its counterpart, **Thermos Day Sauna** (✉ Raamstraat 33, ☎ 020/623–9158), which is nearby. On weekends, the Night sauna really gets going, and getting a private room can be near impossible unless you arrive as it opens. Both places have plunge pools, steam rooms, small gyms, and private rooms. The Night sauna is open daily 11 PM–8 AM; the Day sauna is open weekdays noon–11 PM, weekends noon–10 PM.

ROVING PARTIES

Many of the most popular sleaze parties are one-time or semi-regular affairs held at various locations. These go by different names, such as Trash and Cellar, and change venues often, but the hottest ones have been held at a space called the **Factory.** Many of them require, or at least encourage, leather or uniform attire; others don't. Several businesses regularly sell advance (as opposed to more expensive at-the-door) tickets and distribute information to these events. Check with the leather shops Mr. B, Black Body, and RoB; the sex shop, The Bronx; the gay gym, Mandate; or the C.O.C.

PROSTITUTION

Amsterdam's small but thriving gay Red-Light District is centered around the northern end of **Spuistraat** and **Nieuwezijds Voorburgwal.** Prostitution in the Netherlands, like the use of marijuana, is a slightly confusing topic: It's not officially legal (in other words you will not find a written law sanctioning this activity). However, the government and law enforcement agencies have collectively agreed to turn a blind eye and concentrate their efforts on what are considered more serious societal problems, such as hard-core drug use, violent crime, child pornography, and the like.

The Dutch tax brothels and have instituted health programs for sex-industry employees. The majority of the city's prostitutes (particularly those that advertise regularly in the major newspapers) receive weekly physicals, STD testing, and other sorts of counseling, and are also members of their own trade union. Obviously, this system has its flaws; both underage prostitution (the age of consent for both straight and gay sex is 16) and drug use remain major problems. The spread of such diseases as AIDS, however, has been fought more successfully in the Netherlands than in most other countries, and many observers attribute this to the aboveboard manner in which society treats casual sex (for hire and otherwise).

There are several popular gay-male escort services and bordellos; all of the following advertise regularly in the major gay newspapers. Virtually every service works the word "boy" into its title. Although employees of these operations are not actually under the legal age of 16 (they are required to prove their age before gaining employment), many of them are in their late teens (and those who aren't usually started out as teens). They tend to come from Turkey, Poland, Romania and other nations; in many cases they've fled abusive or unsupportive homes or communities with hopes of finding a better world in Amsterdam.

If you're interested in learning more about prostitution in Amsterdam, consider first contacting **SAD-Schorer Stichting** (✉ P.C. Hofstraat 5, ☎ 020/662–4206; also walk-in consultation clinic at Groenburgwal 44), a lesbigay health referral and counseling service. This is a helpful and nonjudgmental gay health advocate, where you can get direct and honest advice on this topic.

The city has two popular male brothels. **Boys Club 21** (✉ Spuistraat 21, ☎ 020/622–8828) has strip shows and a cocktail bar where you can chat with the employees. **Club Boys for Men** (✉ Spuistraat 44b, ☎ 020/638–1512) proudly advertises that it's just a 10-minute walk from Centraal Station, thus conjuring up images of men training into Amsterdam and speed-walking to a quick tryst. The club's ad also notes that the "boys (are) under medical control," which probably means something far more benign than it sounds. A bonus here is that you can rent out the S/M cellar. Two well-known escort services (which means their employees make out calls only) are **Michael's Boys Escort** (☎ 020/618–1824) and **People Male Escorts** (☎ 020/662–9990). A newcomer to the scene is **High Heels** (☎ 020/670–0046), which, as the name hints, specializes in drag escorts.

CINEMAS

Amsterdam has dozens of erotic movie cinemas; most of them sell day passes, which entitle the bearer to unlimited in-and-out privileges for the day's duration. One local favorite is **Adonis** (✉ Warmoesstraat 92, ☎ 020/627–2959), which has video chambers, a dark room, a movie theater, and a bookshop. **Man to Man** (✉ Spuistraat 21, ☎ 020/625–8797), another busy venue, has two cinemas, one generally showing butch and leather-type films, and the other showing movies with younger guys in them.

SEX SHOPS

If you're thinking about purchasing pornography in the Netherlands, remember a few important things. Although it's legal to sell material depicting sex between persons over 16 in the Netherlands, this material is illegal in many other countries. Laws about what publications may or may not depict and the age of the models pictured vary greatly, and should you attempt to return home with pornography that's illegal in your nation (regardless of whether you purchased it legally in Amsterdam), you may have the material confiscated, and you may be detained. If you're buying videotapes, remember that video players vary from country to country; before you buy, ask a staff person whether the tape you want will be compatible with your VCR at home.

As with sex cinemas, there are many sources of erotica and sex toys throughout the city. Many of them are straight-oriented, which is not to say they aren't gay-friendly but only that most of the erotica is heterosexually themed. Women should check out **Female & Partners** (*see* Women's Amsterdam, *above*). Three popular options for men are **The Bronx** (✉ Kerkstraat 53–55, ☎ 020/623-1548), a clean, well-lighted place with video booths and a nice selection of videos, magazines, and toys; and **Drake's** (✉ Damrak 61, ☎ 020/627-9544), a Dutch outpost of the Los Angeles–based chain of gay porn parlors. Also try the gay bookstore, **Intermale** (*see* Bookstores *in* The Little Black Book, *below*), and **Adonis** cinema (*see above*), which is along Warmoesstraat, site of several other queer sex shops.

LEATHER SHOPS

If you're looking for the latest in leather, uniforms, and other fetish wear, you've definitely come to the right city. Amsterdam has several excellent sources of leather wear, many of them also selling sex toys and accessories. **Mr. B** (✉ Warmoesstraat 89, ☎ 020/422-0003) has a huge selection of apparel and accessories; they also have information and/or sell tickets to a number of sex-and-dance parties (after-hours and otherwise) throughout the city. Even if you're not into leather, consider the fine selection of sex supplies and gay books—mostly erotica, and books on leather and S/M. Nearby and just opposite the Stablemaster Bar, **Master Leathers** (✉ Warmoesstraat 32, ☎ 020/624-5573) carries more of the same.

Elsewhere in the city, **RoB** (✉ Weteringshans 253, ☎ 020/625-4686) is a leather outfitter near the Frederiksplein; **Robin and Rik** (✉ Runstraat 30, ☎ 020/627-8924) is a stylish leather boutique on the edge of the Jordaan; and **Black Body** (✉ Lijnbaansgracht 292, ☎ 020/626-2553), close to the Rijksmuseum, is a sleek industrial space that emphasizes fetish and S/M wear and accessories.

CRUISY AREAS

Cruising is less popular among gays in Amsterdam than it once was; it's definitely less tolerated by authorities. There has not been a severe crackdown on this activity, but the layout of the cruisy section of **Amsterdamse Bos** (Amsterdam Woods), an expansive park south of the city, was recently altered so that there are fewer secluded nooks and hidden areas. Furthermore, as it's so easy to find sex in dark rooms, clubs, and saunas in Amsterdam the need to cruise here is largely absent.

On the other hand, Amsterdam's a very cruisy city in terms of pedestrians checking each other out and smiling; it's not terribly difficult to meet cute locals this way. Just be careful that you're not flattened by a speeding bicycle—or a tram for that matter—while winking at comely passersby. In warm weather the mood is ideal for checking out the crowds; best bets are the **Rembrandtplein** and **Leidseplein,** although the latter has become decreasingly queer over the past couple of decades. There's always plenty of people-watching in **Vondelpark**, and **Oosterpark** (which can be very dicey at night) gets its share of down-and-dirty cruisers. Probably the most infamous cruise ground in the entire country is **Amsterdamse Bos.**

SLEEPS

Amsterdam has a great variety of hotel and guest rooms in every price category. However, as many rooms as there are, it can be difficult to find one from Easter on through the summer, so book as far in advance as you can. No matter what you pay, you can expect spotless rooms and such modern conveniences as phones and TVs. At most hotels you're assured a private bath, although quite a few budget properties offer rooms with shared baths at a discount. All the city's major attractions, dining, and gay nightlife are close to the city center (inside or near the Singelgracht), which is where you'll also find the bulk of accommodations. Most every hotel welcomes lesbians and gays, and quite a few cater predominantly to gay travelers. It's unlawful for any hotel to turn away same-sex couples, and it's rare that gays and lesbians will ever encounter so much as a raised eyebrow. Gay-oriented places are typically small (between 10 and 25 rooms) and modest, with reasonable rates and atmospheres ranging from social and sleazy to quiet and cozy.

Many of the city's hotels are close to the Centraal Station, which is a desirable spot for sightseeing and convenient to getting in and out of the city, but is a relatively long walk (20 minutes) from all of the gay nightlife, except for the leather bars along Warmoesstraat. It's also a busy and rather dull part of the city. The best location is around the Leidseplein, which is a bit of a haul from Centraal Station (a 25-minute walk) but close to gay bars, restaurants, music and theater venues, Vondelpark, and several of the major attractions, including the Rijksmuseum—the closer you can stay to the

Sleeps

Leidseplein, the better. There's also inexpensive hourly bus service to and from the Leidseplein and Schiphol (*see* Getting Around, *above*); a ride takes about 30 minutes; buses only come once an hour. Another great area with a few hotels is the area of the city between Dam Square and the Jordaan—most of these properties are along the three scenic tree-shaded canals, Herengracht, Keizersgracht, and Prinsengracht.

For price ranges, *see* lodging Chart A at the front of this guide.

Apartment and Houseboat Rentals

An ideal option if you're planning to stay in Amsterdam for a week or more, and an excellent alternative to hotels, is the gay-friendly **Amsterdam House** (✉ Amstel 176a, 1017 AE, ☎ 020/626–2577, FAX 020/626–2987; ☎ 904/677–5370 in the U.S. or 800/618–1008, FAX 904/672–6659), which rents out 35 apartments and 10 houseboats, all of them complete with kitchens, baths, direct phones, stereos, cable TV, and, on request, many business services (such as fax, photocopiers, etc.). These are nicely furnished places that are often ideal for friends or two couples traveling together; they come in many configurations and sizes. Rates range from about Fl 150 to Fl 400 nightly. There's also a fine predominantly gay rental service, **Centre Apartments Amsterdam** (✉ Heintje Hoekssteeg 27, 1012 GR, ☎ 020/627–2503, FAX 020/625–1108). This consists of about 15 apartments (three-night minimum) and are about Fl 150 to Fl 250 nightly. The apartments are near Centraal Station and are very well outfitted, many with stereos and VCRs.

Hotels

$$$$ **Amstel Inter-Continental.** There are few hotels more impressive in appearance than this 1867 grande dame on the banks of the Amstel River, a 15-minute walk from the city center. The entire hotel underwent a sumptuous renovation in 1992 by Parisian designer Pierre Yves Rochon. With their Oriental rugs, brocade upholstery, and Delft lamps, the lavish rooms, the most spacious in Amsterdam, definitely recall an earlier era. You're unlikely to complain about the intrusion of the modern world: CD players, fax machines, and VCRs are all standard amenities. The service is top-notch if somewhat stuffy; the pool and health club are out of this world.

✉ *Prof. Tulpplein 1, 1018 GX,* ☎ *020/622–6060,* FAX *020/622–5808. 100 rooms. Restaurant, pool, health club.*

$$$$ **Grand Amsterdam.** On the site of Amsterdam's medieval town hall, this dramatic old property incorporates a number of buildings dating from the 16th century. It has hosted numerous stars and dignitaries, and was the site of Queen Beatrix's wedding. Some rooms overlook a charming old garden courtyard. Each is attractively filled with prize furnishings. It's steps from Centraal Station. Art lovers take note: Among the decorations in the public areas are Jugendstil stained-glass windows and, in the café, a mural by Dutch abstract expressionist Karl Appel, painted to repay a debt to the city. ✉ *Oudezijds Voorburgwal 197, 1012 EX,* ☎ *020/555–3111,* FAX *020/555–3222. 182 rooms. 2 restaurants, pool, health club.*

$$$$ **Hotel de l'Europe.** Built in 1895 and extensively renovated 100 years later, the majestic structure overlooking the flower market and the Amstel River is not only centrally located but also is one of the most elegant hotels in Western Europe. Service is refined but unstuffy. Riverside rooms have French doors that open onto balconies; all have marble baths. For a special occasion, you won't find more romantic accommodations in the city. ✉ *Nieuwe Doelenstraat 2–8, 1012 CP,* ☎ *020/531–1777,* FAX *020/531–1778. 100 rooms. Restaurant, pool, exercise room.*

$$$–
$$$$ **American.** The ornate American, overlooking the Leidseplein, is ideal if you want to be in the center of activity. Many rooms overlook the Singelgracht canal. All are decorated in art nouveau and art deco styles; double-glazed windows keep out the noise from the busy Leidseplein outside. The restaurant, Cafe American, is the hotel's stunning art deco showcase, but the food seldom lives up to the buzz. ✉ *Leidsekade 97, 1017 PN,* ☎ *020/624–5322,* FAX *020/625–3236. 188 rooms. Restaurant, exercise room.*

$$$–
$$$$ **Grand Hotel Krasnapolsky.** This imposing 1866 hotel right on Dam Square and across from the Royal Palace is popular with conventioneers (it's hosted gay groups before), and although the rooms are clean and attractive, they don't measure up to the promise of the building's elaborate facade. The hotel has a first-rate business center, however, making this ideal if you're here for that reason. ✉ *Dam 9, 1012 JS,* ☎ *020/554–9111,* FAX *020/622–8607. 430 rooms. 5 restaurants.*

Sleeps

$$$– **Pulitzer.** One of the most distinctive hotels in the city, the
$$$$ gay-friendly Pulitzer consists of 24 17th-century town houses facing very fashionable stretches of both the Prinsengracht and the Keizersgracht canals. Most rooms contain antiques, and many have beam ceilings. The layout can be quirky and challenging to navigate (note the steep stairs to some rooms). You're steps from the Jordaan's charming shops and restaurants. ✉ *Prinsengracht 315–331, 1118 BG,* ☏ *020/523-5235,* FAX *020/627-6753. 220 rooms. Restaurant.*

$$$ **Barbizon.** Of the many business hotels below the Leidseplein, the Barbizon is the most attractive—it also has an extremely gay-friendly management. Behind the attractive 1928 Amsterdam School facade you'll find a smoothly run hotel with spacious (by the city's standards) rooms, a few of which have balconies. Recent major renovations have seen the overhaul of the central lobby, which is a nice spot for high tea, and the addition of a first-rate northern Italian restaurant, Bice (part of the Milan-based chain). ✉ *Stadhouderskade 7, 1054 ES,* ☏ *020/685-1351,* FAX *020/685-1611. 236 rooms. 2 restaurants, health club.*

$$–$$$ **The Ambassade.** Similar in concept to the Pulitzer, the Ambassade is a series of 10 canal-side merchant's houses (most overlooking the prestigious Herengracht, two on the Singel); it's less luxurious than its more expensive competitor, but more homey, with glorious public areas. Rooms can be a bit small, but many have antiques, pitched beam ceilings, and tall windows. ✉ *Herengracht 341, 1016 AZ,* ☏ *020/626-2333,* FAX *020/624-5321. 52 rooms.*

$$–$$$ **Tulip Inn Amsterdam.** Part of a chain that's equally big with business travelers and vacationers, this complex of five 1920s Amsterdam School–style buildings has bright contemporary guest rooms and an elegant art deco lobby. It's in a good location, close to both the Jordaan and the curious mix of sleaze and fine dining along Spuistraat (which is handy, as there's no on-site restaurant). ✉ *Spuistraat 288–292, 1012 VX,* ☏ *020/420-4545, 800/344-1212 in the U.S./Canada,* FAX *020/420-4300. 208 rooms.*

$$ **Hotel Smit.** This affordable, intimate hotel on fashionable P.C. Hooftstraat is close to the diamond district, museums, Vondelpark, and Leidseplein. Rooms are typical of other properties in this price range, but bathrooms are unusually nice with marble details and bathtubs or showers. ✉ *P.C.*

Hooftstraat 24–28, 1071 BX, ☎ 020/671–4785, ℻ 020/662–9161. 65 rooms. Restaurant.

Small Hotels and Guest Houses

$$–$$$ 🏨 **Black Tulip Hotel.** At press time (winter 1997), this plush new hotel is slated to open near the Warmoesstraat bar district in January 1998, offering an upmarket experience for guys into the leather scene. Rooms will be equipped with VCRs, voice mail, and tea/coffee service—*and* slings and bondage hoops. The Fantasy Room is being designed by the guys from the Black Body leather shop. The restored, modernized, 15th-century building will have soundproof walls and an outdoor breakfast area. ✉ *Gelderskade 16, 1012 BH, ☎ 020/427–0933, ℻ 020/624–4281. 9 rooms with phone, TV, and private bath. Breakfast. Gay male.*

$–$$ 🏨 **Freeland.** A recent renovation makes the Freeland one of the better budget choices near the Leidseplein and Jordaan. The 19th-century building is typical of others in the area, but its thick walls and double-pane windows shelter guests from the noise of busy Marnixstraat. ✉ *Marnixstraat 386, 1017 PL, ☎ 020/622–7511, ℻ 020/626–7744. 18 rooms with phone, TV, most with private bath. Breakfast. Mixed gay/straight.*

$–$$ 🏨 **Hotel New York.** The New York is a well-maintained gay hotel; it's been popular for many years and a recent renovation has made it only more so. Rooms are functional but clean. It's in a quiet and well-to-do part of Amsterdam, not far from the Jordaan, Centraal Station, or the Shipping District. ✉ *Herengracht 13, 1015 BA, ☎ 020/624–3066, ℻ 020/620–3230. 20 rooms with phone, TV, private bath. Breakfast. Mostly mixed gay male/lesbian.*

$–$$ 🏨 **Hotel Sander.** It's a bit of a walk to gay nightlife, but this handsome 19th-century hotel on a quiet street near Vondelpark and the Museumplein is ideal if you're seeking peace and privacy. Rooms are typically modest but clean with modern bathrooms and in-room safes. There's a garden terrace in back. Very friendly staff. ✉ *Jacob Obrechtstraat 69, 1071 KJ, ☎ 020/662–7574, ℻ 020/679–6067. 20 rooms with phone, TV, private bath. Breakfast. Mixed gay/straight.*

$–$$ 🏨 **Orfeo.** Hosts Peter Königshausen and Avi Ben-Moshe opened this gay hotel in 1969, back when its location just off the Leidseplein was about as gay as any property in the city. Although most of the nightlife is now a few blocks

In case you want to see the world.

At American Express, we're here to make your journey a smooth one. So we have over 1,700 travel service locations in over 120 countries ready to help. What else would you expect from the world's largest travel agency?

do more

AMERICAN EXPRESS

http://www.americanexpress.com/travel

Travel

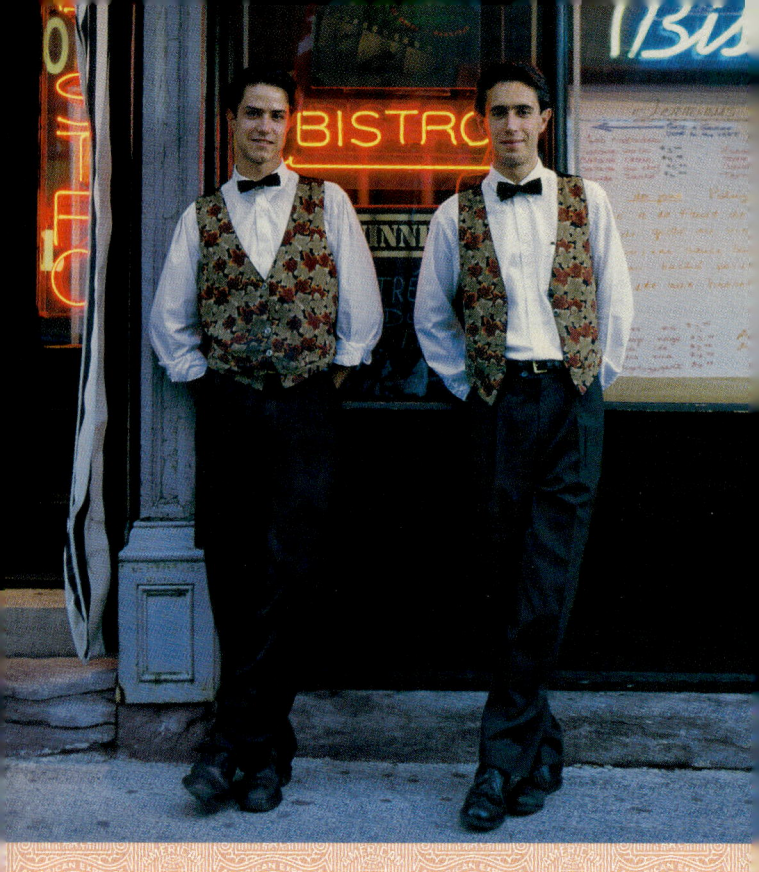

In case you want to be welcomed there.

We're here to see that you're always welcomed at establishments everywhere. That's why millions of people carry the American Express® Card – for peace of mind, confidence, and security, around the world or just around the corner.

do more® AMERICAN EXPRESS

Cards

In case you're running low.

We're here to help with more than 118,000 Express Cash locations around the world. In order to enroll, just call American Express before you start your vacation.

do more

AMERICAN EXPRESS

Express Cash

And just in case.

We're here with American Express® Travelers Cheques and Cheques *for Two.*® They're the safest way to carry money on your vacation and the surest way to get a refund, practically anywhere, anytime.
Another way we help you...

do more

AMERICAN EXPRESS

Travelers Cheques

©1997 American Express Travel Related Services Company, Inc.

away, this is still a great spot—steps from restaurants, cinemas, and several major attractions. Rooms are comfortable but simple, and the crowd is extremely social and outgoing—lots of Americans, Brits, and other international visitors stay here. Guests congregate in the homey common lounge and bar, or mingle in the Finnish sauna. ⊠ *Leidsekruisstraat 14, 1017 RH,* ☎ *020/623–1347,* ℻ *020/620–2348. 24 rooms with phone, many with TV and private bath. Breakfast. Gay male.*

$–$$ 🏨 **Prinsen.** The charming Prinsen, which was built by Rijksmuseum architect P. J. Cuypers, is on an elegant tree-lined street that feels miles from the action but is actually less than a five-minute walk from the Leidseplein. Rooms are among the best you'll find in this price range, with clean modern baths and pleasant pastel hues. In back you can relax in the delightful garden. ⊠ *Vondelstraat 36–38, 1054 GE,* ☎ *020/616–2323,* ℻ *020/616–6112. 40 rooms with phone, TV, private bath. Continental breakfast. Mixed gay/straight.*

$ 🏨 **Arena.** Slackers, backpacking students, and alternateens flock to this former convent that now serves as a hip and grungy budget hotel, youth hostel, restaurant, lounge, and music club—the entertainment facilities are reason enough to visit, plus there's a huge garden. You can either pay for a bed in one of the common rooms or spend only a bit more for a private room. Although a ways out of the City Center (three metro stops), it's a likely spot to meet some pretty cool fellow travelers. ⊠ *'S Gravesandestraat 51–53, 1092 AA,* ☎ *020/694–7444,* ℻ *020/663–2649. 600 beds, some in common areas, some in private rooms with shared baths, and some in private rooms with private baths. Mostly straight.*

$ 🏨 **Chico's Guesthouse.** Two men who live in de Pijp, the up-and-coming neighborhood southeast of the City Center (close to Sarphetti Park) rent three extremely inexpensive guest rooms out of their home in a quiet early-20th-century working-class neighborhood. They also let a private apartment with a kitchen and private entrance. Although the accommodations are modest (but clean), a stay here will give you a very good sense of what it's like to live in Amsterdam. ⊠ *St. Willibrordusstraat 77, 1073 VA,* ☎ *020/675–4241. 3 rooms share a bath; 1 apartment. Mostly gay male.*

$ 🏨 **Greenwich Village.** Even though this hotel borrows its name from the New York City neighborhood, few of its staff members speak great English (the owner is Czech). The place is basic and lacks much in the way of charm, but it is popular with young Euro-queers on a budget (there's a large dorm-style room with several beds). ⊠ *Kerkstraat 25, 1017 GA,* ☎ *020/626–9746,* 📠 *020/625–4081. 10 rooms with phone, TV, private bath; plus 1 dorm-style room. Breakfast. Mixed gay/straight.*

$ 🏨 **Hotel Aero.** This is the best of the gay-popular properties along busy Kerkstraat—the owners also run the Camp Cafe (*see* Eats, *above*) and Bronx adult bookstore next door. Rooms and public areas (*see* Eats, *above*) are furnished with an eclectic mix of antiques; those rooms on the upper floors have picturesque views of the city's skyline. ⊠ *Kerkstraat 49, 1017 GB,* ☎ *020/622–7728,* 📠 *020/638–8531. 19 rooms with phone, TV, private bath. Breakfast. Mixed gay/straight.*

$ 🏨 **Hotel Unique.** One of several old-style queer hostelries along Kerkstraat, this one has been popular with gays since 1948. It's set inside two adjoining 1737 buildings. No frills. ⊠ *Kerkstraat 37, 1017 GB,* ☎ *020/624–4785,* 📠 *020/627–0164. 18 rooms with phone and TV, some with private bath. Breakfast. Mostly mixed gay male/lesbian.*

$ 🏨 **ITC Hotel.** With the prettiest location of any of the gay-oriented hotels, this 1760s canal house is on a picturesque stretch of Prinsengracht, steps from the trendy restaurants and shops along Utrechtsestraat. John and Grant, the friendly hosts, know plenty about the city; the downstairs lounge also has an extensive queer library. Rooms are nice by budget standards, with many looking over the canal. ⊠ *Prinsengracht 1051, 1017 JE,* ☎ *020/623–1711,* 📠 *020/624–5846. 15 rooms with phone and TV, most with private bath. Breakfast. Mostly mixed gay male/lesbian.*

$ 🏨 **Monopole.** This clean, modern but basic queer hotel, above the bar of the same name, is within a short walk of about a dozen more bars and the bustle of the Rembrandtplein. If all you need is a place to sleep and store your belongings, this will do perfectly. The four brightest, largest rooms front on the canal. ⊠ *Amstel 60, 1017 AC,* ☎ *020/624–6271. 11 rooms with shared bath. Breakfast. Mostly gay male.*

$ 🏨 **Quentin.** This friendly hotel overlooking the Singelgracht canal has been fashioned out of three stately old houses, one from the 1600s and the others from the 1800s. Although rooms contain functional furnishings, many of them look out upon the canal. The staff is friendly and helpful. ⊠ *Leidsekade 89, 1017 PN,* ☎ *020/626–2187,* 📠 *020/622–0121. 45* *rooms with TV, most with phone and private bath. Mixed gay/straight.*

$ **Rainbow Palace.** It's a short walk to most gay bars, but the Rainbow Palace has many assets: Nearby attractions include Dam Square, the Jordaan, the C.O.C., and the Homomonument, and the rooms are terribly cheap. It's one of about a dozen hotels fashioned out of the top floors of the impressive Art Nouveau Utrecht Building, so bear in mind that you must climb a quaint but frighteningly narrow and steep flight of stairs just to reach the lobby. Other similar and gay-friendly options in this building are **Clemens** (✉ No. 39, 1016 DC, ☎ 020/624–6089, 10 rooms) and **Pax** (✉ No. 37, ☎ 020/624–9735, also 10 rooms). ✉ *Raadhuisstraat 33, 1016 DC, ☎ 020/625–4317, ℻ 020/420–5428. 9 rooms with phone and TV, some with private bath. Breakfast. Mostly gay male.*

THE LITTLE BLACK BOOK

Tips on Traveling to the Netherlands

CLIMATE

Late fall and winter in the Netherlands is long, wet, raw, and dreary. If you come at this time, bring clothing that's suitable for chilly, rainy days. Beginning around March, temperatures begin to climb into the 50s and 60s F (10s–20s C), until summer arrives bringing generally clear, beautiful weather, with temperatures rarely greater than 70°F (21°C). March and April, of course, are when tulips are in bloom, making it a popular time to visit.

CURRENCY AND EXPENSES

Prices in the Netherlands are low compared with other Western European countries, and even costs in Amsterdam are no worse than you'll find in major U.S. or Canadian cities, and less than what you'll find in the United Kingdom, Australia, and New Zealand. At press time (winter 1997), one dollar was worth about 1.70 guilders (abbreviated in this book as Fl, but also seen commonly as Hfl, Dfl, and F); one pound sterling, about 2.65 guilders; and one Canadian dollar, 1.30 guilders.

A 17.5% VAT (value-added tax) is levied on all purchases, but residents of non–European Union countries are entitled to a refund (usually 10% to 15%, depending on any commissions) on purchases greater than Fl 300 that are personally carried out of the country within 30 days. Ask your shopkeeper for details on how this works; sometimes you can obtain the refund directly from the shop; other times you have to obtain this at Schiphol on your way home.

Tipping has picked up in popularity and acceptance in the Netherlands in recent years, and it's wise to round to 5% to 15% on most restaurant bills, leave a little extra change when buying drinks at bars, and add about 10% for taxis.

ATMs that are connected to such U.S. networks as Cirrus and Plus are prevalent all around Amsterdam as well as in other Dutch towns and cities.

LANGUAGE

The Dutch, especially those living in larger cities, are well versed in many languages. English, German, and French are the most widely spoken languages after Dutch. Dutch itself is an extremely difficult language to learn, but it definitely will pay off to pick up a few basic phrases, and to familiarize yourself with how letters and vowels are pronounced. English-speaking visitors sometimes think that because the entire city of Amsterdam is fluent in English, locals don't appreciate hearing things pronounced correctly. They do, and pronouncing Dutch names and places correctly (Den Haag instead of The Hague) will help you fit in better. See the vocabulary section at the end of this guide for useful Dutch vocabulary and pronunciations of place-names.

OPENING AND CLOSING TIMES

Laws have loosened greatly in Amsterdam and other major Dutch cities during the '90s, and many stores are now permitted to stay open on Sundays from noon till 5, and one night weekly until 9 PM (usually Thursday). Not all stores do this, but many do. Otherwise, shops are open typically from 9 until 5 or 6.

PASSPORTS AND VISAS

U.S., Canadian, and British citizens need passports but not visas to enter the Netherlands.

PHONES

The Netherlands's country code is 31. Dial only the area code and not the preceding zero when placing a call from another nation to the Netherlands (i.e., you dial 20 instead of 020 to reach Amsterdam). No area code is needed when placing intercity calls. If you're calling outside Amsterdam, you'll need to dial the area code before the phone number.

Coin-operated public phone booths are being replaced with equipment that requires phone cards. Pay phones in bars and restaurants take Fl 25 or Fl 1 coins. Phone cards may be purchased from post offices, railway stations, and newsagents for Fl 10 or Fl 25. Dial 0800/0410 for an English-speaking operator.

For local directory assistance, call 0900/8008. For operator assistance, dial 0800/0410.

Direct-dial international calls can be made from any phone booth. To reach an **AT&T** long-distance operator, dial 0800/022–9111; for **MCI,** dial 0800/022–9122; for **Sprint,** dial 0800/022–9119.

VISITOR INFORMATION BEFORE YOU GO

Contact the **Netherlands Board of Tourism** in **North America** (✉ 355 Lexington Ave., 21st Floor, New York, NY 10017, ☎ 212/370–7360, FAX 212/370–9507; 90 New Montgomery St., Suite 305, San Francisco, CA 94105, ☎ 415/543–6772, FAX 415/495–4925; 225 N. Michigan Ave., Suite 326, Chicago, IL 60601, ☎ 312/819–0300, FAX 312/819–1740; 9841 Airport Blvd., 10th Floor, Los Angeles, CA 90045, ☎ 310/348–9333); in **Canada** (✉ 25 Adelaide St., Suite 710, Toronto, Ontario, M5C 1Y2, ☎ 416/363–1577, FAX 416/363–1470); or in the **United Kingdom** (✉ 25–28 Buckingham Gate, London, SW 1E 6LD, ☎ 0171/828–7900).

At Your Fingertips

AIDS Hotline (☎ 060/222220). **Amsterdam Gay Business Guild** (✉ Lijnbaansgracht 210H, 1016 XA, ☎ FAX 020/620–8807, e-mail havana@euronet.nl). **British Consulate** (✉ Koningslaan 44, ☎ 020/676–4343). **C.O.C. Amsterdam** (lesbigay community center; ✉ Rozenstraat 14, ☎ 020/626–3087). **C.O.C. national headquarters** (✉ Nieuwezijds Voorburgwal 68–70, 1012 SE, Amsterdam, ☎ 020/623–4596, FAX 020/626–7795). **Gay and Lesbian Switchboard** (open daily 10–10, ☎ 020/623–6565, Web site www.dds.nl/plein/homo). **Emergency** (☎ 0611). **GC&GD** (free STD and AIDS testing and counseling; ✉ Groenburgwal 44, 020/555–5822). **GWK** (money exchange; ✉ Centraal Station, ☎ 020/627–2731; ✉ also attached to the VVV office at Leidsestraat 106, by the Leidseplein, no phone). **HIV**

Vereniging (HIV and AIDS resource; ✉ Eerste Helmerstraat 17, ☎ 020/616–0160). **Homodok** (gay and lesbian archive; ✉ Oudezijds Achterburgwal 185, ☎ 020/525–2601). **International Women's Library** (✉ Obiplein 4, ☎ 020/625–0820). **Lesbich Archief** (Lesbian Archive; ✉ Eerste Helmerstraat 17, ☎ 020/618–5879). **Police** (non-emergency, ☎ 020/559–9111). **SAD-Schorer Stichting** (lesbigay health referral and counseling service; ✉ P.C. Hofstraat 5, ☎ 020/662–4206; also walk-in consultation at Groenburgwal 44). **U.S. Consulate** (✉ Museumplein 19, ☎ 020/664–5661). **VVV Amsterdam Tourist Office** (✉ Stationsplein 10, by the Centraal Station, ☎ 06/340–340666, FAX 020/625–2869; also inside Centraal Station, by reservations office; and at Leidsestraat 106, by the Leidseplein). **VVV Logiesservice** (a same-day hotel-booking service run by the government tourism office; ✉ Stationsplein 10, by the Centraal Station; also inside Centraal Station, by reservations office; and at Leidsestraat 106, by the Leidseplein). **Vrouwen Bellen Vrouwen** (Women Call Women, general women's referral and info hotline; ☎ 020/625–0150).

Gay Media

Although there are a few gay papers and magazines in the Netherlands, some of them are printed only in Dutch. The one queer paper with English and Dutch coverage is the monthly *Gay News* (☎ 020/679–1556, Web site www.gaynews.com), which you'll find free in bars and shops all over the city. It's an extremely useful resource with a detailed listing of bars and many interesting articles. Some of the staff at the *Gay News* left to form a similar English/Dutch lesbigay paper, **Gay and Night** (☎ 020/622–5364), which also comes out monthly. *Trout* (☎ 020/420–6775), begun by some of the people from the failed *Time Out Amsterdam* venture (they ceased publishing a weekly guide in 1996), is a small, info-packed booklet, which comes out every two weeks and is geared specifically toward alternative types—those into independent films and music, squats, drug culture, partying, cutting-edge art, and such. Much of the information has a gay bent to it, but not all. For genXers and independent thinkers visiting Amsterdam, it's a wonderful resource that costs Fl 2.50). The same folks have also begun publishing a specifically gay 'zine, **Queer Agenda,** which is distributed free in gay bars, at the VVV, and in other convenient locations; it carries loads of homo-themed arts and entertainment news. **SAD Schorerstichting** (*see* At Your

Fingertips, *above*) publishes booklets on HIV prevention, safer-sex practices, and other health issues. They also distribute a helpful and fun booklet, **Gay Tourist Info**, with all sorts of great tips and suggestions on how to enjoy all that the city has to offer; it's written in English.

As for Dutch-language publications, the lesbigay magazine **Culture and Camp** (☎ 020/679–9188, e-mail rainbow@neturl.nl) has plenty of bar listings and information. **De GAY Krant** (☎ 499/391–000, e-mail red@gayworld.nl) is the leading queer newspaper, covering both the Netherlands and Belgium; some of the coverage is in English. **Expreszo** (☎ 020/623–4596, e-mail nvihcoc@xs4all.nl) is big with younger gay guys (and to a lesser extent, women); it's published by the national C.O.C. Bimonthly **Squeeze** (☎ 010/452–5082) is the country's Dutch-language glossy.

BOOKSTORES

Amsterdam has plenty of sources of lesbian and gay books, newspapers, and magazines. Unless noted, you'll find a decent selection of English-language publications in all of these stores. **Vrolijk** (✉ Paleisstraat 135, ☎ 020/623–5142, e-mail vrolijk@xs4all.nl), which was begun around the corner from its current location as a squat in 1984, is the city's main lesbigay bookstore. It's a two-level shop with a friendly and helpful staff. A spacious, well-organized bookstore with mostly male titles, from novels to nonfiction, **Intermale** (✉ Spuistraat 251, ☎ 020/625–0009) also has an extensive selection of erotica and porn, and plenty of travel guides. Women should check out **Xantippe Unlimited** (✉ Prinsengracht 290, ☎ 020/623–5854), which has an extensive selection of feminist and lesbian books and magazines. Along Westermarkt, you can also drop by **Vrouwen in Druk** (✉ Westermarkt 5, ☎ 020/624–5003), which stocks secondhand feminist and women's books, with a good selection of English titles. If you're looking specifically for porn and blue videos, Amsterdam has quite a selection (*see* Action, *above*).

Of general-interest bookstores, Amsterdam has two terrific sources of English-language books. Most extensive is the multistory **American Book Center** (✉ Kalverstraat 85, ☎ 020/625–5537, Web site www.abc.nl), which has a tremendous lesbian and gay section of both books and magazines; this section is on the lower level, and many of the staff down here are gay and can help you find or special-order specific titles.

The store also has an unusually good selection of science fiction, travel, and New Age. All students receive a 10% discount. An outpost of the British-based chain **Waterstone's** (⊠ Kalverstraat 152, ☎ 020/638–3821) is also a good option, but the lesbigay section is much smaller than that of the American Book Center. **Athenaeum Neiuwscentrum and Boekhandel** (⊠ Spui 14–16, ☎ 020/624–2972) is one of the best sources of foreign newspapers and magazines.

Working Out

The main gay-men's gym is **Mandate** (⊠ Prinsengracht 715, ☎ 020/625–4100), a relatively small but high-tech fitness center, with a nice sauna, and, on the ground floor, a trendy little coffee and juice bar. It overlooks the Prinsengracht canal, just around the corner from the gay nightlife area along Kerkstraat. Rates are Fl 18 for one visit but drop the more you go, to as low as Fl 63 for six visits. Cruisy, but not to be confused with a bathhouse.

One of the city's largest and trendiest fitness centers, newly renovated **Splash** (⊠ Looiersgracht 26–30, ☎ 020/624–8404) is extremely popular with gays and lesbians. The clean contemporary facility is on a charming street in the Jordaan, right beside de Rommelmarkt. Amenities include a handsome chrome juice bar, Turkish baths, saunas, a cardio-fitness center, a wide variety of aerobics classes, and personal trainers. Splash is not cheap for one day's visit (about Fl 35), but rates drop quickly if you visit for one week (Fl 65) or two weeks (Fl 95).

2 *Out in* the Netherlands

Haarlem, Zandvoort, Leiden, Den Haag, Rotterdam, Utrecht, and Maastricht

IF YOU HAVE EVEN A FEW HOURS' free time during your visit to Amsterdam, try to see at least one or two of the culturally rich, aesthetically pleasing cities nearby. What follows are detailed suggestions for six of the country's most engaging and gay-friendly cities. In none of them will you encounter the nonstop buzz of Amsterdam's bars, nor will you find that social and political attitudes are so uniformly progressive elsewhere in the Netherlands. Still, at least in the cities covered below, acceptance of homosexuals is the norm, and gay culture definitely exists—even if it takes a little foraging to locate it.

Haarlem and Leiden, the closest of these cities to Amsterdam, make for practical short visits. They both have enough attractions to warrant a full day's exploration. Haarlem is also close to the country's premier gay seaside resort, Zandvoort. Den Haag, Rotterdam, and Utrecht—the busiest and most densely populated cities comprising what is commonly known as the Randstad (literally "edge city")—each have enough museums and charming streets to justify a full day's visit. Furthermore, Rotterdam and Den Haag each have several popular gay and lesbian bars. Although not covered here, other cities considered part of the Randstad and easily toured in conjunction with any of the three aforementioned cities include Gouda, Delft, and Dordrecht. About 40% of the nation's population lives and/or works within the Randstad, making it a region of formidable economic, political, and cultural significance.

The Randstad

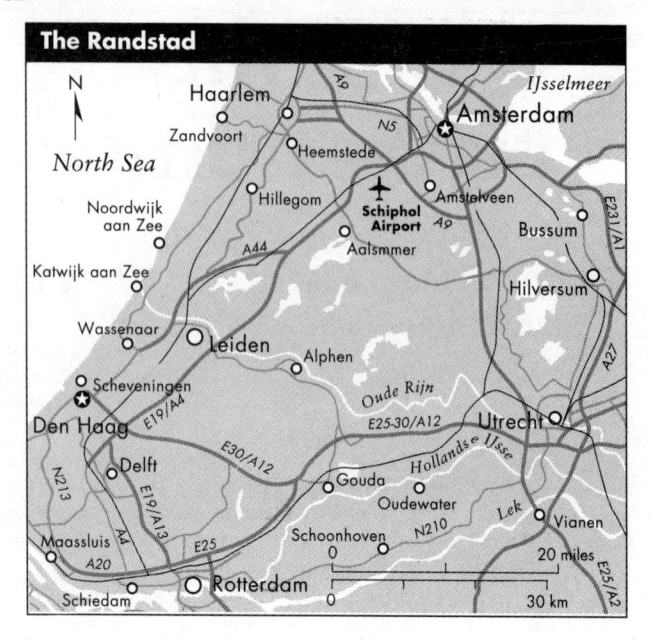

One farther-afield Dutch city that also deserves consideration, both because of its relatively strong queer following and because it's such a magical place, is Maastricht, the provincial capital of Limburg. Although it's at the very southeastern tip of the country, nearly three hours away by train, it is relatively convenient to Belgium (as well as to Germany and Luxembourg) and might make for a good stop on the way to another country.

All of the destinations covered in this chapter are easy to reach by train. Regular and frequent service runs from Amsterdam's Centraal Station to each of these cities, and once you arrive, you'll find that each city's station is within a five- to 20-minute walk of the museums, restaurants, and gay bars.

A Note About Price Categories in Eats and Sleeps Sections

For price ranges noted throughout this chapter, *see* dining and lodging Chart A at the front of this guide.

HAARLEM AND ZANDVOORT

Dutch master painter Frans Hals helped put Haarlem's name on the map as an important 17th-century hub of fine arts, but this quiet and beautifully preserved city 20 km (13 miles) west of Amsterdam dates from the 10th century. It's as well known today for its revealing medieval architecture as it is for being the nation's main center of flower trade.

Upon arriving at Haarlem's rail station, look back to admire its stunning 1908 Art Nouveau design. Walk 10 minutes south along Kruisstraat, which becomes pedestrian-only Barteljorisstraat, to reach the heart of the city, **Grote Markt.** On Saturdays on this busy square you can attend one of the country's best flower markets. The 14th-century **Stadhuis** (Town Hall) stands importantly on the western edge of the square. To the east, note **Grote Kerke of Sint Bavo** (Great Church of St. Bavo, ☏ 023/533-0877), a mammoth cathedral that was constructed throughout the 15th and 16th centuries and contains the Müller Organ, one of the largest pipe organs in the world—both Handel and, as a child, Mozart, have performed on it.

A few noteworthy attractions, including the stone 1598 **Waag** (Weigh House) and the 14th-century **Waalse Kerk** (Walloon Church) are a short distance east of Grote Markt. Steps from the market square, one of the most moving sites in Haarlem is the **Corrie ten Boom House** (✉ Barteljorisstraat 19, ☏ 023/531-0823), a modest house in which the ten Boom family lived during World War II, and from which they actively resisted the Nazi Occupation by harboring fellow Jews inside. The ten Booms eventually were captured by the Germans, and most of them died in concentration camps. Inside the home are documents, photos, and personal effects of the family, preserved living quarters and hiding places, and other bits of lure captured in *The Hiding Place,* a memoir by the surviving daughter Corrie ten Boom about this horrific period. Just east of here is the **Teylers Museum** (✉ Spaarne 16, ☏ 023/531-9010), which dates from 1778, making it the nation's oldest museum. You'll find sketches by Rembrandt, Raphael, and Michelangelo, as well as archaeological artifacts, and various tools and machines of the past few centuries.

Haarlem's must-see cultural attraction, the **Frans Hals Museum** (✉ Groot Heilig Land 62, ☏ 023/531-9180), is a 10-minute walk south of Grote Markt. Set inside an early 17th-century complex of almshouses for men, the museum celebrates the works and life of the famed artist. Though Hals was born in Antwerp around 1580, he earned his fame and prestige while living and painting in Haarlem. Inside are several of his most important works, including the eight group portraits for which he is best known. The collection also includes works by other masters of the Haarlem School, including Jacob van Ruisdael and a dozen other lesser-knowns.

Zandvoort aan Zee (meaning Zandvoort by the sea, and commonly referred to as simply Zandvoort) is Holland's gay resort. Although it's about a 40-minute train ride west of Amsterdam, it's just a quick bump from Haarlem. Sunbathing here is practical from about April through September. Like most beach resorts, Zandvoort has no substantial cultural offerings, and the brooding North Sea and its plain dark-beige beaches bear little resemblance to the jewels of the French Mediterranean, but the scads of cute barely-if-at-all-clad men and women provide plenty to look at.

From Zandvoort's train station turn left and walk for about 15 or 20 minutes south to reach the queer section. In summer, the beach is very easy to find, given the trail of gays and lesbians trekking between the station and the beach. The queer section is marked by a few very informal gay outdoor bars, which provide everything you need to enjoy the surroundings (beer, terrace seating, and cute patrons). Nudism is particularly prevalent at the gay section of the beach.

Getting Around

Frequent train service runs between Amsterdam and Haarlem, and farther on to Zandvoort aan Zee. The ride to Haarlem is about 20 minutes, and it's another 20 minutes by train to the beach.

Eats

HAARLEM

One of the most famous and enchanting restaurants in Holland is ✗ **Peter Cuyper** (✉ Klein Houtstraat 70, ☎ 023/532–0885, $$$), which is a short walk from the Frans Hals Museum and specializes in haute French and Dutch cooking. In summer, you can take your meal on a festive outdoor patio. On the lighter side, ✗ **Cafe Mephisto** (✉ Grote Markt

29, ☏ 023/532-9742, $) is a great source of *broodjes* (sandwiches), salads, soups, and snacks.

ZANDVOORT
Most of the throngs of gay and lesbian day-trippers to Zandvoort either bring food from Amsterdam or munch on the light snacks and sandwiches sold at the bars along the beach. The town has not cultivated a dining scene to any serious degree.

Scenes

HAARLEM
Haarlem's gay nightlife is oriented primarily toward locals, although outsiders are always welcome. You can pick up basic information on local events and parties at the **C.O.C.** (✉ Gedempte Oudegracht 24, ☏ 023/532-5453), which is a 20-minute walk from the train station. The one queer bar, **Cafe Wilsons** (✉ Gedempte Raamgracht 78, ☏ 023/532-5854), is on the ground floor of a Victorian town house; it's a popular disco with a patio, and you can also grab a light meal here. Since this is the only true game in town, it draws an eclectic crowd of men and women.

ZANDVOORT
Zandvoort's gay bars generally shut down from the end of September through April.

One of the most popular venues, **Adonis** (✉ Tjerk Hiddestraat 20, ☏ 023/571-3110), draws a mostly male clientele and is close to the beach but actually in town. Otherwise, most of the queer bars are party shacks along the beach without fixed addresses or phone numbers; furthermore, their names often change from year to year. It's best just to amble along and catch a glimpse of which establishments are drawing whom. One mainstay you can count on, however, is **Havana Aan de Zee** (✉ Paulus Loot Boulevard 1c, ☏ 023/571-4321), is an informal place, but more substantial than the bars down along the sand (it's actually on the road just before the beach).

LEIDEN

Of the towns near Amsterdam, Leiden (45 km/28 miles south of Amsterdam) holds the most appeal for visitors to the Netherlands. Rembrandt was born here (the house was destroyed during a World War II air raid), and the medieval city contains the oldest and most prestigious university in the country. In fact, Leiden bears a striking resemblance to Oxford, with its concentration of historic and rather regal buildings, and its bustle of students and professors. With some excellent museums, lively cafés, and captivating narrow lanes and canals, Leiden makes one of the best and easiest excursions in the Netherlands. The academic presence infuses the town with a groovy, open mind-set in which you're likely to feel quite comfortable.

As you leave Leiden's train station and stroll south toward the city center, you'll come immediately to two of the city's smaller museums, one definitely worth a stop and the other with limited appeal. Do visit the **Molenmuseum de Valk** (Windmill Museum de Valk; ✉ 2e Binnenvestgracht 1, ☎ 071/516–5353), a seven-story windmill, one of the few remaining in this town that used to have as many as two dozen of them. You can tour the interior's restored living quarters and climb to the top of the tower—this is a good place to get any curiosity you have about the nation's long-standing and integral relationship with windmills out of the way. The other attraction near the station, the **Rijksmuseum Voor Volkenkunde** (State Ethnological Museum; ✉ Steenstraat 1, ☎ 071/516–8800) contains exhibits detailing the cultures of former Dutch colonies—it's not unlike the Tropenmuseum in Amsterdam, but is not nearly so engaging or imaginatively executed.

There are two further sites between here and the City Center. **Lakenhal** (Cloth Hall; ✉ Oude Singel 28–32, ☎ 071/516–5361) is a 17th-century former cloth hall. It is now a museum tracing Leiden's rich history as a hub of wool and cloth trade and a general repository of priceless artifacts and art relevant to local history. Inside are paintings by Rembrandt, Jan Steen, Gerrit Dou; a famous triptych, *Last Judgment,* created by Lucas van Leyden; and several small galleries of ceramics, tiles, silver and pewter, and period furnishings. Of interest, perhaps, to aspiring medical students, the **Museum Boer-**

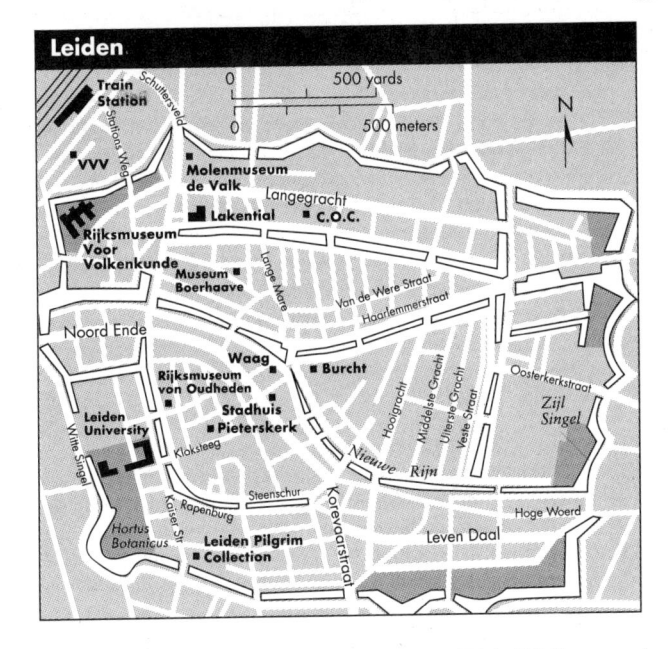

haave (⊠ Agnietenstraat 10, ☏ 071/521–4224) traces the science of medicine since the 17th century.

Leiden's center is at the confluence of the now-canaled Oude Rijn and Nieuwe Rijn rivers; they run east–west through the city. Paralleling the Oude Rijn Canal (a.k.a. the Oude Singel), Haarlemmerstraat, a fast-pace pedestrianized lane of mostly generic shops, offers some pleasant browsing and people-watching. A few steps south, at the precise point where the two canals meet, stand the mid-17th-century **Waag** (Weigh House) and the 16th-century **Stadhuis** (Town Hall). Just east of the Stadhuis, the imposing **Burcht** (just off of Nieuw Markt) is the rudimentary framework of the 12th-century embattlement, from which Leiden was once defended; it sits atop a slight bluff, and there are fine views of the city from its towers. Nieuwe Rijn runs from here in a southeasterly direction—its shops and cafés are considerably more engaging than those on Haarlemmerstraat. On Wednesday and Saturday a lively farmers' market is held along the banks of the canal.

Even if you can't trace your roots to the founding of Plymouth Colony in Massachusetts, you may want to stop for a moment at **Pieterskerk** (St. Peter's Church; ⌧ Pieterskerkhof, ☎ 071/512-4319) and, a few blocks south, the **Leiden Pilgrim Collection** (⌧ Vliet 45, no phone). The church, which overlooks Leiden's central square and dates from the 1400s, has been deconsecrated but contains the graves of Jan Steen, Rembrandt's parents, and the leader of the Puritan Pilgrim Fathers, John Robinson, who died before the 1620 *Mayflower* voyage from Plymouth, England, but who was largely responsible for the success of the movement. Many of the Pilgrim Fathers lived for a time in the still-standing houses near the church. At the Pilgrim Collection, which is contained within the walls of Leiden's archives, you can learn more about Robinson and the Pilgrim Fathers.

Southwest of here are the majority of **Leiden University**'s 16th- and 17th-century buildings, most of which are closed to the public but are still worth admiring from the outside. The university, founded in 1575, has sheltered its share of leading thinkers and scientists of that era, René Descartes foremost among them. Just south of this complex, the **Hortus Botanicus** (Botanical Garden; ⌧ Rapenburg 73, ☎ 071/527-5188), the oldest on the continent, makes for a beautiful stroll. The blocks north and east of here, along Rapenburg and back toward the Nieuwe Rijn, are loaded with everything from fashionable clothing shops to festive student-infested pubs. The western edge of this district is dominated by Leiden's most-visited points of interest, the **Rijksmuseum van Oudheden** (State Museum of Antiquities; ⌧ Rapenburg 28, ☎ 071/516-3163). Inside are numerous galleries absolutely crammed with artifacts from the ancient Greek, Roman, and Egyptian periods. Most dramatic is the towering Temple of Taffeh, a 1st-century AD Egyptian temple donated in 1969 to the Netherlands in recognition of the latter's extensive contributions in helping to excavate myriad Nubian archaeological digs in Ethiopia.

Head west of this section along Noordeinde, and you'll come upon a modern-feeling neighborhood of homes, which were constructed following a major German bombing during World War II. Unfortunately, the home in which Rembrandt was born, right by the Weddesteeg Bridge (over de Rijn, which is a broad river at this point), was one of those leveled in the assault. Miraculously, however, the studio in which Rembrandt painted off and on for 26 years before moving to Amsterdam survived the war; you reach it by crossing the Weddersteeg Bridge and turning right along Korte Galgewater. The studio is No. 4A and is now a private residence. This lane runs parallel to the river and will lead you back the short distance to the center of town.

Getting Around

Leiden is just 20 minutes from Amsterdam by train and extremely easy to navigate on foot. From Leiden it's only another 20 minutes by train to Den Haag.

Eats

One of the most gay-friendly restaurants in Leiden, ✗ **Cafe van Engelen** (✉ Nieuwe Rijn 1, ☏ 071/512–3798, $–$$$) has two levels. Upstairs is a slick bar and terrace overlooking the canal where you can fill up on the great sandwiches, such as the *Berlijn* (with smoked salmon, horseradish, guacamole, and dill), and locally revered apple pie. Downstairs is a more formal dining room–cum–art gallery where the menu changes often but features a range of contemporary Continental and Dutch dishes. Fans of Mexican fare should consider skipping the many overrated such restaurants in Amsterdam in favor of ✗ **Topolobampo** (✉ Noordeinde 27, ☏ 071/513–1914, $$), a romantic restaurant just west of the fancy shopping street, Rapenburg. Rustic decor fills each of the restaurant's rooms including Mexican folk art and furniture; top dishes include tamales *de Jalisco* (with spicy minced meat and cabbage) and warm fish salad with a sweet mango dressing. The excellent souvlakia, *tzatziki* (a cucumber-lemon-garlic yogurt dip), and many vegetarian dishes make ✗ **Olympia** (✉ Botenmarkt 19, ☏ 071/513–1929, $$) a popular choice among locals. A great option for an inexpensive lunch while shopping along Haarlemmerstraat, ✗ **Déli France** (✉ Haarlemmerstraat 176–178, ☏ 071/513–1116, $) is an airy and cozy café and bakery with excellent baguettes (try the one filled with coq au vin), croissants, and espresso; several marble tables are set on the sidewalk.

Scenes

Although Leiden has a substantial queer population, much of it student-based, locals tend to train in to Amsterdam, or even to Den Haag, for serious clubbing. Nevertheless, Leiden's **C.O.C.** (✉ Langegracht 65, ☏ 071/522–0640, Web site www.dsl.nl~nvihcoc) has frequent visitor-friendly social events. The C.O.C. is a short walk from the train station: As you leave the station and walk down Stationweg toward the center of town, turn left by the Molenmuseum de Valk. Continue along Langegracht for a few blocks; the C.O.C. is on the right, just before you hit the Aldi grocery market. The center keeps irregular hours, so call first, but dykes should keep in mind that the last Sunday afternoon (around 4 PM) of each month is **Vrouwencafe** (Women's Café), which is an extremely popular event. Weekend evenings there's always something going on here; it tends to be more lesbian-oriented on Fridays, and mixed-gender on Saturdays.

Leiden also has one of the coolest clubs you'll find in the Randstad, **Odessa** (✉ Hogewoerd 18A, ☎ 071/512–3311), which is just a few hundred yards east of Leiden University's campus. The loud and upbeat bruin cafe, a study in shabby-chic, always welcomes a mix of gays and straights, but Thursdays tend to be more gay male and Mondays more lesbian. The crowd is young, hip, and into the alternative music and arts scene. Theater and music posters line some walls and local art covers the others; the beam ceilings and dim lighting impart an appropriately old-fashioned ambience. You can dance your heart out many nights (to a mix of pop, techno, and disco), and in warm weather folks congregate on the rear terrace, which overlooks the Nieuwe Rijn Canal. Odessa is in a thicket of student-popular bars, all of which are ostensibly gay-friendly but nevertheless predominantly straight; go ahead and visit a few of them (they often have good live music), but conduct yourself discreetly if you want to be perfectly safe.

DEN HAAG

The Netherlands's capital, Den Haag (The Hague in English) is in many respects the nation's most conservative city. With a parade of suit-clad politicians and business executives marching up and down the streets, the city has a formal mood. Certainly it lacks the raucous spirit and rowdy venues of Amsterdam, 57 km (36 miles) to the northeast. Adding an additional layer of propriety is the refined 19th-century architecture—although parts of the city date from the 1300s, Den Haag was not developed seriously, and into the nation's political center, until the 1800s.

Den Haag

- Madurodam
- Prof. B. M. Telders Weg
- Jthan De Witt Laan
- Verhuell Weg
- TO SCHEVENINGEN
- Scheveningse Bosjes
- Haags Gemeentemuseum
- Plesman Woeg
- Scheveningse Weg
- Jacob Cats Laan
- 0   330 yards
- 0   300 meters
- Vredespaleis
- Patlijn Laan
- Schev Weg
- Nassau plein
- Laan van Meerdervoort
- Java straat
- Surinamestraat
- Bali straat
- Ram weg
- Tromp straat
- Anna Paulowna straat
- Bazar straat
- de Ruyter
- Bazariaan
- Alexander straat
- Schelp kade
- Kerkstraat
- Frederik str.
- Wassenaarseweg
- Koningtimegracht
- Konings kade
- Kortenaerkade
- Maurits kade
- Denneweg
- Dr. Kuyperstr.
- Prinssesseweg
- Noodeinde
- Amaliastr.
- Park straat
- Willem straat
- Zuid-Holland laan
- Jan van Nassau straat
- Kazerne straat
- Prinse straat
- Molen straat
- Lange Voorhout
- Haagse Bosjes
- Prince William V Gallery
- Museum Bredius
- Mauritshuis
- Nobel str.
- Buitenhof
- Kneuterdijk
- Lange Vijverberg
- Prinsessegracht
- Konings kade
- Grote Markt
- Hoogstr.
- Hofvijver
- Korte Voorhout
- Koekamp laan
- Binnenhof
- Korte Vijverberg
- Lange Houtstr.
- Ridderzaal
- Lange Poten
- Herengracht
- Bezuidenhoutse weg
- Spuistraat
- Den Haag CS Station
- VVV

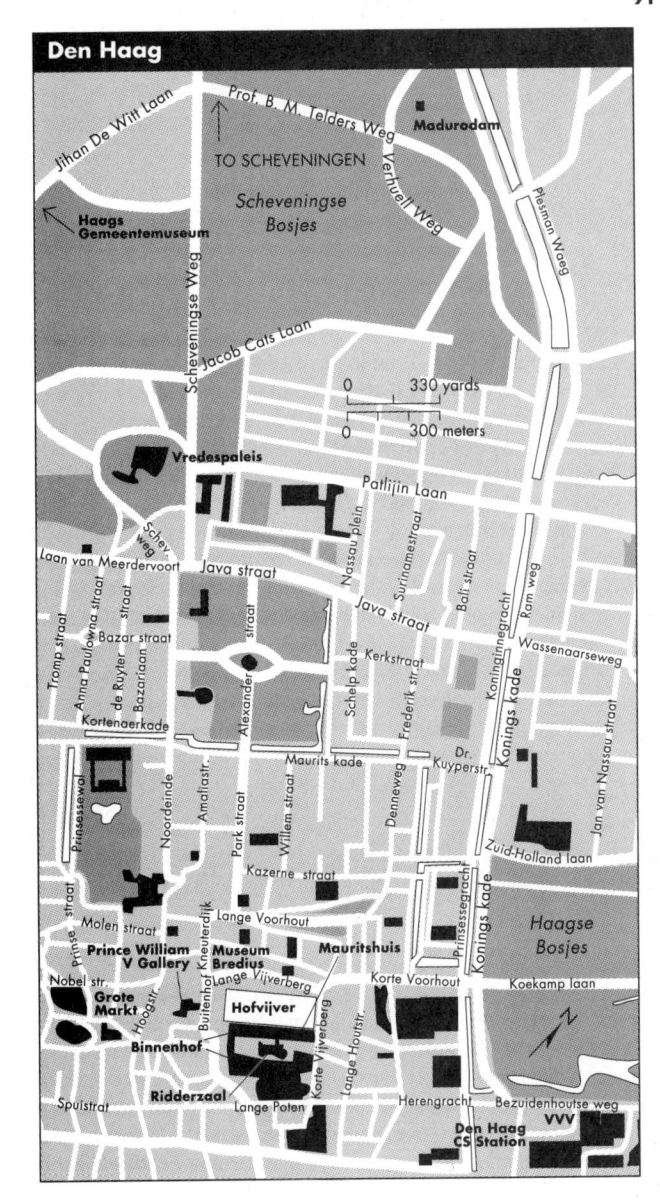

Den Haag receives a bum rap for being dull and bureaucratic, but just because its charms are somewhat less apparent than Amsterdam's or Utrecht's, don't be fooled into thinking it lacks culture or style. This gracious city has an excellent variety of museums and great shopping—most of which is within walking distance of the Centraal Station. And although the nightlife is tame, there are enough bars here to facilitate a brief but entertaining club crawl (even on weekends, however, the streets are unsettlingly quiet). Furthermore, the barflies in Den Haag are among the most amiable you'll find in the Netherlands.

Count William II built a castle in what is now the center of Den Haag in the 13th century; the surrounding community, under William's rule, came to be known as the "Count's Hedge" ('s Gravenhage), but the Dutch refer to it conversationally as "Den Haag." On the site of the actual castle, a five-minute walk northwest of the Centraal Station, is the **Binnenhof** (Inner Court), the seat of the Dutch Parliament. Stand in the Binnenhof to observe each of the Parliament's two chambers (the equivalent of the U.S. Senate and House of Representatives). The **Eerstekamer** (First Chamber) dates from Den Haag's early-19th-century appointment as a joint capital with Brussel of the United Kingdom of the Netherlands (which in 1830 dissolved into the two nations, the Netherlands and Belgium). Members of the **Tweedekamer** (Second Chamber) lobbied for the creation of new digs a few years ago; they now convene in an ugly modern (1994) structure outside of which is a long granite monument hailing the right of all Nederlanders to live free from discrimination on the basis of race, gender, religion, and sexual orientation. The former Tweedekamer, incidentally, has been lavishly converted into a tacky ballroom (much to the horror of many Dutch taxpayers).

The Binnenhof overlooks the impressive **Ridderzaal** (Knight's Hall), which dates from the city's less-than-humble 13th-century beginnings. It's a certifiably big deal when Queen Beatrix arrives at Ridderzaal and presents her annual address to open Parliament (the third Tuesday of September). For a suitably regal view of this complex, stand by the **Hofvijver** (Court Lake), a long reflecting pool on the north side of the Binnenhof.

Immediately northeast of Parliament, **Mauritshuis** (✉ Korte Vijverberg 8, ☎ 070/365–4779) houses the astounding collection of Flemish and Dutch art amassed during the late 18th century by Prince William V of Orange. These holdings, which include important pieces by Rembrandt (three self-portraits as well as *The Anatomy Lesson*), Vermeer (*Girl with the Pearl, View of Delft,* and *Diana with Her Companions*), Frans Hals, Van Dyck, and Rubens, are arranged inside a stunning 17th-century mansion—there's also one of Warhol's exuberant works of *Queen Beatrix* thrown in with a nice sense of juxtaposition. Walk just west of the Binnenhof to find the **Gevangenenpoort Museum** (Prisoner's Gate Museum; ⊠ Buitenhof 33, ☏ 070/346–0861), which contains many of the implements of torture and punishment used during the building's tenure as a prison (it was closed in the 19th century after a few centuries of good old-fashioned brutality). Next door, the small but highly acclaimed **Prince William V Gallery** (⊠ Buitenhof 35, ☏ 070/362–4444) contains works by Rembrandt, Paulus Potter, and many others. Walk just north of the Hofvijver to visit the **Museum Bredius** (⊠ Lange Vijverberg 14, ☏ 070/362–0729), an 18th-century mansion once owned by collector Abraham Bredius and which now is filled with his impressive art collection (which includes still more works by Rembrandt and Jan Steen). Den Haag has several gracious parks, including the rather cruisy **Haagse Bosjes,** which is east of Parliament and just north of Centraal Station. By day this is also a beautiful place for a stroll amid the trails and gardens.

Southwest of the Binnenhof, **Spuistraat** runs west from Hofweg and has been converted into a pedestrian-only covered shopping arcade with many high-end boutiques. Follow it to **Grote Markt** for more of the same kinds of stores, as well as some good restaurants and what's believed to be the oldest gay bar in the Netherlands, Cafe de Vink.

The rest of the city's most important sites are northwest of the city center, still within walking distance (a tram is quicker, but you'll want to check at Centraal Station for information on tram routes and stops). The International Court of Justice operates out of the ornate **Vredespaleis** (Peace Palace; ⊠ Carnegieplein 2, ☏ 070/320–4137), a 1903 structure built with a $1.5 million gift from Andrew Carnegie. Still best known for possessing the world's largest collection of works by Piet Mondrian, the **Haags Gemeentemuseum** (Hague Municipal Museum; ⊠ Stadhouderslaan 41, ☏ 070/351–

2873) is a short walk northwest of Vredespaleis; it also contains an eclectic array of both fine and decorative arts, ranging from antique glass and silver to Dutch and Chinese porcelain. Note that the museum is undergoing a full renovation and will be closed through October 1998.

These two sites are on the fringes of the huge **Scheveningse Bosjes,** the city's largest park, which is a great place to walk and enjoy nature and contains the **Madurodam** (✉ George Maduroplein, ☎ 070/355–3900), a Dutch village in miniature (on a scale of 1:25) containing detailed reproductions of every major building in the Netherlands. Touristy as it is, Madurodam is quite a spectacle. Immediately northwest of the park begins the seaside resort community **Scheveningen,** whose many miles of beach front the North Sea.

Getting Around

Trains depart Amsterdam's Centraal Station regularly for Den Haag; the ride takes about 45 minutes. Trains pull into Den Haag HS (Hollands Spoor Station); from here you can catch a frequently running train for the quick, two-minute hop to Den Haag CS (Centraal Station).

Eats

Den Haag has no shortage of pricey formal restaurants, most of them catering to politicos and visiting dignitaries. The most worthwhile of these is ✗ **Saur** (✉ Lange Voorhout 47, ☎ 070/346–2565, $$$–$$$$), a sumptuous eatery renowned for its fine seafood. This is a pretty straight spot, however—not the place to cut loose with a gaggle of gay friends or get overly intimate with a partner. For very good Continental cooking and a memorable old-fashioned atmosphere, try the nearby ✗ **Zwarte Ruiter** (✉ Grote Markt 27, ☎ 070/364–9549, $$), a high-ceilinged restaurant with a metal bar, two-tiered seating (the best section is on a catwalk overlooking the flurry of guppies, yuppies, and fashion plates below), and a blackboard menu that might list baked salmon with bacon and olive butter, or thin-sliced beef with imported Pecorino cheese. The best of Den Haag's gay-popular eateries is ✗ **HnM Eetcafe** (✉ Molenstraat 21a, ☎ 070/365–6553, $–$$), a romantic and extremely cute bistro with mismatched chairs, soft lighting, burgers, pastas, and a tasty steak *frites* (with french fries).

Den Haag 95

Scenes

Den Haag has about as many bars as Rotterdam, and together these two cities are the nation's top gay nightlife centers after Amsterdam. However, they are extremely different in mood; Den Haag's bars are friendly but rather mellow and restrained—an accurate mimicking of the city in which they're located. (Rotterdam's bars are mostly sexy and sleazy; they also have a substantially working-class following—but more on that in Rotterdam Scenes, *below.*) Den Haag has no exclusively lesbian bars, but women are quite welcome at all of the places described below and have a particularly strong presence at Cafe de Vink, Boko, de Landman, and Strass Dans (*see below*).

Almost all of Den Haag's gay bars are within a 15-minute walk of the Binnenhof and Centraal Station, making a tour of them very practical. A good place to start is **Cafe de Vink** (⊠ Schoolstraat 28, ☎ 070/365-0357), a "gezellig" (cozy) bar that's had a gay following since 1931 (even during the Nazi Occupation), making it the longest-running queer bar in the Netherlands. De Vink is a dark homey spot with Barbra photos on the walls, stained-glass, traditional Dutch music blaring (it's big with the sing-along crowd), and a convivial older crowd of both men and a few women. Bartenders are sweet and outgoing. Nearby are a pair of neighborhood bars popular with politicians and business types (both open and closeted—take your pick). The **Triompf** (⊠ Kettingstraat 4-6, ☎ 070/346-7107) has chandeliers and sweeping curtains and is particularly busy in the early evening.

A 10-minute walk northeast of here, just above the Binnenhof, are Den Haag's most popular gay bars, which are a few doors apart. **Boko** (⊠ Nieuwe Schoolstraat 1, ☎ 070/364-2374) is a trendy stand-and-model bar in the same mold as April and Havana in Amsterdam. Peach and turquoise walls, a stone archway separating the dance floor from the bar, long banquette seating, and ornate chandeliers make this a more stylish spot than most Dutch bars. On weekends it's packed with a hip crowd, mostly male but with some women. **Stairs** (⊠ Nieuwe Schoolstraat 11, ☎ 070/364-8191), on the other hand, gets no awards for its decor—low lighting, black walls, and lots of dark nooks and crannies—but the decor is hardly what the leather-and-jeans crowd is here for. The dance floor is usually packed and pulsing on weekend evenings, especially after 11 PM. It's all a bit of a surprise in a city as placid as this one.

Just around the corner from Stairs, **de Landman** (⊠ Denneweg 48, ☏ 070/346–7727) is more of a neighborhood bar. It's packed from late afternoon to early evening and pulls in a mix of men and women, gay and straight. Dozens of black-and-white celeb photos (Ella Fitzgerald, Eva Gabor, and the like), as well as an enormous portrait of Queen Beatrix, hang above the bar. Smoke-filled and chatty, this is just the place to meet some local color.

Probably the most mixed gay male and lesbian venue is the late-night **Strass Dans** (⊠ Javastraat 132, ☏ 070/363–6522), which is only open on weekends and doesn't truly get going until most of the other bars close. There's great dancing here, as well as some terrific drag shows.

ROTTERDAM

Bombed to pieces during World War II, Rotterdam was rebuilt in the years that followed and is now one of the most thoroughly contemporary cities in Europe. Although the blocks of gleaming glass-steel-and-concrete office blocks convey none of the charm typical of Amsterdam (77 km/48 miles to the north) or Utrecht (58 km/36 miles to the northeast), the city is stark but hardly gloomy. Companies prosper within the walls of these immense structures—Rotterdam is the busiest port city in the world. Nonstop commerce is conducted from a mammoth 48-km-long (30-mile-long) swath of piers and wharves, **Europoort.** If you have an appreciation for modern architecture, Rotterdam may hold as much appeal for you as any Dutch city. Given the abysmal record of commercial building during the second half of this century, Rotterdam scores high marks for its many notable structures.

The Boymans-van Beuningen Museum (*see below*) is one of the top art museums in Western Europe, but apart from this, there are few major historical sites and museums, so if that's your thing, you won't need too much time here. The gay club scene, however, is second (albeit a distant second) only to Amsterdam in variety and energy; it may very well surpass Amsterdam in cruisiness.

Rotterdam

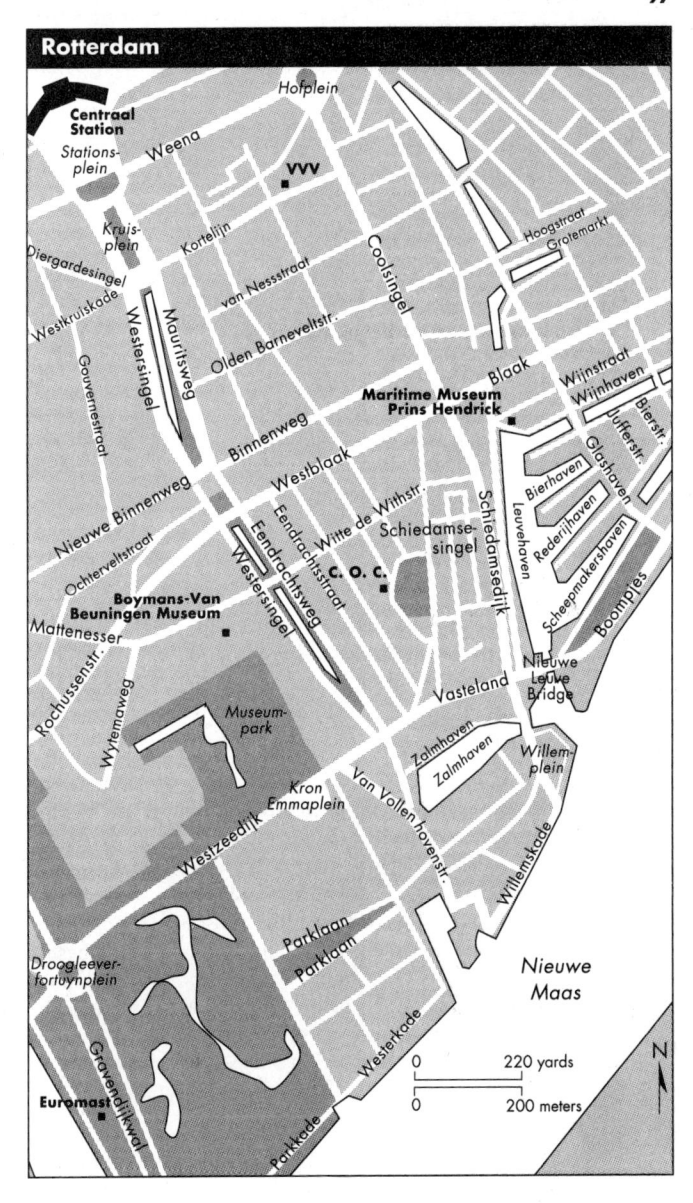

98   **Out in the Netherlands**   Chapter 2

It's hardly surprising, given the city's impressive maritime history, which spans four centuries, that Rotterdam's **Prins Hendrik Maritime Museum** (✉ Leuvehaven 1, ☎ 010/413–2680) is one of the most impressive such facilities you're likely to find anywhere. At the base of the city's Leuvehaven Harbor, which opens onto the busy Nieuwe Maas River, the Museum consists of both interior exhibits and moored historic ships. The neighborhood just west of the harbor, through which Schiedamse is the main thoroughfare, holds the bulk of the city's gay scene.

The **Boymans-van Beuningen Museum** (✉ Museumpark 18–20, a block west of Westersingel, ☎ 010/441–9400) is up there with Amsterdam's Rijksmuseum on the shortlist of the Netherlands's must-see museums. Its outstanding collection spans the past five centuries and includes works by Hieronymus Bosch, Hans Memling, Jan Steen, and Rembrandt, as well as such 19th- and 20th-century artists as Cézanne, Dalí, Munch, and Picasso. There's enough important and engaging art within these walls to keep an ardent follower enthralled for several days.

Southwest of the museum, via Westzeedijk, the 600-foot-tall **Euromast tower** (✉ Parkhaven 20, ☎ 010/436–4811) affords astounding views of the Randstad and the North Sea. Unfortunately, the roughly Fl15 admission is nearly as steep as the tower itself.

Getting Around

Rotterdam has an extensive metro and tram system, but the few attractions and all of the gay bars are within an easy 20-minute walk of Centraal Station. The city's streets may feel quiet and eerie at night, as few people live in the center of Rotterdam. For the most part, though, this is a safe place. Best of all, modern architects had the good sense to construct the majority of the gleaming skyscrapers with overhangs protecting the sidewalks below; in a nation infamous for its long rainy winters, this is no small convenience. In general, sidewalks are broad and well-lighted—further testimony to the generally good sense of the postwar planners.

Eats

As in any city comprising a significant number of office buildings, Rotterdam is a land of expense-account power-lunching and hotel dining—the sorts of places tourists (es-

Rotterdam

pecially queer ones) may wish to avoid if here only for an excursion.

For the best concentration of restaurants, most of them affordable and ranging from traditional Dutch to Asian, wander along the pedestrianized **Stadhuisplein** (just west of Coolsingel, a block south of Weena); there are dozens of cafés and eateries, many with outdoor seating, along this span midway between Centraal Station and the gay nightlife district. For eateries with a somewhat more boho atmosphere and a younger and queerer crowd, walk along Witte Withstraat, just west of where the gay bars are; this area also has several popular "coffeeshops"(hash bars).

For a proper dinner, consider romantic ✕ **Le Vilette** (✉ Westblaak 160, ☏ 010/414–8692, $$$), which is close to the Boymans-van Beuningen Museum and specializes in haute French cooking. There are very few restaurants in the heart of the gay area, but ✕ **Olympia** (✉ Schiedamsevest 2, ☏ 010/433–4949, $–$$) serves quite tasty Greek food and has a friendly staff.

Scenes

Other than a few local dives outside the city center, virtually all of Rotterdam's limited but potent nightlife is concentrated in a small gay district, centered along crescent-shape Schiedamsesingel. Overall, this neighborhood was left largely unscarred by the war, and much of the architecture dates from the 19th century. As a result, it retains the small scale and almost quaint feel typically in other Dutch cities. Invariably, those who have lived in Rotterdam for any period of time complain that the city has a fairly paltry bar scene, but the establishments here are popular, and finding a little action (at least for guys) is about as easy here as it is along Amsterdam's Warmoesstraat.

Before heading to some of the more popular and late-night-oriented clubs, consider beginning your evening at **de Bak** (✉ Schiedamsevest 146, ☏ 010/433–4783), a convivial pub and "eetcafe," where you can quaff some lager and munch on light food. The bar is plastered with homoerotic photos and posters, the space is cozy with bars and tables, and the crowd is kind of butch but diverse, with a mix of dykes and fags, ages 18 to 68. A darker and cruisier basement section opens after 10; you can sometimes buy hash down here. A short block east, **Loge 90** (⌧ Schiedamsedijk 4, ☏ 010/414–9745) is a quiet neighborhood tavern—not worth going out of your way for, but friendly and casual.

The best bars are just around the corner, centered around the **C.O.C.** (⌧ Schiedamsesingel 175, ☏ 010/414–1555), which, like other Dutch lesbian and gay community centers, provides plenty of information on local social groups, events, and the like.

Cosmos (⌧ Schiedamsesingel 133, ☏ 010/412–3668) is one of the most popular bars along this stretch. It's an attractive compact space with a hammered brass bar, great music, racy drag and strip shows, and dim lighting. After midnight it's almost impossible to move in here without sliding up against somebody (this seems to be the idea); guys frequently exchange looks and smiles before repairing upstairs to the Cosmos Sauna. Here there are both a Turkish and Finnish sauna, dark rooms, a video room showing porn flicks, and plenty of cute young men. The management bills this place a leather bar, but you'll meet all kinds. A bit more hard-core about its leather-and-Levis following, **Shaft** (⌧ Schiedamsesingel 137, no phone) doesn't open until 11 PM on weekends (at 9 PM other nights), and keeps rocking until around 5 AM. The cavernous old club has an ear-splitting sound system and plenty of space for cruising and ogling; it's justly renowned for its enticing theme parties—the pant-less T-shirt-and-sneakers parties are particularly popular.

Considerably more guppiesh, **Boy** (⌧ Schiedamsesingel 173, ☏ 010/414–2284) is the other major hot spot along this stretch. In front is a stylish contemporary cocktail bar (staffed by some awfully hunky bartenders); behind this is a dance floor with predictable but fun music. Women hang here more than at the Cosmos and Shaft, but the crowd is mostly male, young, and somewhat trendy.

One additional sauna that's a few blocks west of here, actually northwest of Euromast, **Spartacus** (⌧ 'S Gravendijkwal 130b, ☏ 010/436–6285) gets going late most evenings and draws a rougher, more local crowd than Cosmo.

Sleeps
The budget-oriented ⌶ **Heemraad Hotel** (⌧ Heemraadsingel 90, 3021 DE, ☏FAX 010/477–5461, $) is mixed but gay-friendly and not far from much of the gay scene.

UTRECHT

Although it's surrounded by the trappings of modern industry and sprawling Dutch suburbia, Utrecht's historic city center is among the most alluring in Western Europe. As with many cities near Amsterdam (40 km/25 miles northwest of Utrecht), the city is laced with canals, but its waterways are sunken one story below street level. A sidewalk extends along these depressed canals, from which you can admire the historic architecture and gain access to several underground restaurants and clubs—many of the outdoor tables sit directly overlooking the water, and at night, when street lamps glow above them, the canals make for a highly romantic stroll. Utrecht was a river port when the canal system was developed in the 14th century, and these canal-level cellars of the street-level businesses were used as warehouses.

Even on weekends, the City Center, in which you'll find most attractions and restaurants, is fairly quiet, ideal for exploring but hardly a hub of nightlife or counterculture. The gay community is thinly settled and not particularly visible, although like other Randstad population centers, this is a tolerant place. Only the University of Utrecht, the largest in the nation, gives the city a palpable sense of energy. Utrecht is much older than Amsterdam, having been established as an outpost of the Roman Empire during the 1st century AD. By the 7th century it had developed into one of Europe's most influential bishoprics, and during medieval times the city prospered as much as any in the Netherlands. The economic success is still evident by the considerable number of grand structures that date from the 15th and 16th centuries.

The city's historic center is anchored by **Domplein,** less than a 10-minute walk east of the train station and the adjacent Hoog Catherijne shopping mall. The Domplein is a medieval square dominated by the 367-foot-tall **Domtoren** (Dom Tower; ☎ 030/231–0403), the tallest church tower in the Netherlands, built in the 1380s. Although only half of the original cathedral still stands (the nave came tumbling down during an apparently awe-inspiring storm in the early 17th century), you can tour the grounds and the adjacent **Domkerk** (Dom Church; ☎ 030/231–0403), and climb nearly to the top of the tower, where you'll be rewarded with astounding views of the countryside. Adjacent is the **Klooster-**

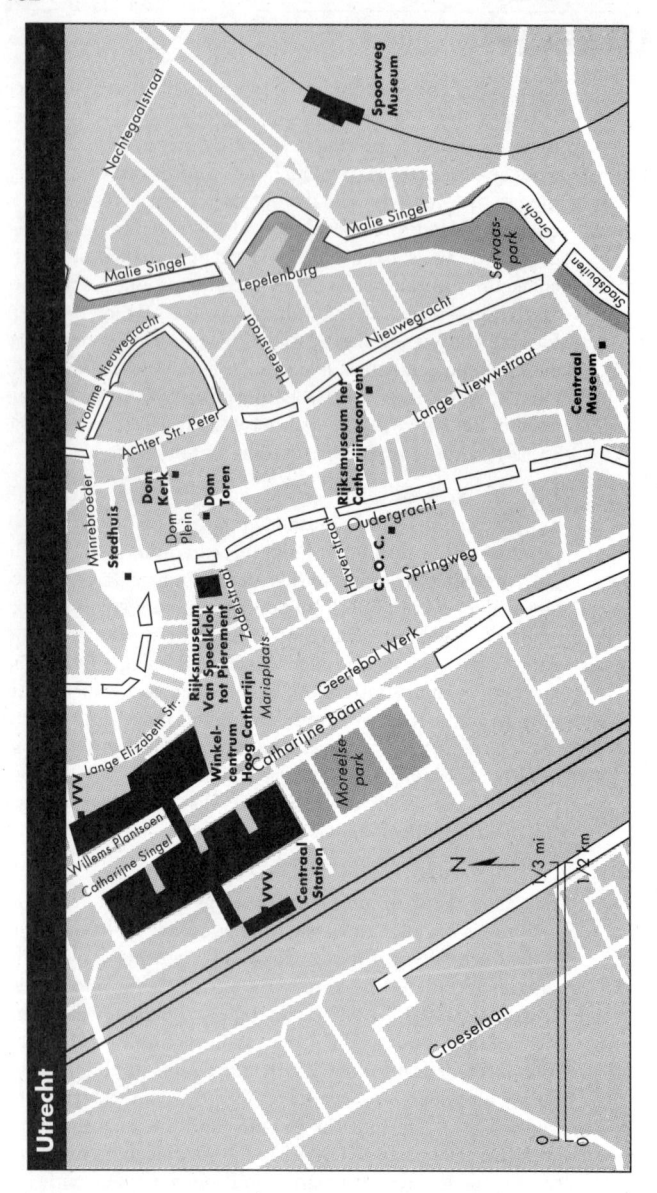

Utrecht

102

gang, serene cloisters that date from the 14th century and connect the cathedral to a small chapter house.

It's just a short walk west, back toward the Centraal Station, to reach one of the city's most curious attractions, the **Rijksmuseum van Speelklok tot Pierement** (State Museum from Musical Clock to Street Organ; ✉ Buurkerkhof 10, ☎ 030/231–2789), which is set inside a converted church and treats guests to the sights and sounds of countless musical instruments dating from the present back more than 200 years.

From Domplein, you can wander about a half mile south alongside one of the two main sunken canals, **Oudegracht,** to reach one of the city's most engaging attractions, the **Centraal Museum** (✉ Agnietenstraat 1, ☎ 030/231–7296), whose holdings range from important works of art to odd bits of local memorabilia. Paintings by members of the 16th- and 17th-century Caravaggio-inspired Utrecht School hang here, as well as remnants of a 12th-century Viking ship, and troves of textiles, furnishings, and artifacts.

From here you can walk east along the grassy north bank of Stadsbuitengracht, through Servaas Park, where a bridge crosses the other famous sunken canal, **Nieuwegracht.** This makes for a pretty walk, and just north of Servass Park, you can walk over to the **Spoorweg Museum** (Railway Museum; ✉ Maliebaanstation, ☎ 030/230–6206), a former rail station that's now filled with old trains and buses, plus miniature model railroads and numerous artifacts. If you're a devotee of the history and workings of public transportation, give it a go; otherwise, this isn't one of the city's most riveting sites.

You can head back up toward Domplein along Nieuwegracht, on your way perhaps pausing to visit the **Rijksmuseum het Catharijneconvent** (✉ Nieuwegracht 63, ☎ 030/231–7296), in which you'll find the nation's largest collection of medieval art, as well as countless religious artifacts.

Back at Domplein, you walk back over to Oudegracht and wander north along it, passing the imposing **Stadhuis** (Town Hall) and walking by dozens of funky cafés and engaging shops. This part of town has the highest level of energy.

Getting Around

There's frequent train service from Amsterdam's Centraal Station to Utrecht's terminal, which is inside the dizzyingly large Hoog Catharijne shopping mall, an insipid 1970s complex with about 200 run-of-the-mill shops. Although the rail service runs 24 hours, service is limited to about once an hour late at night. From here it's about a five-minute walk east—turn right at the top of the stairs from your train platform, and walk through the mall—to reach Lange Elizabethstraat, which will lead you right to historic Utrecht's heart, Domplein.

Eats

Other than grabbing a bite at one of the gay bars that serves a light menu, you won't find an ostensibly gay restaurant in Utrecht. On the other hand, there are tons of restaurants along Oudegracht and Nieuwegracht, as well as on the streets running perpendicular between them. These places are all quite blasé about same-sexers, and many of them draw a hip student crowd. On the trendy side, elegant ✕ **Het Grachtenhuys** (✉ Nieuwegracht 33, ☎ 030/231–7494, $$$) offers nouvelle Dutch cooking from a prix-fixe menu—choose either the four- or five-course meal. For an inexpensive but filling meal, try ✕ **Oude Munt Kelder** (✉ Oudegracht 12, canal level, ☎ 030/231–6773, $) for traditional Dutch pancakes. Nearby, lots of countercultural types frequent ✕ **De Werfkring** (✉ Oudegracht 123, ☎ 030/231–1752, $), a vegetarian eatery.

Scenes

As in other cities with only a handful of gay commercial establishments, much of the gay social scene in Utrecht—for locals and visitors alike—revolves around the **C.O.C.** (✉ Oudegracht 221, ☎ 030/231–8841), which has its own pub, **Pann Cafe** (☎ 030/293–3722). This charming brick building overlooking the canal is a short walk south of Domplein. Typically the center and the café are open on weekends and for certain events (call first if it's important to you); the crowd tends to be very mixed in age and split male/female.

There are three small but lively gay bars slightly north of Domplein, all within a short distance of each other. **Wolkenkrabber** (✉ Oudegracht 47, ☎ 030/231–9768) is a quaint and narrow bruin cafe filled with candles in red globes and a mix of bar stools and seats and tables. This is a fairly quiet con-

Pick up the phone.

Pick up the miles.

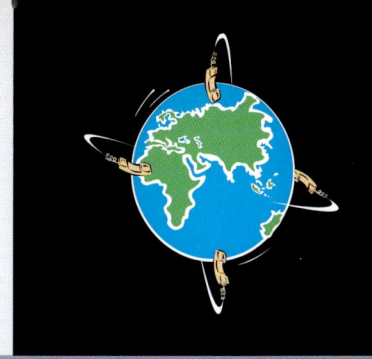

Use your MCI Card® to make an international call from virtually anywhere in the world and earn frequent flyer miles on one of seven major airlines.

Enroll in an MCI Airline Partner Program today. In the U.S., call **1-800-FLY-FREE**. Overseas, call MCI collect at **1-916-567-5151**.

1. To use your MCI Card, just dial the WorldPhone access number of the country you're calling from. (For a complete listing of codes, visit www.mci.com.)
2. Dial or give the operator your MCI Card number.
3. Dial or give the number you're calling.

# Austria (CC) ♦	022-903-012	# Netherlands (CC) ♦	0800-022-91-22
# Belarus (CC)		# Norway (CC) ♦	800-19912
From Brest, Vitebsk, Grodno, Minsk	8-800-103	# Poland (CC) ÷	00-800-111-21-22
From Gomel and Mogilev regions	8-10-800-103	# Portugal (CC) ÷	05-017-1234
# Belgium (CC) ♦	0800-10012	Romania (CC) ÷	01-800-1800
# Bulgaria	00800-0001	# Russia (CC) ÷ ♦	
# Croatia (CC) ★	99-385-0112	To call using ROSTELCOM ■	747-3322
# Czech Republic (CC) ♦	00-42-000112	For a Russian-speaking operator	747-3320
# Denmark (CC) ♦	8001-0022	To call using SOVINTEL ■	960-2222
# Finland (CC) ♦	08001-102-80	# San Marino (CC) ♦	172-1022
# France (CC) ♦	0-800-99-0019	# Slovak Republic (CC)	00-421-00112
# Germany (CC)	0130-0012	# Slovenia	080-8808
# Greece (CC) ♦	00-800-1211	# Spain (CC)	900-99-0014
# Hungary (CC) ♦	00▼800-01411	# Sweden (CC) ♦	020-795-922
# Iceland (CC) ♦	800-9002	# Switzerland (CC) ♦	0800-89-0222
# Ireland (CC)	1-800-55-1001	# Turkey (CC) ♦	00-8001-1177
# Italy (CC) ♦	172-1022	# Ukraine (CC) ÷	8▼10-013
# Kazakhstan (CC)	8-800-131-4321	# United Kingdom (CC)	
# Liechtenstein (CC) ♦	0800-89-0222	To call using BT ■	0800-89-0222
# Luxembourg	0800-0112	To call using MERCURY ■	0500-89-0222
# Monaco (CC) ♦	800-90-019	# Vatican City (CC)	172-1022

Is this a great time, or what? :-)

Automation available from most locations. (CC) Country-to-country calling available to/from most international locations. ♦ Public phones may require deposit of coin or phone card for dial tone. ★ Not available from public pay phone. ▼ Wait for second dial tone. ÷ Limited availability.
■ International communications carrier. Limit one bonus program per MCI account. Terms and conditions apply. All airline program rules and conditions apply. ©1997 MCI Telecommunications Corporation. All rights reserved. Is this a great time, or what? is a service mark of MCI.

Urban planning.

CITYPACKS

The ultimate guide to the city—a complete pocket guide plus a full-size color map.

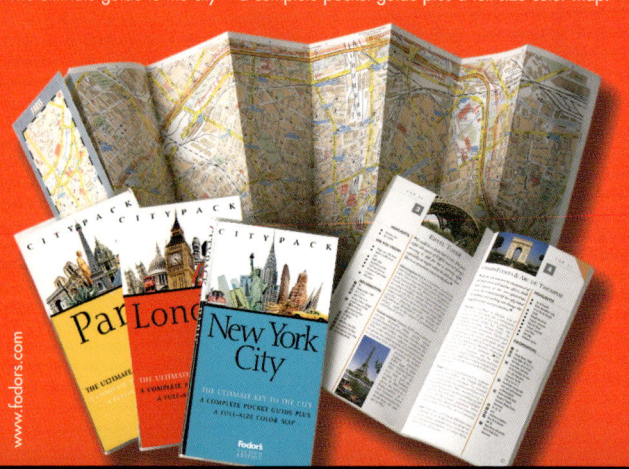

www.fodors.com

Fodor's *The name that means smart travel.*™
At bookstores, or call 1-800-533-6478.

versational bar, where friends gather before heading downstairs directly alongside the canal to **Roze Wolk** (✉ Oudegracht 45, ☎ 030/232–2066), the Wolkenkrabber's louder and darker sister. Despite its historic and romantic setting, this is a lively and festive disco with great music and women's nights held from time to time (both of these bars are mixed male/female other times). Open only on weekends.

Back up a flight of stairs at street level and across the canal, **Bodytalk** (✉ Oudegracht 64, ☎ 030/231–5747) is another mixed male/female venue with a downstairs weekends-only disco, the **Cellar** (✉ Oudegracht 62, same phone). Bodytalk is a friendly low-key place with frequent sing-alongs and a crowd whose median age is slightly older than Wolkenkrabber's. There's also a pleasant open-air terrace. The Cellar draws what few leather men you'll find in Utrecht but welcomes all looks and styles.

MAASTRICHT

Maastricht is the un-Dutch Dutch city: At the very southeastern tip of the country, it is closer to many German and Belgian cities than to Amsterdam (from which it is 207 km/130 miles). The oldest city in the Netherlands, it was founded by the Romans around the middle or end of the first century BC and has been occupied by France, Spain, and Austria at various times throughout history. Today it has one of the nation's best-preserved medieval cores. Maastricht is also, uncharacteristically, surrounded by hills. During Belgium's split from the Netherlands in 1830, the Dutch military laid a strong claim on Maastricht, and so it remained a part of this nation with which it shares few traits. In 1992 it was the site of the signing of the Treaty of Maastricht, a pact further stipulating the diplomatic logistics and goals of the European Union.

Maastricht's train station is in the newer (i.e., 19th-century) eastern side of the city, a short walk from the medieval center. As you come out of it, head west on Stationstraat until you cross the 13th-century **Sintservaas Brug** (St. Servatius Bridge), from which you'll have outstanding views of River Maas below, as well as the ancient skyline.

Once across the bridge, you'll be in the heart of the city center, many of whose streets are cobbled pedestrian lanes lined

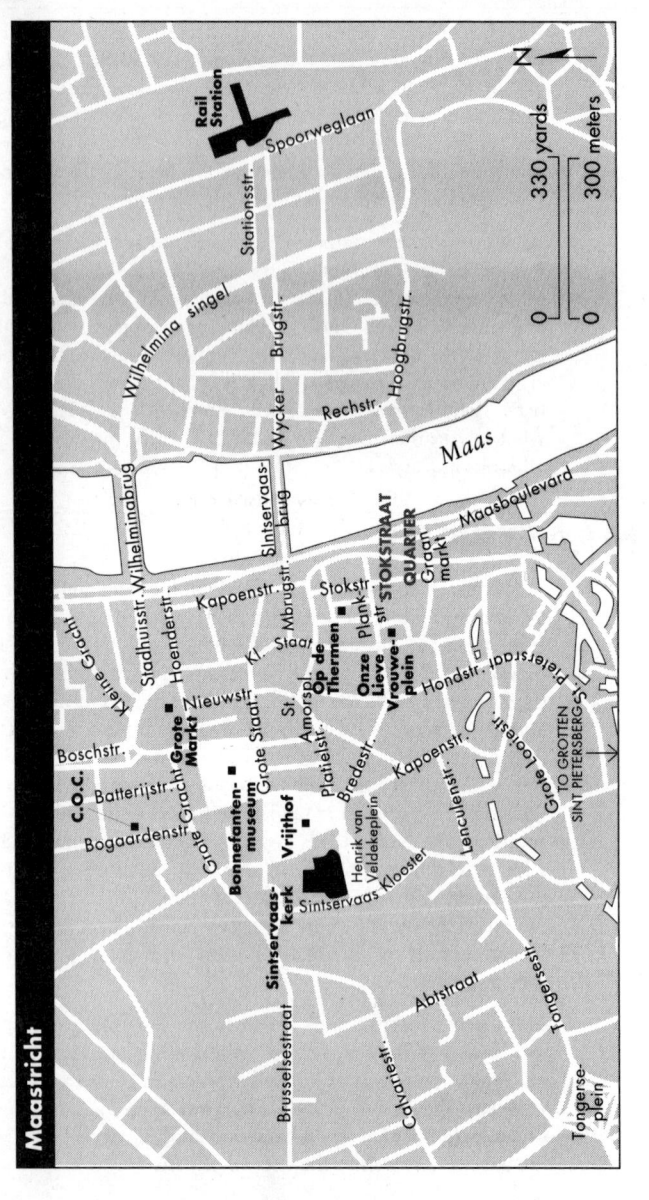

Maastricht

with high-quality shops and restaurants. The City Center is grounded by three major squares, each quite charming and picturesque. To the north, you'll come upon the **Grote Markt** (Market Square), which is dominated by the 1662 **Stadhuis** (Town Hall). Although most Stadhuises only warrant an exterior examination, Maastricht's is open to visitors and contains an outstanding collection of decorative and fine arts. On Wednesday and Friday mornings, a noisy and fragrant farmers' market is held on the square. To the immediate southwest, the **Bonnefantenmuseum** (✉ Ave. Ceramique 250, ☎ 043/329–0190) is the region's top museum. The eclectic holdings range from works by Van Dyck, Rubens, the Bruegels, and other Flemish masters to a fine contemporary art collection; also check out the many archaeological finds that shed some light on the region's two millennia of history.

Of the three squares, the smallest and most enchanting is dominated by **Onze Lieve Vrouwe Basiliek** (Basilica of Our Beloved Lady); this cobbled tree-shaded plaza is a 10-minute walk south of Grote Markt (with so many winding lanes along the way to tempt you, the walk may take longer). The church dates from the 11th century, but archaeological evidence around the square suggests that a Roman Temple may once have occupied the site. Walk immediately east to reach **Op de Thermen,** the former site of a Roman villa and a complex of ancient bathhouses. This is the heart of Maastricht's **Stokstraat Quarter,** and the streets around this medieval basilica are dotted with restored 17th- and 18th-century town houses, as well as art galleries and fancy shops.

The western edge of the city center is dominated by what is considered to be the oldest cathedral in the Netherlands, the 10th-century **Sintservaaskerk** (Church of St. Servatius; ✉ Vrijthof, ☎ 043/325–2121). The treasury here contains a rich collection of medieval religious artifacts. The church looms over the **Vrijthof,** a tree-filled square with outdoor cafés and the constant buzz of pedestrians.

Maastricht may be without the usual art museums and traditional attractions of most other Dutch cities, but it does possess one of the most unique sites in Holland, the **Grotten Sint Pietersberg** (Caves of Mount St. Peter). There are two main entrances to these caves, which wend their way underground for some 200 km (125 miles), but the easiest access from Maastricht is the **Grotten Noord** (Northern Entry), which is about 1½ km (1 mile) southwest of the city center via Hubertuslaan. You can only enter the caves via a guided tour, so it's best to consult with the VVV regarding opening times and directions before visiting. One general rule: The caves are open daily from early April to late September but only on weekends the rest of the year. These caves are man-made—the result of mining for marl (a form of limestone used commonly in local construction). More than 20,000 passages within this immense mountain have been hollowed out by miners over the past two millennia. Of particular note inside are the carvings and graffiti on the walls created by everybody from meditating theology students to, *allegedly*, Napoléon.

Getting Around

There's frequent direct rail service from Amsterdam's Centraal Station to Maastricht; the ride takes about 2½ hours. Maastricht is less than two hours from Brussel by train, so you may wish to combine a trip here with one to Belgium (*see* Chapter 3).

Eats

With its checkered history of occupation by nations with culinary reputations superior to the Netherlands', Maastricht has a fabulous dining scene. This may be the last place in the Netherlands where men still don jackets and ties at the better restaurants, so pack accordingly. Despite the slightly formal air, Maastricht is not at all stuffy, and the mix of locals and jet-setters, young and old, gives both the dining and nightlife scenes a definite air of intrigue. Although Maastricht has no visibly gay dining scene, queer visitors are a bold hue of the municipal fabric—you and your same-sex partner will rarely feel out of place. Despite having a reputation for pricey restaurants, Maastricht has a wealth of cafés for every budget. The highest concentration of eateries overlook the three squares mentioned above, Grote Markt, Onze Lieve Vrouweplein, and Vrijthof.

A high-end favorite is ✗ **'t Pakhoes** (✉ Waterpoort 4, ☎ 043/325–7000, $$$), whose classic Belgian and French cooking and formal setting rival the best restaurants in Brussel and Paris. Named for the regiment of American soldiers who liberated Maastricht at the end of World War II, ✗ **Old Hickory** (✉ Meerssenerweg 372, ☎ 043/362–0548, $$–$$$) offers some of the finest seafood and game in the region, most of it prepared with both traditional and contemporary French recipes. In the shadows of one of the city's oldest churches, ✕ **La Villa** (✉ Onze Lieve Vrouweplein 28, ☎ 043/321–9889, $$–$$$) is a hip bistro offering a tasty array of nouvelle French and Dutch specialties. The friendly staff and perfectly seasoned fare at ✕ **Raz Bari Tandoori** (✉ Boschstraat 105, ☎ 043/325–1521, $$–$$$), which is just north of the Grote Markt, make this one of the best Indian restaurants in town; try the chicken *tikka masala* (boneless chicken served in a mild curry of yogurt and spices). In the south end of the City Center, the plant-filled ✕ **Plaka** (✉ St. Bernardusstraat 4a, ☎ 043/325–4256, $$) has an extensive menu of Greek specialties, from broiled octopus to hefty salads. Nearby ✕ **Alexandria** (✉ Koestraat 21, ☎ 043/321–5155, $) is a cheap and cheerful pizzeria, also with short-order burgers, gyros, and other light foods.

Scenes

You'll see more gays walking along Maastricht's boutiques-filled streets than you will at the few bars and clubs. However, the few nightlife venues in the city are festive and fun. West of the River Maas, your only option is the hard-to-find **C.O.C.** (✉ Bogaardenstraat 43, ☎ 043/321–8337), which is on a nondescript modern residential street just off of Grote Gracht, west of Grote Markt. Inside what appears to be a small apartment building is a foyer filled with posters and notices of upcoming events in the gay community; down a hall are some C.O.C. offices and **Cafe Rose,** a cozy bar with timber ceilings, music posters, alternative and dance music, and a youthful and outgoing crowd. There are usually things going on here after 10 PM Thursday through Sunday, and visitors are quite welcome.

Maastricht's two commercial gay establishments are steps from the train station, east of the River Maas. **La Ferme** (✉ Rechstraat 29, ☎ 043/321–8928) is a convivial bruin cafe, very compact and typically brimming with guys (and maybe a few dykes) of all ages. This is mostly a neighborhood hangout, although during the touristy summer months you'll spy a more eclectic crowd. It doesn't open until 10 PM, but **La Gare** (✉ Spoorweglaan 6, ☎ 043/325–9090), although not huge, is a more substantial nightclub, drawing more of a mix of men and women. There's a small dance floor with the usual dance tunes, and plenty of space for lounging and cruising.

Sleeps

Because Maastricht is so far from Amsterdam, you may want to consider spending the night here. Unfortunately, if you're here on a tight budget, you won't have an easy time finding affordable digs. Although Maastricht has no gay hotels or B&Bs, all of the mainstream properties are quite hospitable. At the top of the line, the luxurious ☆ **Hotel Derlon** (✉ Onze Lieve Vrouweplein 6, 6211 HD, ☎ 043/321–6770, FAX 043/325–1933, $$$$) has spacious individually furnished rooms and overlooks one of the prettiest squares you're likely to find anywhere. Steps from the city's two gay bars, family-owned ☆ **Hotel Bergere** (✉ Stationsstraat 40, 6221 BR, ☎ 043/325–1651, FAX 043/325–5498, $$) is a handsome 19th-century building with pleasantly appointed rooms—as nice as you'll find in this price range.

THE LITTLE BLACK BOOK

Tips on Traveling Throughout the Netherlands

See Tips on Traveling to the Netherlands *in* Chapter 1.

At Your Fingertips

C.O.C. (gay and lesbian center: Den Haag, ✉ Scheveningseveer 7, ☎ 070/365–9090; Haarlem, ✉ Gedempte Oudegracht 24, ☎ 023/532–5453; Leiden, ✉ Langegracht 65, ☎ 071/522–0640, Web site www.dsl.nl~nvihcoc; Maastricht, ✉ Bogaardenstraat 43, ☎ 043/321–8337; Rotterdam, ✉ Schiedamsesingel 175, ☎ 010/414–1555; Utrecht, ✉ Oudegracht 221, ☎ 030/231–8841). **VVV** (the tourist office: Den Haag, ✉ Koningin Julianaplein 30, just north of the Centraal Station, ☎ 06/340–35051; Haarlem, ✉ Stationsplein 1, just outside the rail station, ☎ 06/320–24043; Leiden, ✉ Stationsplein 210, turn right just outside the rail station, ☎ 071/514–6846; Maastricht, ✉ Kleine Staat 1, just west of the River Maas, near the Sintservaas Brug, ☎ 043/325–2121; Rotterdam, ✉ Coolsingel 67, a five-minute walk from the rail station [turn left as you leave the station], ☎ 06/340–34065; Utrecht, just northeast of the rail station, ✉ Vredenburg 90, ☎ 06/340–34085).

Gay Media

There are no queer newspapers specifically for any Dutch cities outside of Amsterdam; however, all of the national gay papers, including the bilingual (English-Dutch) *Gay News* (☎

020/679–1556, Web site www.gaynews.nl), have coverage of the entire country. Dutch-language national publications include **Culture and Camp** (☎ 020/679–9188, e-mail rainbow@neturl.nl); **De GAY Krant** (e-mail red@gayworld.nl); and **Expreszo** (☎ 020/623–4596; e-mail nvihcoc@xs4all.nl).

BOOKSTORES

There are no specifically lesbian and gay bookstores in the Netherlands outside of Amsterdam. Furthermore, most of the general-interest stores you'll find carry only a limited number of English-language titles. The one exception is a terrific one: The **American Book Center** (✉ Lange Poten 23, Den Haag, ☎ 070/364–2742, Web site www.abc.nl), like its Amsterdam branch, is an outstanding source of literature and has quite a few queers titles.

3 Out in Belgium

Antwerpen, Gent, Brugge, and Brussel

IF YOU'RE VISITING AMSTERDAM for more than four or five days, consider hopping over to Belgium for a night or two, or perhaps just for a day-long jaunt. The most popular Belgian cities—Brussel, Antwerpen, Gent, and Brugge—are three to four hours from Amsterdam by train, which is by far the most popular, convenient, and economical way to approach these cities from Amsterdam, at least for quick trips.

Although Belgium and the Netherlands are unmistakably linked culturally and historically, the latter has very much its own personality, landscape, and style of entertainment. From a legal and political standpoint, the Netherlands is considerably more tolerant of lesbians and gays than Belgium, a country steeped in conservative Catholic tradition and famous for its stiff notions of propriety and order (queer porn shops were unheard of in Belgium until several years ago). In the cities covered here, however, you'll have little trouble fitting in, walking comfortably down the street with a same-sex partner, and finding reasonably friendly bars. Fellow Europeans may speak disparagingly of Belgium's official lack of enlightened social policies, but travelers from the United States and the United Kingdom will rarely detect the dark forces typical of many right-wing towns and cities back home. Still, do not come to any Belgian city expecting the nonstop revelry of Amsterdam—bars even in a major international metropolis such as Brussel are generally small, neighborhoody, and cliquey.

Aesthetically, Belgium has a great deal to recommend it: Antwerpen, Gent, and Brugge all retain a delightful me-

Out in Belgium

dieval character. Brussel, since blossoming after World War II into Europe's great center of diplomacy and commerce, feels modern, cosmopolitan, but also rather characterless and bureaucratic in places. Nevertheless, the city has a charming historic section, which, conveniently, meshes with the queer bar and restaurant district.

Lovers of 16th- and 17th-century painting and of medieval architecture and cobbled lanes should not miss Belgium. And if you need one final justification for visiting, consider the incredible food. You might hear that the best cooking is in Brussel, whose French restaurants rival those of Paris (honest!). But the Flemish cities of Antwerpen, Brugge, and Gent all have outstanding international cuisine, too—menus far more inventive and ingredients fresher and better chosen than those you'll find in the Netherlands (it appears that when the two countries split up in 1830, Belgium made off with all the cookbooks).

Although few Belgian city dwellers will blink an eye at lesbians and gays wandering by, discretion is still the rule. You must ring a buzzer to gain entrance to most gay bars, and you don't often see rainbow flags or political banners or any visible evidence of queer life in Belgium. As in many European countries, the gay scene has flourished particularly among young people and students; as a result, many of the trendy art spaces, literary cafés, and fashionable discos—even when catering to a predominantly straight crowd—are gay-friendly. A general tip is that disco bunnies, leather men, and sleaze hounds will have a great time in Antwerpen. Brugge is for lovers and has a nearly invisible gay nightlife. Gent is a bigger, somewhat grittier version of nearby Brugge, and has a few lively bars. Brussel is worth a visit, has an okay club scene, and has plenty of first-rate restaurants and luxury hotels, but most of these cater to business travelers and fail to register on the romance scale.

Making the Most of Your Time

The following itineraries work well for either men or women. One is for a couple in search of seclusion and the other for either a single traveler or for a few single friends looking for action. The couple should take a train from Amsterdam to Antwerpen in the morning; arrive around noon (store your bags at the station) and explore the Old City, perhaps catching lunch near the Grote Markt. By early evening, get back to the station and continue on to Brugge, where you can enjoy dinner, go for an evening walk around this enchanting medieval city, and spend the night somewhere cozy. In the morning, explore Brugge a bit longer, and then make the 30-minute trip to Gent, where you'll find several more hours of engaging exploration and a few choice options for dinner. If you leave by 9, you'll be back in Amsterdam by shortly after midnight.

If you're looking for a wilder time, catch a train to Antwerpen, where you should spend the entire day and overnight, enjoying dinner at one of the gay-popular restaurants near the Grote Markt. If you're a dyke, there's a nice bar in this area. Guys should walk (or cab it) to either of the two bar districts (there's one for leather and sleaze; another more for the young guppie set). The next morning (or early afternoon, if you had a late night), take the train to Brugge, where you can spend several hours enjoying the city. After dinner, catch the four-hour train back to Amsterdam. If you have limitless energy, you might cap your day in Brugge by hopping over to Gent for a brief dinner-and-pub adventure, before returning to Amsterdam—just be sure you're armed in advance with the departure time of the final return train (or, if you play your cards right, meet a new friend and perhaps enjoy a final night in Gent!).

If you want to devote two nights to Belgium, spend the final evening in Brussel. If you're primarily interested in nightlife, arrive on a weekend, which is when you'll find the best party scene. The next day, you can spend the day exploring Brussel's city center before heading back to Amsterdam. One final suggestion: To combine your Belgian adventure with a visit to any Dutch cities, work it in with an overnight to Maastricht (*see* Chapter 2). Maastricht is the only Dutch city far enough from Amsterdam to necessitate an overnight, and it's only an hour or two from the Belgian cities covered here (it's minutes from the Belgian border, near Liège).

A Note About Place-Names and Language

Flemish, which is the practical equivalent of Dutch, is spoken in Antwerpen, Brugge, Gent, and the rest of Flanders (French is spoken in most of the southern half, with German spoken mostly in the eastern tip of Belgium). Officially, Brussel is bilingual, but at most restaurants, hotels, and nightclubs, French is spoken more often than Flemish. Most younger Belgians, as well as most employees in the tourism and hospitality industry, speak Flemish (which is nearly identical to Dutch), French, and very good English (and often German), but it definitely helps to master a few basic Flemish/Dutch phrases while in Flanders, and some French words while in Brussel. See the vocabulary section at the end of this guide for useful Dutch vocabulary and pronunciations of place-names.

Names of the four cities in this chapter are written in Flemish/Dutch, which is typically how you'll hear them referred to and see them written about during your stay in Amsterdam. In English, Antwerpen is known as Antwerp (Anvers in French), Brugge as Bruges (as it is in French), Gent as Ghent (Gand in French), and Brussel as Brussels (Bruxelles in French). Because you'll typically see them this way, street addresses and place-names are given in Flemish/Dutch throughout the sections on Antwerpen, Brugge, and Gent, and in French throughout the Brussel section.

A Note About Price Categories in Eats and Sleeps Sections

For price ranges noted throughout this chapter, *see* dining and lodging Chart B at the front of this guide.

ANTWERPEN

Compared with Amsterdam, **Antwerpen** is a rather quiet, reserved city, but compared with the rest of Belgium, it buzzes with activity (and more than its share of debauchery). Antwerpen is also highly walkable: From the Centraal Station, it's a five-minute walk to where most of the gay bars are, and from 15 to 30 minutes on foot to almost every attraction. Architecturally, the city is a survey of highs (with only a few lows) of the past five centuries, with an emphasis squarely on the 19th century. Relatively few of the modern office blocks that dominate Brussel have scarred Antwerpen's dashing medieval facade, although you will find some disturbingly ugly streets outside the historic city center.

Antwerpen has long been one of Europe's major commercial and shipping centers (it's the second-busiest port city on the continent), with a virtual lock on the diamond trade; about 85% of the world's uncut diamonds pass through the city. In terms of prestige and wealth, the city peaked during the first half of the 16th century, during the reign of Emperor Charles V, who made Antwerpen the principal port of his vast

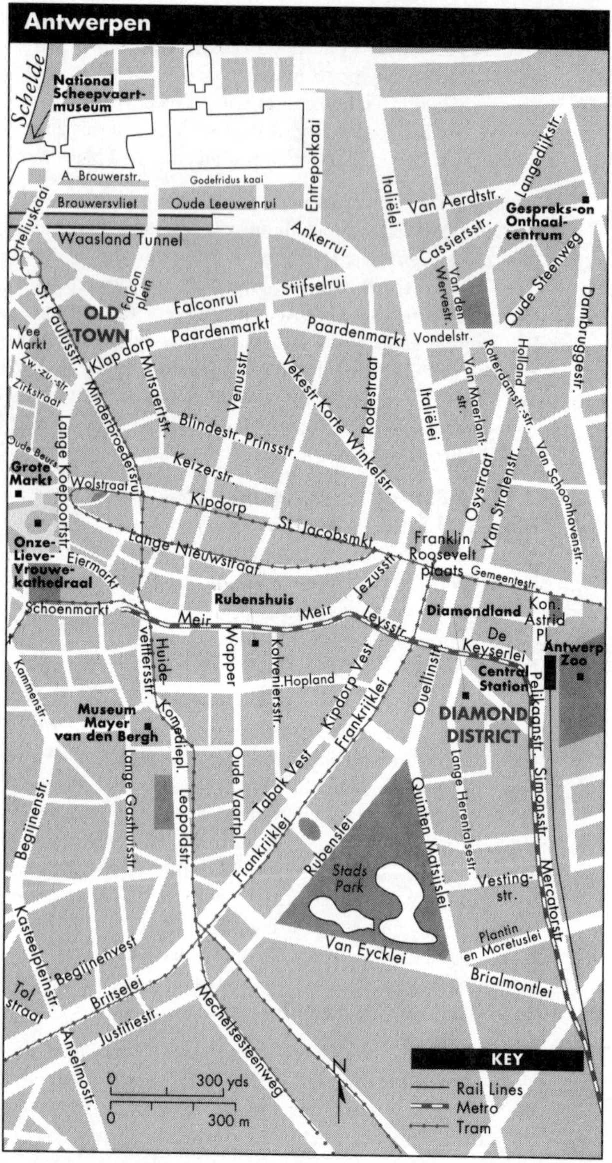
Antwerpen
Schelde
National Scheepvaart-museum
A. Brouwerstr.
Godefridus kaai
Brouwersvliet
Oude Leeuwenrui
Entrepotkaai
Waasland Tunnel
Orteliuskaai
Ankerrui
Italiëlei
Van Aerdtstr.
Langedijkstr.
Gesprekss-on Onthaal-centrum
Cassiersstr.
Van den Wervestr.
Oude Steenweg
Dambruggestr.
Falcon plein
Stijfselrui
Falconrui
OLD TOWN
St. Paulusstr.
Vee Markt
Paardenmarkt
Vondelstr.
Klapdorp
Mutsaertstr.
Venusstr.
Vekestr.
Korte Winkelstr.
Rodestraat
Italiëlei
Van Maerlant-str.
Rotterdamstr.
Holland str.
Zirkstraat
Minderbroedersrui
Blindestr.
Prinsstr.
Lange Koepoortstr.
Oude Beurs
Grote Markt
Wolstraat
Keizerstr.
Kipdorp
Osystraat
Van Stralenstr.
Van Schoonhovenstr.
St Jacobsmkt.
Franklin Roosevelt plaats
Gemeentestr.
Onze-Lieve-Vrouwe-kathedraal
Eiermarkt
Lange Nieuwstraat
Jezusstr.
Rubenshuis
Diamondland
Kon. Astrid Pl.
Schoenmarkt
Meir
Leysstr.
De Keyserlei
Antwerp Zoo
Huidevettersstr.
Wapper
Kolveniersstr.
Kipdorp Vest
Hopland
Central Station
Kammenstr.
Museum Mayer van den Bergh
Komediepl.
Frankrijklei
Quellinstr.
DIAMOND DISTRICT
Pelikaanstr.
Lange Gasthuisstr.
Leopoldstr.
Oude Vaartpl.
Tabak Vest
Quinten Matsijslei
Lange Herentalsestr.
Simonsstr.
Begijnenstr.
Frankrijklei
Rubenslei
Stads Park
Vesting-str.
Mercatorstr.
Kasteelpleinstr.
Begijnenvest
Van Eycklei
Plantin en Moretuslei
Brialmontlei
Tol straat
Britselei
Justitiestr.
Mechelsesteenweg
Anselmostr.
N
0
300 yds
0
300 m
KEY
Rail Lines
Metro
Tram

domain. In the 1560s, Antwerpen and Paris were the only European cities with more than 100,000 citizens. But when commerce declined following Charles's abdication in 1555 (his successor, Philip II of Spain, was an ardent Roman Catholic without the same sympathy for the Protestants of the Netherlands), such master painters as Rubens, Jordaens, and Van Dyck earned the city acclaim as an arts center. Diamond cutting and oil painting remain integral to Antwerpen's identity, but much of the population derives its livelihood from trade and industry. The city is elegant but refreshingly gritty, international but possessing a strange mix of provincial arrogance and small-town friendliness, and highly cultured but with a love of partying and with a busy red-light district. Although much smaller than Brussel's, the city's gay population is probably more visible and definitely more intent on cutting loose; it lacks, however, the activist bent of the community in Brussel.

If you approach Antwerpen from the spectacular neo-baroque **Centraal Station,** your first impression will be one of seediness and bustle. The blocks immediately around the station are sullen, as is the small **gay entertainment district** a few hundred yards north of the station, beginning at the intersection of Gemeentestraat and Von Schoonhovenstraat (by Koningen Astridplaats). Many businesses are along Von Schoonhovenstraat, with others a bit north (and a couple of blocks east) along Dambruggestraat, which is where you'll find the **Gespreks-on Onthaalcentrum** (G.O.C., which acts as the city's lesbian and gay community center, just as the C.O.C.'s do in the Netherlands; ✉ Dambruggestraat 204, ☎ 03/233–1071); the center is typically staffed Tuesday through Friday in the evening and often sponsors parties (call for details). To reach most of the city's important attractions, wander west from the station along De Keyserlei, which intersects with **Meir,** a broad avenue lined with tony shops.

Along this route consider two interesting detours. The banal blocks just southwest of the Centraal Station comprise the city's commercial **Diamond District**—many of the small shops and stalls hawking gems are beneath the elevated rail tracks and possess all the charm and mystique of a low-budget flea market. If diamond hunting is your thing, however, you'll love it.

Farther along Meir, however, you'll come upon one of Belgium's must-see attractions, the magnificent Italian baroque–

style **Rubenshuis** (✉ Wapper 9, ☎ 03/232–4747), which was largely reconstructed from Rubens's own designs. This was Rubens's home when he was at the pinnacle of his fame: traveling on diplomatic missions, painting some of his finest portraits and major commissions. Only a few of his 2,500 works hang in the mansion today (300 were sold off by Helen Fourment, his young widow, following his death in 1640), which also contains a re-created studio and details of his life and career. The narrow streets south and west of Rubenshuis are also filled with engaging shops and cozy cafés. From here it's just a short walk to another arts highlight, the **Museum Mayer Van den Bergh** (✉ Lange Gasthuisstraat 19, ☎ 03/232–4237), which contains the amazing 4,000-piece collection amassed by the art connoisseur Mayer Van den Bergh during the 19th century. The highlights of the collection are two paintings by Bruegel: the witty, miniature *Twelve Proverbs,* and *Dulle Griet,* also known as "Mad Meg," which pictures an irate woman wearing helmet and breastplate, a sword in one hand, and food and cooking utensils in the other, striding across a field strewn with the ravages and insanity of war.

Meir leads eventually to Antwerpen's charming **Old Town,** which is anchored by the triangular **Grote Markt** and, to the southeast, the **Onze-Lieve-Vrouwekathedraal** (Our Lady's Cathedral; ✉ Handschoenmarkt, ☎ 03/231–3033), whose 404-foot spire looms over this beautifully preserved medieval neighborhood. The exploring is particularly good from the Grote Markt west to the River Schelde, along the banks of which you'll find the **National Scheepvaartmuseum** (National Maritime Museum; ✉ Steenplein, ☎ 03/232–0850). The museum is housed inside the 9th-century **Steen,** an ancient fortress overlooking the river.

The area north of the city center quickly gives way to a thriving but dreary red-light district and then a rather rough industrial neighborhood. A small but extremely popular queer leather-bar entertainment district (*see* Scenes, *below*) is centered here.

Getting Around

Antwerpen is closest to Amsterdam of the Belgian cities covered in this chapter, about two and a half hours by train. From here it's another 30 minutes to Brussel and Gent, and about an hour to Brugge. The Centraal Station is a healthy 1½-km (1-mile) walk from the Old Town center, but it's a pleasant stroll. If you're in a hurry or the weather is uncooperative, try a cab or the subway (which you can take to Groenplaats for access to Old Town).

Eats

Antwerpen probably has the most sophisticated and constantly evolving cuisine of any city in northern Belgium; if dining is a high priority, don't miss it. You'll pay more here for a meal (as you will in any Belgian city) than in Amsterdam, but the results will speak for themselves. Many of the best and, in many cases, most gay-friendly restaurants are on the narrow, winding lanes around the Grote Markt—in fact, just about any restaurant in this area is tolerant and hip. You should avoid eating near the gay entertainment district by the Centraal Station, which has little to offer from a culinary standpoint.

For a truly fine-dining experience, make a reservation at the formal (wear a jacket and tie), very straight, but supremely elegant ✕ **De Matelote** (✉ Haarstraat 9, ☎ 03/231–3207), a two-level restaurant whose mezzanine is reached by a sweeping staircase; the menu features some of the finest seafood (a Flemish specialty) in the city. In a historic building with huge windows overlooking the Grote Markt, ✕ **Ultimatum** (✉ Grote Markt 8, ☎ 03/232–5853, $$) has one of the best restaurant settings in the city. A bonus is the terrific bistro-style menu and cute (male and female) servers—this is the gayest restaurant in Old Town, and it's especially pink later in the evening on weekends, when there's live music in the adjacent lounge and bar.

Another first-rate gay-popular choice is ✕ **In de Schaduw van de Kathedraal** (✉ Handschoenmarkt 17, ☎ 03/232–4014, $$), an intimate nouvelle Continental restaurant that looks directly out at the cathedral square. ✕ **Facade** (✉ Hendrik Conscienceplein 18, ☎ 03/233–5931, $–$$) is known for its tasty veggie fare, bohemian atmosphere, good music, and artsy crowd. You'll find plenty of young trendy types, both gay and straight, at ✕ **Ulcke van Zurich** (✉ Oude Beurs 50, ☎ 03/234–0494, $–$$), which is just a block or two north of the Grote Markt and set inside a charming old house; the food is light and affordable, and served until quite late in the evening.

Scenes

Antwerpen's bar scene is small but packs a punch. Queers are more than welcome at many of the centrally located hetero taverns and clubs in Old Town, but the main gay-male bar district is 20 minutes away (but convenient to Centraal Station) in a neighborhood that's rather bleak and even has a dicey feel at night. The most popular bars here are along Von Schoonhovenstraat, with some fairly sleepy neighborhood bars along nearby Dambruggestraat. Bars tend to be narrow, modern, and loud, with dance floors the size of postage stamps. On the plus side, they are cruisy and down-to-earth. The popular leather-bar district is a good 15 minutes on foot from either the main gay district or Old Town.

If you're looking for a friendly mixed gay-straight hangout close to the Grote Markt, check out the funky **Swingcafé** (⌧ Suikerrui 13–15, ☏ 03/233–1478), which has live jazz music most nights and a nice selection of beer. **Babbelbox** (⌧ Grote Pieterpotstraat 18, ☏ 03/234–0369) is another popular and centrally located mixed gay-straight pub.

Also in Old Town, **Shakespeare** (⌧ Oude Koornmarkt 24, ☏ 03/231–5058) is a slick lesbian bar near the Grote Markt that's comfy inside and draws a great mix of women, all ages and types. The dance floor is not large, but the Euro pop and dance music is pretty decent. You'll have to walk a short way south of the city center to reach **Lady's Pub** (⌧ Waalsekaai 56, ☏ 03/238–5490), a neighborhood lesbian bar.

In the gay district, **Den Bazaar** (⌧ Van Schoonhovenstraat 22, ☏ 03/232–9197) is most popular among wired club kids; it's a cramped, smoke-filled place with young voguers, stand-and-model boys, and a few amusing attitude queens. In back you'll find a small but busy dance floor and a great juke box. More elegant and drawing a better mix of ages, **50/50** (⌧ Van Schoonhovenstraat 40, ☏ 03/225–1173) has a comfy lounge with sofas in back and a nice bar up front. **Borsolino** (⌧ Van Schoonhovenstraat 48, ☏ 03/226–9162) will show you roughly what Antwerpen might have looked like in the '80s, with extensive use of mirrors and brash lighting (to say nothing of the ear-splitting music); the staff is very friendly, the crowd campy (and includes a few women, unlike most of the other gay bars). For Abba-inspired music with the ambience of a Second Empire drawing room, drop by **Twilight** (⌧ Van Schoonhovenstraat 54, ☏ 03/232–6704) and admire the Eros statuary, elaborate chandeliers, and towering floral arrangements; in warm weather head for the charming courtyard in back.

The one disco that's not too close to the gay district or the Grote Markt but is worth a trip on weekends is **Café d'Anvers** (✉ Verversrui 15, ☏ 03/226–3870), which is a 10-minute walk north of the Old Town area. It draws a young and hip crowd of both fags and dykes, and quite a few straights.

The most famous of the hangouts in the leather-bar district, **The Boots** (✉ Van Aerdtstraat 22, ☏ 03/233–2136) is open Fridays and Saturdays and has a video bar, several very frisky dark rooms, glory holes, an S/M cellar, and (surprise) terribly cruisy bathrooms. The Boots is a private club, which means that you'll have to buy a one-time membership card at the door—the staff are quite nice about this, charge very little, and don't require that you be introduced by another member. Tiny but action-packed **Hanky Code** (✉ Van den Wervestraat 69, ☏ 03/226–8172) has a pleasant terrace that fills up with hunky and horny guys on warm evenings. **Captain Caveman** (✉ Geulincxstraat 28, ☏ 03/233–4487) is one more option that's no less raunchy than the others. All of these places encourage leather, uniforms, rubber, or other such attire, but also welcome a simple jeans-and-white-T-shirt ensemble; anybody otherwise gussied up, however, will be turned politely away.

If you're not into the leather scene but are looking for a little action, Antwerpen has great saunas. The busiest and most nicely furnished of the bunch is **Spa 55** (✉ Sanderusstraat 55, ☏ 03/238–3137), an impressive five-floor bathhouse that draws a cross-section of guys; it's about a 15-minute walk south of Grote Markt. Another option, up near the leather scene, is **City Sauna** (✉ Olijftakstraat 35, ☏ 03/234–1925), which is comfortable but not as nice as Spa 55. For erotica, stop by the centrally located **Libidos-Erotheek** (✉ Gemeentestraat 11, ☏ 03/233–1001), which is the largest queer porn palace in Belgium; it's right around the corner from the Van Schoonhovenstraat bars.

Sleeps

Antwerpen has a full slate of hotels, from dreary but cheap glorified youth hostels (there are a proliferation around the Centraal Station) to stately old grandes dames. Few of them advertise or market to gays and lesbians, but virtually all of them are perfectly gay-friendly.

Very close to the city center and about a 20-minute walk from the queer bar district, the 🏨 **Hotel Cammerpoorte** (✉ Nationalestraat 38–40, B-2000, ☎ 03/231–9736, FAX 03/226–2968, $$) has spare modern rooms at decent rates; bathrooms are clean and updated. The extremely gay-popular 🏳️‍🌈 **Hotel Florida** (✉ De Keyserlei 59, B-2018, ☎ 03/232–1443, FAX 03/233–0835, $) is beside the train station, a few minutes from the gay district, and has dull but clean rooms at prices that are very tough to beat.

GENT AND BRUGGE

Flanders, known mostly for its art cities of **Brugge** and **Gent**, still evokes the Middle Ages with its perfectly restored buildings and streets (further aided by the considerable number of faux-medieval embellishments created in these cities, especially Brugge, during the past century). Both cities prospered dramatically during the 13th and 14th centuries as the world's cloth-manufacturing centers (Flemish tapestries and lace are cherished to this day). Flemish painting—in fact, the practice of painting with oil—began in Brugge in the 1420s. Jan Van Eyck and Hans Memling were the earliest practitioners of the technique (which was subsequently exported to Italy by Petrus Christus, a student of Van Eyck's). Today they and the other early Flemish masters are well represented in the city's museums.

Queens of all genders: Stop for a moment wherever you are to savor this Marie-Antoinette-esque anecdote, which involves the French queen Jeanne of Navarre. In 1301 Queen Jeanne lamented how she was being upstaged by the women of Brugge, who loved to spend money on their clothes: "I thought I alone was queen," she said, "and here I am surrounded by hundreds more." She got her comeuppance a year later, when the men of Brugge, fed up with financing the French royal couple's lavish entertaining bills, massacred the French garrison and went on to defeat the French at the Battle of the Golden Spurs.

The region is ideal for exploring on foot or by bicycle; the terrain is flat, and scenic towpaths run along the area's many canals. Brugge is the more idyllic of the two cities—you can't help but realize after visiting that it exists almost solely to entertain tourists. That said, it's difficult not to succumb to its considerable appeal. Gent, meanwhile, is a workaday city that happens to have a wonderful medieval city center, but its outlying neighborhoods are dull. Of the two, Gent also has the better nightlife and a considerably more visible queer community.

Gent

Gent is the seat of Flanders's regional government. All told, it contains as many picturesque lanes and breathtaking medieval buildings as does Brugge; you just have to wander through some less eye-pleasing sections to find them all. Although Brugge was barely touched by industry during the late 19th century, Gent flourished in this regard, giving rise to numerous factories and industrial areas. If planning only a short visit to Flanders, try to factor in at least an afternoon in Gent to see its contributions to the world of art and architecture. Its three medieval towers—**Sint-Niklaaskerk** (St. Nicholas's Church; ⊠ To the west of the Goudenleeuwplein), the **Belfort** (Belfry; ⊠ Sint-Baafsplein, ☏ 09/233–3954), and **Sint-Baafskathedraal** (St. Baaf's Cathedral; ⊠ Sint-Baafsplein)—are in the heart of the city center and visible from St. Michael's Bridge. In the latter you can see Jan Van Eyck's famed masterpiece, *The Adoration of the Mystic Lamb,* trumpeted—and rightly so—as Gent's number-one artistic treasure. A polyptych altarpiece completed in 1432, it has one of the stormiest histories of any piece of Western art—it was successively stolen, either in whole or in part, by Napoléon, an anonymous thief, and the Germans, but made it back home after being discovered by American troops in an abandoned salt mine in Austria. For an astounding view of the city, ride the elevator to the top of the Belfort. These three towers loom above the most impressive blocks in Gent, around which you'll see ancient guild houses and many other prominent buildings.

Leading from the center, past the Stadhuis (Town Hall), Hoogpoort is lined with several artsy restaurants and bars; follow it across the river Leie to reach the ancient (circa 1180, but heavily altered in the 19th century) Castle of the Counts of Flanders, **'s Gravensteen** (⊠ Sint-Veerleplein, ☏ 09/225–9306). From the battlements there's a terrific view over the rooftops of old Gent; inside, an *oubliette* (secret dungeon) lies deep within the bowels of the building. A final city center highlight is **Museum voor Volkskunde** (Folklore Museum; ⊠ Kraanlei 65, ☏ 09/223–1336), which comprises a cluster of 16th-century almshouses, each of which has been refitted to depict a different facet of 18th- and 19th-century life in Gent, from a cooper's shop to a tavern.

Gent

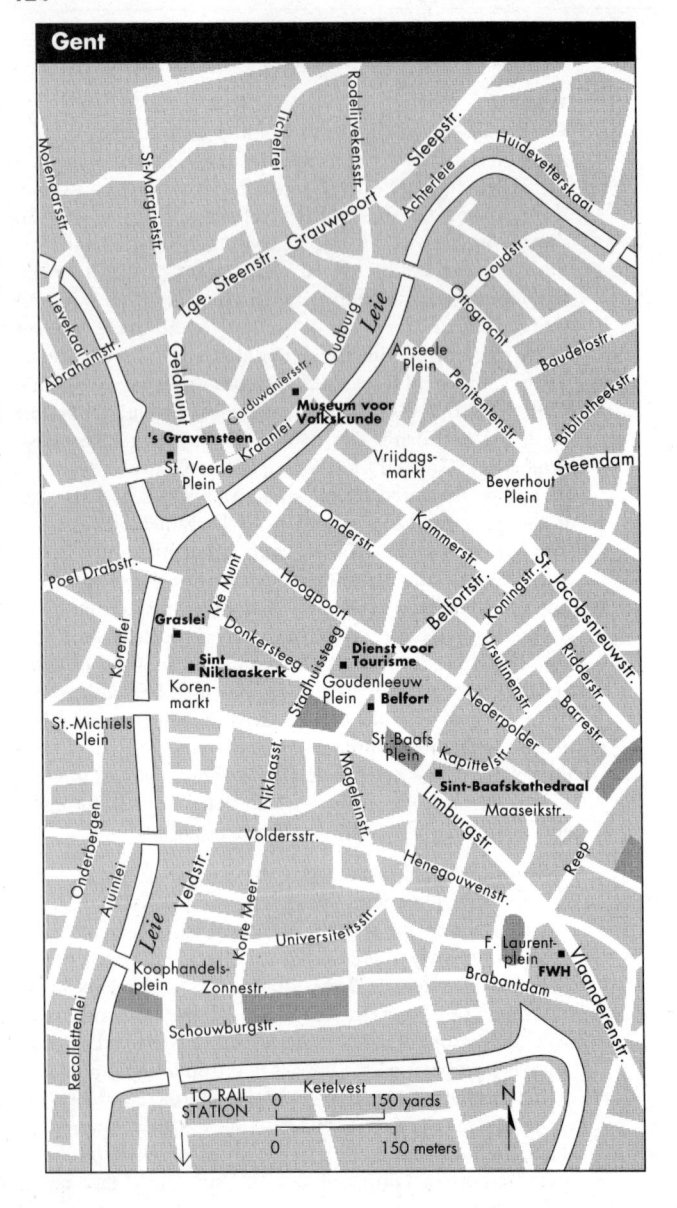

Brugge

Relatively compact and a pleasure to navigate, Brugge feels a bit Disneyesque in places (it may have more candy shops and lace-souvenir stores per head than any town in Western Europe). This is not a city without sites, but you can do perfectly well by wandering along the narrow cobbled streets without an agenda or a map, peeking down streets. Brugge abounds with cafés and has several of the country's better museums, and in summer it swells with crowds of families and schoolchildren on break. No visit to Belgium would be complete without at least a walk through the heart of the city.

Although it's a 20-minute walk from the train station to the city center, the stroll is engaging, especially if you go by way of the placid **Minnewater Park,** named for the small harbor (a.k.a. "the Lake of Love") that passes through it. This narrow body of water was the city's commercial port during the Middle Ages; today it's a place for swooning couples (mostly heterosexual) to stroll around arm in arm. From here it's a short distance north to the **Begijnhof** (Beguinage; ⌧ Monasterium de Wijngaard, Oud Begijnhof, ☏ 050/330011), a well-preserved 13th-century compound of small houses in which lay women resided for many decades. Many of the original inhabitants were the widows of Crusaders; it is now occupied by Benedictine nuns. One of the houses is now a small museum, and the grounds make for a tranquil stroll, but visitors should take care to respect the nuns' peace and privacy.

Continue walking north for 10 to 15 minutes to reach the **Markt,** which has been the center of the city's activities since 958. Old guild houses line the north and west sides of the square. In the center stands a statue of Jan Breydel and Pieter De Coninck, the city's medieval heroes, who led the people of Flanders to victory (albeit short-lived) over their aristocratic French oppressors. To the east, restaurant-lined Breidelstraat leads to a second smaller ancient square, the **Burg,** which is flanked by the grandiloquent 14th-century **Stadhuis** (Town Hall), a white sandstone Gothic jewel. Most of the city's major streets radiate from these two squares. About midway between the Begijnhof and the Markt and Burg, the **Onze-Lieve-Vrouwekerk** (Church of Our Lady; ⌧ Gruuthusestraat at Mariastraat) and its 400-foot spire tower over many of the city's most treasured sites. The nearby **Groeninge Museum** (⌧ Dijver 12, ☏ 050/448711) surveys six centuries

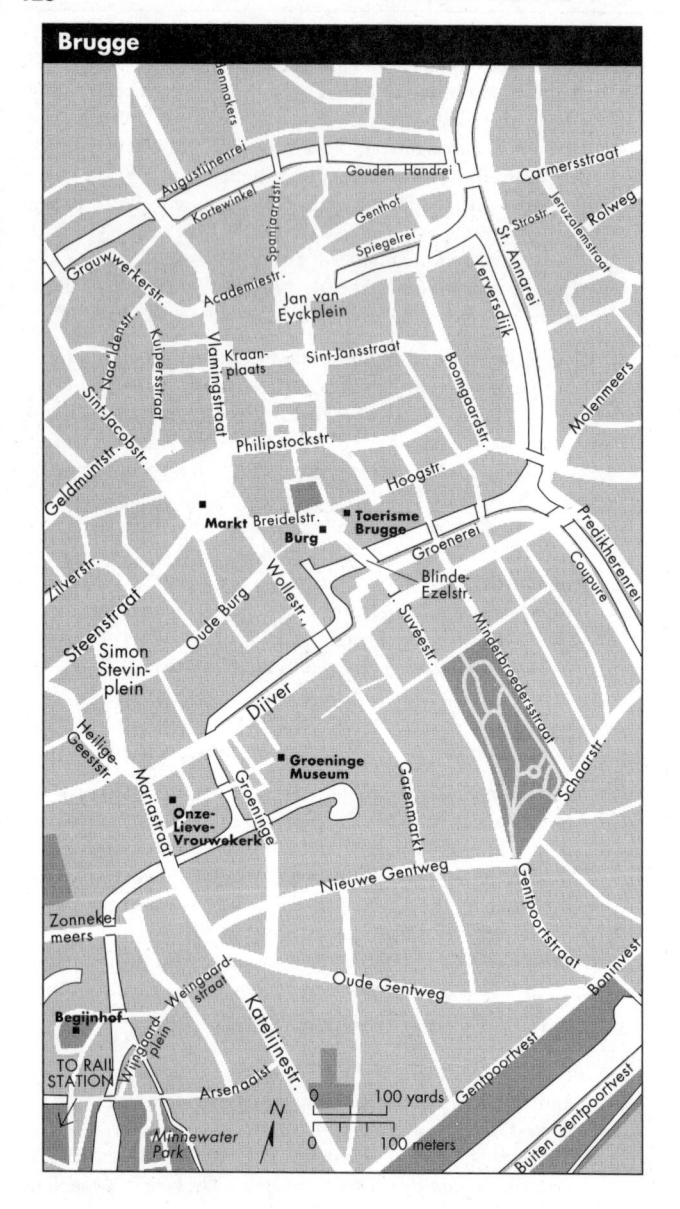

Brugge

of Flemish, Dutch, and Belgian art. Among the standouts are the works of the so-called "Flemish Primitives"—Jan Van Eyck (including his astonishingly realistic Madonna with Canon Van der Paele), Hieronymus Bosch, Pieter Bruegel (both Elder and Younger), and Hans Memling, as well as works up through the 20th century.

Getting Around

By train, Gent is about 30 minutes from Brussel or Antwerpen, and Brugge is another 25 minutes. Alas, in Gent, the train station is a fairly unmemorable 20-minute walk from the historic city center; consider hopping a cab or taking Tram 1, 11, or 12 to Centrum.

Eats

In this unbelievably romantic land, fancy formal restaurants are abundant but certainly not the only purveyors of outstanding cuisine. Nevertheless, if you're willing to break the bank, take your honey to ✕ **Den Gouden Harynk** (✉ Groeninge 25, ☏ 050/337637, $$$$), an intimate café filled with museum-quality antiques and the aroma of fine Fleming and French cooking. For some of the best mussels and seafood in the city, stop by ✕ **Breydel-De Coninck** (✉ Breidelstraat 24, ☏ 050/339746, $$), a simple but comfy eatery revered more for its food than for its ordinary atmosphere. The one fairly gay restaurant in Brugge, ✕ **Miramar** (✉ Mariastraat 13, ☏ 050/347262, $-$$) serves great salads, sandwiches, apple pie, and a variety of teas; there's a small garden with tables in back.

In Gent, ✕ **Buddhasbelly** (✉ Hoogpoort 30, ☏ 09/225-1732, $) is a great vegetarian eatery with a boho sensibility. Just up and across the street, ✕ **Ludwig** (✉ Hoogpoort 37, ☏ 09/223-7165, $) is an elegant little bar and café that's popular with family. Also quite gay-friendly, ✕ **Rococco** (✉ Corduwanierstraat 57, ☏ 09/224-3035, $-$$) is set in an elegant 18th-century house with a hip cocktail bar and reasonably priced menu. For something a bit more substantial, plan a meal at ✕ **Buikske Vol** (✉ Kraanlei 17, ☏ 09/225-1880, $$-$$$), a nouvelle Belgian restaurant known for its innovative cooking.

Scenes

Brugge is geared mostly for couples, not singles, so the nightlife is predictably tame with no flashy queer discos or anything-goes dark rooms and spas. You'll find one true gay bar, **Passe-Partout** (⌧ Sint Jansstraat 3, ☏ 050/334742), a mixed lesbian/gay bruin café that's extremely festive and friendly from late afternoon until well into the night. Another possibility is **Ma Rica Rokk** (⌧ 't Zand 6–8, ☏ 050/332424), a straight but rather chic disco with a somewhat queer following (there's at least one Judy Garland poster on the wall, if that's any indication); it's on a relatively modern stretch of restaurants and bars that's popular with students, hipsters, and other lively souls. **Chaplin** (⌧ 't Zand 24, ☏ 050/347997) is another gay-friendly pub along this street.

Revelers will have somewhat better luck in Gent, whose friendly queer scene doesn't exactly rival Antwerpen's but at least offers a few interesting choices. **Paradox** (⌧ Vlaanderenstraat 22, ☏ 09/224–1037), which is both a disco and a pub, draws an eclectic mix of local guys. The **Cherry Lane Disco** (⌧ Meersenierstraat 3, ☏ 09/233–7491) is a better disco for lesbians, although plenty of gay men and straights party here, too. **Dandy's** (⌧ Princes Clementinalaan 195, ☏ 09/220–5181) is a popular sleaze venue, with strip shows and rent boys. It's very close to the train station.

Sleeps

Even at the most gay-friendly properties in Brugge, the clientele tends to be mostly straight, most of the time. However, this is a fairly tolerant city, and the options reviewed below are at least comfortable for same-sex couples. Keep in mind that the city is overwhelmed by visitors in summer, so try to book ahead. In a pinch, there are several hotels along 't Zand, a square built above one of the city's main underground parking lots; this area is very close to the train station, Minnewater Park, and some of the gay-friendly pubs, but it lacks the ancient charm typical of those accommodations in the heart of the city.

For an overnight, Brugge is one of the most romantic cities in Europe, although room rates are expectedly high. If considering a luxury property, don't be put off by the modern ⌸ **Holiday Inn Crowne Plaza Brugge** (⌧ Burg 10, ☏ 050/345–834, FAX 050/345–615, $$$$); it's an impressive space and its innovative design blends nicely with its historical surroundings; it couldn't be more centrally located, and it has a nice pool and fitness center, too. For more moderate budgets, consider ⌸ **Egmond** (⌧ Minnewater 15, ☏ 050/

341–445, ℻ 050/342–940, $$–$$$), a small cozy inn, many of whose rooms have fireplaces, skylights, and other romantic details; all rooms have views of the gardens in Minnewater Park. Of budget options, ☎ **De Pauw** (✉ Sint-Gilliskerkhof 8, ☎ 050/337–118, $) is another very small property that's comfortably furnished. The ☎ **Hotel Hans Memling** (✉ Kuipersstraat 18, ☎ 050/332–096, $) is a simple but pleasant budget property that's probably the only major hotel in the city with a substantial gay following.

In Gent, the outpost of the ritzy French chain ☎ **Sofitel** (✉ Hoogpoort 63, ☎ 09/233–3331, ℻ 09/233–1102, $$$–$$$$) is an inviting hotel in the heart of the old city—it's not far from good bars and restaurants. ☎ **The Flandria** (✉ Barrestraat 3, ☎ 09/223–0626, $$) is a clean gay-popular mid-range property that's not far from the city center—it's perfect if you simply need a convenient tourist-class accommodation while in town.

BRUSSEL

Folks in Amsterdam may snicker a little if they hear that you've planned a big trip to Brussel, which you may hear described as everything from dull to stiff to aesthetically challenged. In truth, although you might not rank Brussel among the most fascinating city capitals of Europe, you may be pleasantly surprised with its offerings.

The capital of Europe and the center of EU and NATO politics ("Brussels" is now shorthand for the European Commission, the guiding body of the EU), the city does attract its share of expats, suit-clad bureaucrats, and the like—but a constant influx of expense-account visitors help to support the city's astonishing selection of fine restaurants and elegant shops. True, the city lacks the gutsy licentious mood of Amsterdam. It's also exceptionally clean, safe, and pleasant to explore on foot (pickpockets, who can be extremely sneaky and resourceful, are the one plague of visitors—guard your belongings vigilantly).

Considering Brussel's cultural conservatism, it was ironic that in 1988 the American choreographer Mark Morris was invited to take up residency with his dance company at the Théâtre Royal de la Monnaie, Brussel's state opera house. Openly gay, and often outspoken about his gayness and his dance pieces,

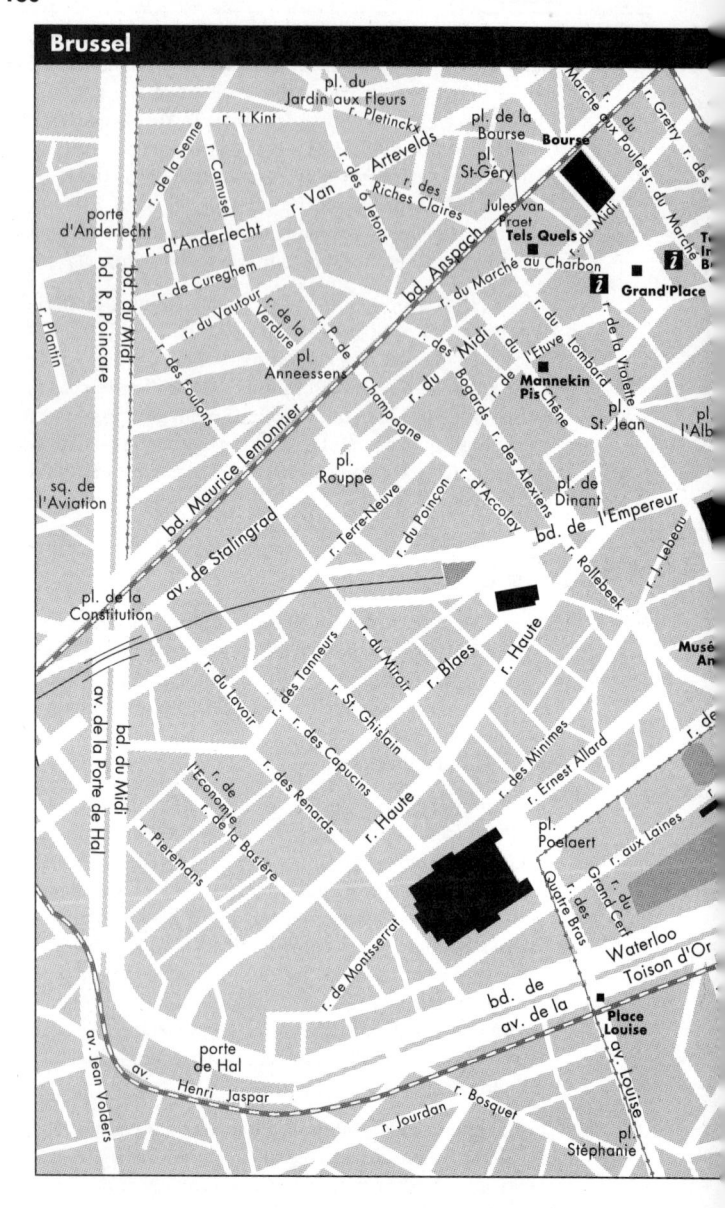

Brussel

pl. du Jardin aux Fleurs
r. 't Kint
r. Pletinckx
r. de la Senne
r. Camusel
r. Van Artevelds
r. des 6 Jalons
r. des Riches Claires
pl. de la Bourse
pl. St-Géry
Bourse
Marché aux Poulets
r. du Marché
r. Grétry
porte d'Anderlecht
r. d'Anderlecht
Jules van Praet
Tels Quels
r. du Midi
bd. R. Poincaré
bd. du Midi
r. de Cureghem
r. du Vautour
r. de Verdure
bd. Anspach
r. du Marché au Charbon
r. Plantin
r. des Foulons
pl. Anneessens
r. de Champagne
r. des Bogards
r. du Midi
r. d'Étuve
r. Lombard
Mannekin Pis
r. du Chêne
r. de la Violette
Grand'Place
pl. St. Jean
pl. l'Alb
sq. de l'Aviation
bd. Maurice Lemonnier
pl. Rouppe
r. Terre-Neuve
r. du Poinçon
r. d'Accolay
r. des Alexiens
pl. de Dinant
bd. de l'Empereur
av. de Stalingrad
r. J. Lebeau
r. Rollebeek
pl. de la Constitution
r. des Tanneurs
r. du Miroir
r. Blaes
r. Haute
Musé An
r. du Lavoir
r. St. Ghislain
r. des Capucins
r. des Renards
r. des Minimes
r. Ernest Allard
r. de l'Économie
r. de la Basière
r. Pieremans
pl. Poelaert
r. aux Laines
r. du Grand Cerf
r. des Quatre Bras
r. de Montsserrat
Waterloo
bd. de
av. de la
Toison d'Or
Place Louise
porte de Hal
av. de la Porte de Hal
av. Henri Jaspar
r. Bosquet
av. Louise
av. Jean Volders
r. Jourdan
pl. Stéphanie

131

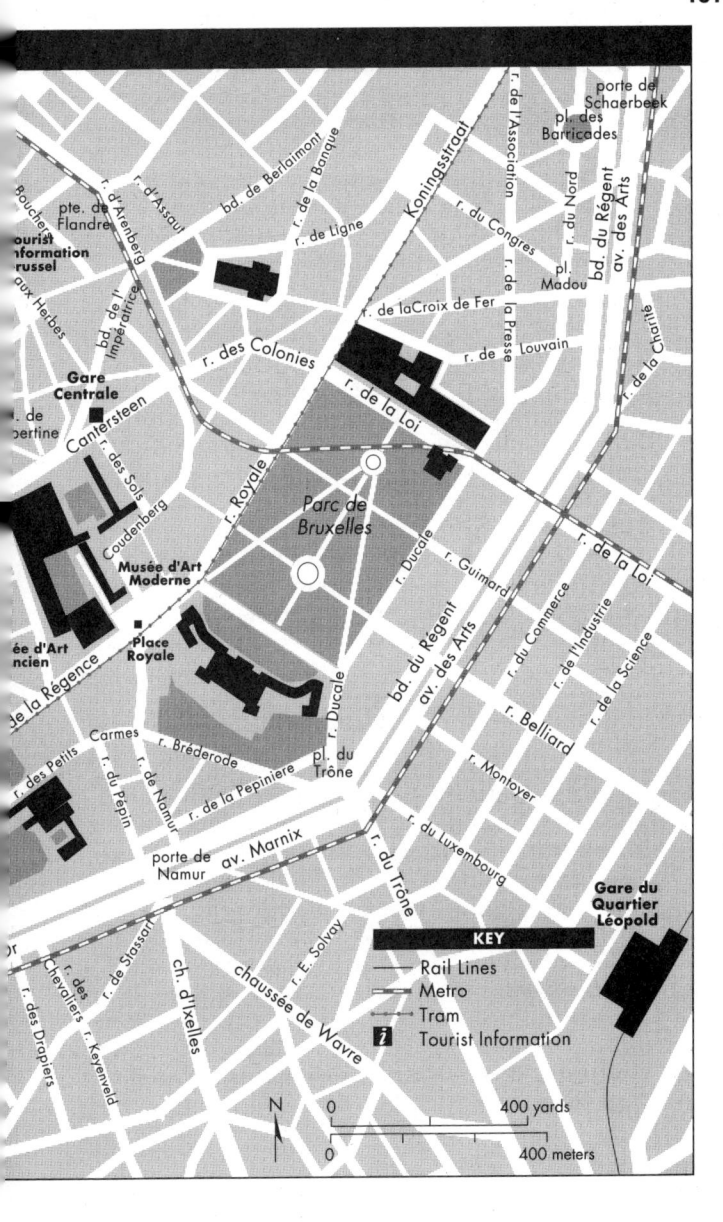

Morris scandalized the Belgian dance critics shortly after his arrival, when, asked to share his philosophy of dance, he quipped, "I make it up, and you watch it. End of philosophy." Anyone who's seen Morris perform knows that his dances are nowhere near as flip as this answer suggests, but by and large, the Belgian critics didn't take kindly to Morris's work, an astonishing fact considering he created his masterpiece to date, the evening-length *L'Allegro, Il Penseroso, ed Il Moderato,* set to music by Handel, while at the Monnaie.

As for complaints about Brussel's architecture, the main political and commercial center is, in fact, characterized by rather cumbersome office blocks built mostly during the '60s and '70s. But these recent buildings are hardly Brussel's only architectural legacy. Upper Town has stunning Art Nouveau architecture—the work of Victor Horta (1861–1947) and his pupils, who designed hundreds of town houses whose sensuous facades are decorated with the style's characteristic sinewy ironwork. Meanwhile, Lower Town contains one of the best-preserved medieval sections of any major city in Europe. In the end, the city's negatives are balanced by quite a few superlatives. And best of all, even if you don't have time for an extended visit, you can get a handle on the city's major attractions, most interesting neighborhoods, and compact gay nightlife in the span of a day or so. If you arrive at the Gare Centrale, you'll be within a 20-minute walk of everything a visitor should see, including most of the hotels.

Brussel is divided into two halves, Lower Town and Upper Town, which are determined not by direction but by altitude: Upper Town begins just east of Rue Royal, where a fairly steep slope rises just beyond the city's 1,000-year-old core. Most of the wealthy neighborhoods, fancy shopping, and grand hotels are in Upper Town, as are several museums. Lower Town is characterized in part by working-class neighborhoods, some of them genuine slums. However, the section of Lower Town nearest the Gare Centrale and the neighboring Grand'-Place (the same as a Grote Markt in a Flemish or Dutch community) is filled with ancient buildings, narrow lanes, and tremendous energy—it's also where you'll find the closest quadrant Brussel has to a gay district, centered around rue du Marché au Charbon and rue des Pierres.

Begin your explorations around the **Grand'Place** (just down the hill from Gare Centrale), which has been the soul of the city center for many centuries and is one of Europe's loveliest city squares. There's now a flower market here daily and a peculiar little caged-bird market on Sunday mornings; there are also music concerts, festivals, and many other activities staged here throughout the year, including the *Ommegan*, a historical pageant that reenacts Emperor Charles V's reception into the city in 1549 (it takes place on the first Tuesday and Thursday in July). Around the square you'll find the city's office of tourism, the enormous Gothic **Hôtel de Ville** (City Hall), and many ornate **guild houses,** built in elaborate baroque style following the 1695 bombardment of the city. Just off the square, rue Charles Buls leads to rue des Brasseurs, which is where poet Paul Verlaine shot and wounded his lover, fellow poet Arthur Rimbaud in 1873 (Verlaine ended up jailed in Brussel). Back on the north side of the square is the **Musée Communal** (✉ Maison du Roi, ☏ 02/279–4355), which has historical artifacts relating to the city's history; it's moderately interesting, worth a stop only if you have some extra time. Walk down the hill along rue de l'Etuve to the corner of rue du Chêne to see **Manneken Pis,** a statue of a pudgy little boy peeing into a fountain that has been the topic of conversation for centuries—at least since 1377 (hence his being known as "Brussel's Oldest Citizen"), though the statue itself is a copy of a 1619 piece that was stolen by French soldiers in 1747. It's meant to symbolize the mischievous and playful spirit of this city that in truth possesses neither of these two qualities. The blocks immediately west of here are where you'll find many of the gay bars, restaurants, and other businesses and organizations, but as far as such districts go, this is fairly invisible and blends in with its surroundings.

From Gare Centrale, it's a short stroll southeast to the lower slopes of the Upper Town to reach the twin **Musée d'Art Ancien** (✉ Rue de la Régence 3, ☏ 02/508–3211), which is dedicated to the Flemish-Dutch painting traditions, dating from the 15th to 19th centuries. Among the painters represented are Hans Memling, Petrus Christus, Pieter Bruegel the Elder (*Landscape with the Fall of Icarus*), Rubens, Van Dyck. The 1,200-work collection also includes works by the 19th-century French masters such as Jacques-Louis David (*Assassination of Marat,* one of his most celebrated paintings), Ingres, Gauguin, Bonnard, Vuillard, and Seurat. An underground passage from the Museum of Ancient Art connects directly to the neighboring **Musée d'Art Moderne** (✉ Pl. Royale 1, ☏ 02/508–3211). Belgian artists are the main event here, with works by the surrealists James Ensor (1860–1949) and René Magritte (1881–1967), with 26 of his works. Most of the major early 20th-century art movements, including fauvism, surrealism, and futurism, are represented. The museums overlook the supremely elegant **place Royale,** a fittingly lavish 18th-century square that acts as gateway to the Upper Town's posh residential and shopping districts. For the best antiquing and café-hopping, wander around the streets emanating from the **Grand Sablon,** another ritzy square. Continue toward the monolithic **Palais de Justice** (Palace of Justice; ✉ Pl. Poelaert), and turn left to reach **place Louise,** where you'll discover more high-end shopping.

Before you leave the city, be sure to sample authentic Belgian pralines (cream- or liqueur-filled); they're the best you'll taste anywhere in the world. **Godiva** and **Neuhuis** are pricey but highly esteemed; **Leonidas** is more affordable and some say just as good. Each of these shops have numerous branches around the city.

Getting Around

Brussel is served by three main train stations, **Gare du Nord, Gare Centrale,** and **Gare du Midi.** If you're just visiting for the day, you should use Gare Centrale, which will put you in the heart of the main tourist, diplomatic, and commercial center of the city, just steps from the historic parts of town and many gay bars and cafés. Brussel is three hours from Amsterdam by train, about an hour from Brugge, and a little over 30 minutes from Gent and Antwerpen.

Brussel is a large city and residents and long-term visitors make good use of the extensive subway, tram, and bus system. For a quick excursion, however, you can easily get around on foot. Most of major hotels and nightlife are within a 15-minute walk of each other; in a pinch you can hail a cab, but this is a pricey way of getting around.

Eats

Brussel has over 1,600 restaurants—some of them the finest in the world (serving some of the richest food you'll eat anywhere). Even at casual cafés you're likely to find varied, appealing menus. Pricey expense-account gourmet restaurants dot the city center, but you needn't dress to the nines or endure the formality of a mostly straight, stuffy restaurant for great food.

Set along the pedestrian arcade that's quite famous for its excellent seafood restaurants, ✗ **L'Annexe** (✉ Rue des Bouchers 71–73, ☏ 02/512–3856, $$–$$$) is probably the best gay-oriented restaurant in Belgium, with wonderful contemporary French and international cuisine and an elegant dining room. Lots of EC queer politicos mingle over dinner and cocktails here. Sandwiched between a few of the queer bars in the gay district, ✗ **Le Troisième Acte** (✉ Rue des Pierres 28, ☏ 02/502–5649, $–$$) is an affordable bistro that's ideal for a romantic rendezvous before heading out to dance.

✗ **H2O** (✉ Rue du Marché au Charbon 27, ☏ 02/512–3843, $$) is both a popular bar and restaurant that draws a young cool crowd for nouvelle cooking; art exhibitions and concerts are staged here frequently. Scads of queer cyber fans surf, mingle, and nosh at trendy ✗ **L'Amour Fou** (✉ Chaussée d'Ixelles 185, ☏ 02/514–2709, $), a cheerful café with inexpensive but rather sophisticated food, hip drinks, jazz and classical music, and eight computer terminals. ✗ **Café Metropole,** ✗ **Falstaff,** ✗ **Orange Bleu,** and ✗ **Le Belgica** are all known as popular watering holes (*see* Scenes, *below*), but don't overlook them as fairly affordable ($–$$) dining options; Falstaff, in particular, is a great place for late-night noshing. Another good option after the bars close is ✗ **Cap de Nuit** (✉ Pl. de la Vieille Halle-aux-Blés 28, ☏ 02/512–9342), an around-the-clock café that serves sandwiches, fries, and other light food.

Scenes

Despite the fact that it's a much larger city, Brussel's queer nightlife is no livelier or more extensive than Antwerpen's. As you might expect of a rather conservative and business-oriented city, bars are generally rather laid-back and smartly dressed patrons are common. The leather scene is subpar for so large a city, but there are quite a few dapper lounges and pubs, many of them popular with both gays and straights.

Most of the very popular bars are in the heart of the old city, a few blocks southwest of the Grand'Place, along either rue du Marché au Charbon or rue des Pierres. You don't have to walk far from central hotels, the shopping districts, or several good restaurants to survey the nightlife, which is definitely an improvement over the location of the gay bar district in many cities. Remember that in discreet Brussel you'll have to ring a buzzer to gain entry into many of the queer bars.

In the heart of things, **L'Incognito** (⊠ Rue des Pierres 36, ☏ 02/513–3788) is a trendy, well-lighted cocktail-and-cruise bar drawing a mixed-age bunch of stand-and-model guys; the staff is very friendly. **Le Can Can** (⊠ Rue des Pierres 55, ☏ 02/512–7404) is the oldest gay bar in the city; expect a mostly thirties to fifties crowd; sing-alongs, birthday celebrations, and other excuses in mirth are commonplace, and a zero-attitude policy prevails. Along the same stretch, **Het Rijk Der Zinnen** (⊠ Rue des Pierres 14, ☏ 02/511–2659) draws a fairly young male crowd for mingling and, many nights, live music. Also popular is **Le Tels Quels** (⊠ Rue du Marché au Charbon 81, ☏ 02/512–4587), which is inside the local queer political and social center; expect a mixed crowd of guys (and some women) of all ages and backgrounds. By far the most popular dyke bar in the city, **Le Féminin** (⊠ Rue Borgwal 9, ☏ 02/511–1719) is open several nights a week and always draws a nice-size crowd.

Leather hands and Levi's boys love the feisty **Big Noise** (⊠ Rue du Marché au Charbon 44, ☏ 02/512–2525), which has great music and a fairly young rowdy crowd. Somewhat more popular among the die-hard leather aficionados, **The Duquesnoy** (⊠ Rue Duquesnoystraat 12, ☏ 02/502–3883) is a warm and quite cruisy hangout big with Belgian "Bears" and assorted horny guys.

As for what you might call Brussel's "bi society," there are several stylish hangouts in the city center that are popular with gays, lesbians, straights, and everybody in between. **Café Metropole** (⊠ Pl. de Brouckèreplein 31, ☏ 02/219–2384) is a slick mixed gay/straight bar where you'll want to dress a bit to fit in with the chic see-and-be-seen crowd. **Falstaff** (⊠ Rue Henri Maus 17–23, ☏ 02/511–8789; also Rue des Pierres 38, ☏ 02/512–1761) is another mixed venue popular with young hipsters and late-night club kids. **Orange Bleu** (⊠ Rue Antoine Dansaert 29, ☏ 02/513–9829) organizes fashion shows and art exhibits and draws the kind of crowd you'd expect at such events; it's always a popular place for after-work cocktails. **Le Belgica** (⊠ Rue du Marché au Charbon 32, ☏ 02/514–0324) is yet another mixed venue big with fashion plates and their followers.

Brussel

Several of the best discos in the city are gay only one or two nights weekly. Probably the most popular of such parties (at least for guys) take place at **Le Garage** (✉ Rue Duquesnoy 18, ☎ 02/512–6622) on Sundays; this is a beautiful club with a hot crowd, mesmerizing light shows, and a fairly compact but impressive dance floor. It doesn't get crowded until after 1 AM. Another great guys' event drawing many of the same folks as Le Garage is Friday's **Bump** (✉ Rue Blaesstraat 208, ☎ 02/511–9789), but it's only held once a month; call for dates. In the same space, **D-Light Wild** (☎ 050/238627) is a major dyke disco fete that's also held one Friday each month. And on Sundays once monthly, boy-popular **La Demence** (☎ 02/511–9789) is held in the same space. It's best to call ahead or ask at one of the smaller bars about these parties, as they change rather often. **Le Why Not** (✉ Rue des Riches Claires 7, ☎ 02/512–6343) is a gay-male venue that has been straight at various times in recent years but most recently has been reopened by gay owners and continues to draw substantial crowds for various theme nights held at different times; again, call for details or ask around.

Saunas are quite popular in Brussel, with clean and spacious **L'Oasis** (✉ Rue Van Orley 10, ☎ 02/218–0800) being the most popular; it has five floors, a state-of-the-art fitness center, and a fairly upscale crowd. Another popular option is **Macho 2** (✉ Rue du Marché au Charbon 106–108, ☎ 02/513–5667).

Sleeps

With so many political and corporate bigwigs regularly passing through, hotels in Brussel command a hefty sum. There are, however, some mid- to low-end properties near gay nightlife venues and restaurants that provide clean, if ho-hum, rooms.

The ⌸ **Royal Windsor Hotel** (✉ Rue Duquesnoy 5, ☎ 02/511–4215, FAX 02/511–6004, $$$$) is probably the most gay-friendly of the luxury business hotels, located as it is near several gay bars. Rooms have fairly standard upscale furnishings but beautiful marble bathrooms. Of high-end gay-popular options, ⌸ **Metropole** (✉ Pl. de Brouckère 31, ☎ 02/217–2300, FAX 02/218–0220, $$$) is a restored Belle Epoque splendor with a chic café (*see* Scenes, *above*) and lavish furnishings. An excellent choice a 10- to 15-minute walk southeast of the city center and just off fashionable avenue Louise is ⌸ **Clubhouse** (✉ Rue Blanche 4, 1000, ☎ 02/

537–9210, FAX 02/537–0018, $$–$$$), an attractive warmly done hotel that's quite gay-friendly. ⛉ **Hôtel Barry** (✉ Pl. Anneessensplein 25, ☏ 02/511–2795, $–$$) is a simply furnished, gay-friendly hotel that's centrally located and has small but clean rooms with spotless bathrooms. ⛉ **Résidence Osborne** (✉ Rue Bosquetstraat 68, ☏ 02/537–9251, $) is an 1860s town house not far from avenue Louise and with an eclectic mix of budget rooms; it's very gay-friendly.

THE LITTLE BLACK BOOK

Tips on Traveling to Belgium

CURRENCY AND EXPENSES

Prices in Belgium run a bit higher than in the Netherlands, especially at restaurants and hotels. Bars, on the other hand, charge relatively little for drinks, which is nice if you're coming to party. At press time (winter 1997), one dollar was worth about BF32; one pound sterling, BF48; and one Canadian dollar, BF23.

PASSPORTS AND VISAS

If traveling to Belgium from Amsterdam, bring along your passport just in case, but you'll almost never be asked to present it. As with traveling to the Netherlands, American, Canadian, and British citizens need passports but not visas to enter Belgium.

PHONES

Belgium's country code is 32. Dial only the area code and not the preceding zero when placing a call from another nation to Belgium (i.e., you dial 2 instead of 02 to reach Brussel). No area code is needed when placing intercity calls.

For directory assistance, call 1207. For international operator assistance, dial 1224.

Direct-dial international calls can be made from any phone booth. To reach an **AT&T** long-distance operator, dial 0800/10010; for **MCI,** dial 0800/10012; for **Sprint,** dial 0800/10014.

VISITOR INFORMATION BEFORE YOU GO

Contact the **Belgian Tourist Office** in North America (✉ 780 3rd Ave., Suite 1501, New York, NY 10017, ☏ 212/758–8130); or in the United Kingdom (✉ 29 Princes St., London W1R 7RG, ☏ 0891/887–799).

At Your Fingertips
Aide Info Sida (AIDS information and testing service, based in Brussel, ☎ 02/514-2965). **Het AIDS Team** (✉ Tolstraat 13, Antwerpen, ☎ 03/238-6161). **G.O.C. Antwerpen** (lesbian and gay community center for Antwerpen; Dambruggestraat 24, ☎ 03/233-1071). **Dienst Voor Tourisme** (Tourist Office for Gent; ✉ Predikherenlei 2, ☎ 09/225-3641). **Federatie Werkgroepen Homosexualiteit** (FWH, the lesbigay social and political organization for Gent; ✉ Vlaanderenstraat 22, ☎ 09/223-6929; this is also a good referral contact for gay information on the rest of the country). **Homocentrum Idem Dito** (the lesbigay social and political organization for Brugge; no address, ☎ 050/334742; meetings are usually at the bar, Passe-Partout, ✉ Sint Janusstraat 3, ☎ 050/334742). **Infor-Homo** (lesbigay social and political organization for Brussels, ☎ 02/733-1024). **International Gay and Lesbian Association** (international queer-rights political organization; Brussel, ☎ 02/502-2471). **Tels Quels** (Brussel-based lesbigay social and political organization with an extensive queer library and many useful resources; ✉ Rue du Marché au Charbon 81, ☎ 02/512-4587). **Toerisme Stad Antwerpen** (Antwerp City Tourist Office; ✉ Grote Markt 15, ☎ 03/232-0103, FAX 03/231-1937). **Toerisme Brugge** (Brugge Tourist Office; ✉ Burg 11, ☎ 050/448686). **Tourist Information Brussel** (✉ Inside the Hôtel de Ville, Grand'Place, ☎ 02/513-8940).

Gay Media
There are no English-language newspapers and magazines covering Belgium's gay scene. Brussel-based **Gay Mag** (☎ 02/512-3108) is the nation's best French-language paper on the queer scene. Also French-language, **Regard** (☎ 02/733-1024) covers queer life in Belgium with more of a political slant. Brussel's queer social and political organization, **Tels Quels** (*see* At Your Fingertips *and* Scenes, *above*), also publishes a monthly French-language newspaper of the same name. The main Dutch/Flemish-language lesbigay paper is **De GAY Krant** (e-mail red@gayworld.nl). In Gent, the FWH (*see* At Your Fingertips, *above*) publishes a monthly Dutch-language newsletter, **Zizo.** In Brugge, the Homocentrum Idem Dito (*see* At Your Fingertips, *above*) also publishes a monthly Dutch-language magazine, the **Pink News.**

BOOKSTORES

In Antwerpen, not too far from the Grote Markt, **De Groene Waterman** (✉ Wolstraat 7, ☏ 03/232–9394) is a bookstore with many lesbian and gay titles, but little in English. Not far from Brussel's Gare Centrale, **Artemys** (✉ Galerie Bortiergalerij 8, ☏ 02/512–0347) is the best lesbian and feminist bookstore in Belgium and one of the best in Europe; it carries mostly Dutch and French titles, as well as quite a few English ones; many cards, CDs, and posters are also sold here.

DUTCH VOCABULARY

Pronunciation of Place-Names

Antwerpen	**ahn**-tvehr-pehn
Begijnhof	beh-**ghaiyn**-hoff
Brugge	bruhkk
Brussel	**bruhs**-sehl
De Pijp	de **paiyp**
Den Haag	den-**haakh**
Gent	ghent
Haarlem	**hahr**-lem
Het IJ	heht **aiy**
Het Koninklijk Paleis	heht **kohn**-in-klaiyk **pahl**-laiys
Jordaan	yoahr-**dahn**
Leiden	**laiyd**-ehn
Leidseplein	**laiyd**-suh-plaiyn
Maastricht	maah-**streekht**
Nieuwezijds Voorburgwal	**nyew**-vehr-zaiyds foahr-burkh-vahl
Nieuwmarkt	**nyew**-mahrkt
Noord Zee	**noahrd** zay
Oosterpark	**oahst**-ehr-pahrk
Oude Kerk	**owhd**-eh kerhk
Raadhuisstraat	**raaht**-heuhrss-straaht
Reguliersdwarsstraat	**rehk**-u-lehrs-**dvahrs**-straaht
Rijksmuseum	**raiyks**-mew-**zay**-uhm
Rotterdam	**rot**-tehr-**dahm**
Schiphol	**skhip**-ohl
Singel	sin-**ghel**
Singelgracht	sin-ghel-**ghrakht**
Stadhouderskade	**staht**-howt-ehrs-**kaht**-eh
Utrecht	**ew**-trehkt
Warmoesstraat	**vahrm**-ooh-straaht
Zandvoort	**zahnt**-foahrt
Zeedijk	**zay**-daiyk

Basics

English	Dutch	Pronunciation
Yes/no	Ja, nee	yah, nay
Please	Alstublieft	**ahls**-too-bleeft
Thank you	Dank u	**dahnk** oo
You're welcome	Niets te danken	neets teh **dahn**-ken

Dutch Vocabulary

Excuse me, sorry	Pardon	pahr-**don**
Good morning	Goede morgen	**ghoh**-deh **mor**-ghen
Good evening	Goedenavond	**ghoh**-dehn-**ahv**-unt
Goodbye	Dag	dakh

Numbers

one	een	ayhn
two	twee	tvay
three	drie	dree
four	vier	fheer
five	vijf	fhaiyf
six	zes	zehss
seven	zeven	**zeh**-fhehn
eight	acht	ahkht
nine	negen	**neh**-ghen
ten	tien	teen

Days of the Week

Sunday	zondag	**zohn**-dakh
Monday	maandag	**mahn**-dakh
Tuesday	dinsdag	**dins**-dakh
Wednesday	woensdag	**voons**-dakh
Thursday	donderdag	**don**-der-dakh
Friday	vrijdag	**fhraiy**-dakh
Saturday	zaterdag	**zah**-ter-dakh

Useful Phrases

Do you speak English?	Spreekt U Engels?	spraykt oo **ehn**-gls
I don't speak Dutch	Ik spreek geen Nederlands	ihk sprayk **ghayn nayd**-er-lahnts
I don't understand	Ik begrijp het niet	ihk beh-**ghrayp** het neet
I don't know	Ik weet niet	ihk **vayt** neet
I'm American/English	Ik ben Amerikaans/Engels	ihk ben am-er-ee-**kahns**/ehn-gerlss
Where is . . . the train station? the post office? the hospital?	Waar is . . . het station? het postkantoor? het ziekenhuis?	vahr iss heht stah-**syohn** het **pohst**-kahn-toar het **zeek**-uhn-heuhrss
Where is the WC?	Waar is de WC?	**vahr** iss de **veh**-seh?

Where are the toilets?	Waar zijn de toiletten?	**vahr** zaiyn de tvah-**leh**-tern
Left/right	links/rechts	leenks/rehkhts
Entrance/exit	ingang/uitgang	**in**-ghankh/**euhrt**-ghankh
Arrival/Departure	Aankomst/Vertrek	**aahn**-kohmst/**fehr**-trehk
How much is this?	Hoeveel kost dit?	hoo-**fayhl** kohst deet
It's expensive/cheap	Het is te duur/goedkoop	het ees teh **deuhr**/**ghoot**-kohp
I am ill/sick	Ik ben ziek	ihk behn zeek
I want to call a doctor	Ik wil een docter bellen	ihk veel ayhn **dohk**-ter **behl**-len
Help!	Help!	help
Stop!	Stoppen!	**stop**-pen

Dining Out

Bill/check	de rekening	de **rehk**-en-eeng
Bread	brood	brohd
Butter	boter	**boh**-ter
Fork	vork	fork
I'd like to order	Ik wil graag bestellen	Ihk veel ghraakh behs-**tell**-en
Knife	een mes	ehn mehs
Menu	menu/kaart	men-**oo**/kahrt
Napkin	en servet	ehn ser-**feht**
Pepper	peper	**peh**-per
Please give me . . .	mag ik [een] . . .	mahkh ihk [ayhn] . . .
Salt	zout	zowt
Spoon	een lepel	ayhn **leh**-pehl
Sugar	suiker	**seuhrk**-ur

INDEX

✗ = *restaurant*, 🏨 = *hotel*

A

AIDS Memorial Day, *32*
Alexandria ✗, *109*
Allard Pierson Museum, *9*
Alternative culture, *61–63*
Ambassade, The 🏨, *71*
American 🏨, *70*
Amstel Inter-Continental 🏨, *69–70*
Amstelkring, *11*
Amstel Taveerne (club), *53*
Amsterdam, *1–4*
apartment and houseboat rentals, *69*
bookstores, *79–80*
canals west and south of Dam Square, *12–14*, *38–41*
Centraal Station and Dam Square, *7–9*, *37–38*
De Pijp and outside the City Center, *26–27*
east of the City Center, *21–24*
excursions, *31*
exploring, *6–27*
festivals, *31–35*
guest houses, *72–75*
gyms, *80*
hotels, *68–75*
Jewish Quarter, *22*
The Jordaan, *18–21*, *38–41*, *58*
Leidseplein and Rembrandtplein, *14–18*, *41–47*
making the most of your time, *5–6*
nightlife, *48–68*
Old Town, *23*
Red-Light District and Nieuwmarkt, *9–12*, *37–38*
restaurants, *35–48*
transportation in, *29–31*
transportation to, *28–29*
Vondelpark and Museumplein, *24–26*
Amsterdam Pride (party event), *33*
Amsterdamse Bos, *27*
Amsterdams Historisch Museum, *9*
Anne Frankhuis, *14*
Antwerpen, *115–122*, *140*
Aphrodite ✗, *42–43*
April (club), *52*
Arena 🏨, *73*
Argos (club), *56*
Artis zoo complex, *23*

B

Backstage ✗, *46*
Barbizon 🏨, *71*
Barney's Breakfast Bar ✗, *40*
Begijnhof (Amsterdam), *9*
Begijnhof (Brugge), *125*
Belfort, *123*
Belgium, *112–115*
Beurs van Berlage, *7*
Bijbels Museum Amsterdam, *13*
Binnenhof, *92*
Black Tulip Hotel 🏨, *72*
Bojo ✗, *45*
Bolhoed ✗, *40*
Bonnefantenmuseum, *107*
Bookstores
Amsterdam, *79–80*
Belgium, *140*
Netherlands, *111*
Boymans-van Beuningen Museum, *98*
Breydel-De Coninck ✗, *127*
Brugge, *122–129*
Brussel, *129–132*
bookstores, *140*
exploring, *132–134*
hotels, *137–138*
nightlife, *135–137*
restaurants, *134–135*
transportation, *134*
Buddhasbelly ✗, *127*
Buikske Vol ✗, *127*

C

Café Françoise ✗, *46*
Cafe Mephisto ✗, *84–85*
Café Metropole ✗, *135*
Cafe Morlang ✗, *43–44*
Cafe van Engelen ✗, *89*
Camp Cafe ✗, *45*
Cap de Nuit ✗, *135*
Caprese Ristorante Italiano ✗, *37*
Caramba ✗, *39–40*
Casa de David ✗, *43*
Casa Maria (club), *56*

Index 145

Centraal Museum, *103*
Chico's Guesthouse ⌸, *73*
Christophe ✕, *38–39*
Cinemas, *66*
Clemens ⌸, *75*
Climate, *75*
Clubhouse ⌸, *137–138*
C.O.C. Amsterdam, *20, 58*
Cockring (club), *56–57*
Coffee Co. ✕, *46*
"Coffee shops" (pot and hash bars), *62–63*
Concertgebouw, *26*
Corrie ten Boom House, *83*
Cosmo Bar, *49*
Cruising, *67–68*
Currency and expenses
Belgium, 138
Netherlands, 75–76

D

Dance Valley Festival, *33*
Dark rooms, *63–64*
De Keuken van 1870 ✕, *38*
De Kroon ✕, *42*
Déli France ✕, *89*
De Matelote ✕, *119*
Den Gouden Harynk ✕, *127*
Den Haag (The Hague), *90–96, 111*
De Pauw ⌸, *129*
De Spijker (club), *49*
De Spijker Van Der Mei ✕, *47*
De Trut (party event), *59*
De Werfkring ✕, *104*
De Ysbreker ✕, *47–48*
Domtoren and Domkerk, *101*
Downtown ✕, *46*
Dutch vocabulary, *141–143*
D'Vijff Vlieghen ✕, *37*
Dynasty ✕, *42*

E

Egmond ⌸, *128–129*
Engelse Kerk, *9*
Erotic Museum, *10*
Euromast tower, *98*
Exit (club), *52*

F

Facade ✕, *119*
Falstaff ✕, *135*

Flandria, The ⌸, *129*
Frans Hals Museum, *83–84*
Freeland ⌸, *72*

G

Gaiety (club), *53*
Galafest, *33*
Gary's Muffins ✕, *46–47*
Gay Games Amsterdam 1998, *34–35*
Gent, *122–129*
Getto ✕, *37*
Gevangenenpoort Museum, *93*
Grand Amsterdam ⌸, *70*
Grand Hotel Krasnapolsky ⌸, *70*
Greenwich Village ⌸, *73–74*
Groeninge Museum, *125, 127*
Grote Kerke of Sint Bavo, *83*
Grotten Sint Pietersberg, *107–108*
Gyms, *80*

H

Haags Gemeentemuseum, *93–94*
Haarlem, *83–85*
Hash Marijuana Hemp Museum, *11*
Havana (club), *52–53*
Heemraad Hotel ⌸, *100*
Heineken Brewery, *27*
Hemelse Modder ✕, *37*
Het Grachtenhuys ✕, *104*
Het Tuynhuis ✕, *41*
Het Vrouwenhuis, *21*
HnM Eetcafe ✕, *94*
Holiday Inn Crowne Plaza Brugge ⌸, *128*
Homodok archives, *10*
Homomonument, *13–14*
Hortus Botanicus (Amsterdam), *23*
Hortus Botanicus (Leiden), *88*
Hotel Aero ⌸, *74*
Hôtel Barry ⌸, *138*
Hotel Bergere ⌸, *110*
Hotel Cammerpoorte ⌸, *121–122*
Hotel de l'Europe ⌸, *70*
Hotel Derlon ⌸, *110*
Hotel Florida ⌸, *122*
Hotel Hans Memling ⌸, *129*
Hotel New York ⌸, *72*
Hotel Sander ⌸, *71*
Hotel Smit ⌸, *71–72*
Hotel Unique ⌸, *74*
H2O ✕, *135*
Huyschkaemer ✕, *44*

Index

I

Impuls Museum of Science and Technology, *23–24*
In de Schaduw van de Kathedraal ✕, *119*
International Court of Justice, *93*
iT (party event), *54–55*
ITC Hotel ⛉, *74*
Izmir ✕, *44*

J

Joods Historisch Museum, *22*

K

Kam Yin ✕, *38*
Kloostergang, *101, 103*
Koh-I-Noor ✕, *39*
Koninklijk Paleis, *8*
Kort ✕, *42*
Kriterion ✕, *48*

L

Lakenhal, *86*
L'Amour Fou ✕, *135*
Lana Thai ✕, *38*
Language
 Belgium, *114–115*
 Netherlands, *76, 141–143*
L'Annexe ✕, *135*
La Strada ✕, *37–38*
La Villa ✕, *109*
Leather Pride festivities, *33*
Leather shops, *67*
Le Belgica ✕, *135*
Le Garage ✕, *47*
Leiden, *86–90*
Leiden University, *88*
Le Monde ✕, *47*
Le Pêcheur ✕, *42*
Lesbian venues, *59–61*
Lesbisch Archief, *20*
Le Shako (club), *54*
Le Troisième Acte ✕, *135*
Le Vilette ✕, *99*
Le Zinc ✕, *43*
Ludwig ✕, *127*

M

Maastricht, *105–110*
Madame Tussaud's wax museum, *9*
Madurodam, *94*
Malvesijn ✕, *44*
Mankind (club), *58–59*
Manneken Pis, *133*
Mauritshuis, *92–93*
Metropole ⛉, *137*
Miramar ✕, *127*
Moeders Pot ✕, *40*
Molenmuseum de Valk, *86*
Monopole ⛉, *74*
Monopole Taveerne (club), *54*
Montmartre (club), *54*
Musée Communal, *133*
Musée d'Art Ancien, *133*
Musée d'Art Moderne, *134*
Museum Boerhaave, *86–87*
Museum Bredius, *93*
Museum het Rembrandthuis, *22*
Museum Mayer Van den Bergh, *118*
Museum voor Volkskunde, *123*
Music and performance, *62*
Muziektheater/Stadhuis, *21–22*

N

National Scheepvaartmuseum, *118*
Nederlands Filmmuseum and Library, *24*
Nederlands Scheepvaartmuseum, *23*
New York Pizza ✕, *47*
Nieuwe Kerk, *8*

O

Old Hickory ✕, *108–109*
Olympia (Leiden) ✕, *89*
Olympia (Rotterdam) ✕, *99*
Onze Lieve Vrouwe Basiliek, *107*
Onze-Lieve-Vrouwekathedraal, *118*
Onze-Lieve-Vrouwekerk, *125*
Op de Thermen, *107*
Opening and closing times, *76*
Orange Bleu ✕, *135*
Orfeo ⛉, *72–73*
Oude Kerk, *11*
Oude Munt Kelder ✕, *104*

P

Pancake Bakery ✕, *40*
Panini ✕, *45*
Parliament buildings, *92*

Index

Passports and visas
Belgium, 138
Netherlands, 76
Pax 🏨, 75
Peter Cuyper ✕, 84
Phone numbers
Belgium, 139
Netherlands, 77–78, 110
Phone service
Belgium, 138
Netherlands, 76–77
Pieterskerk, 88
Pilgrim Collection, 88
Pizzeria Calzone ✕, 45
Plaka ✕, 109
Portugália ✕, 43
Prince William V Gallery, 93
Prinsen 🏨, 73
Prins Hendrik Maritime Museum, 98
Prostitution, 65–66
Publications
Belgium, 139
Netherlands, 78–79, 110–111
Pulitzer 🏨, 71

Q

Queen's Day, 32
Quentin 🏨, 74–75

R

Rainbow Palace 🏨, 75
Rama Thai ✕, 44
Randstad area, 81–82
Raz Bari Tandoori ✕, 109
Reibach ✕, 41
Résidence Osborne 🏨, 138
Ridderzaal, 92
Rijksmuseum, 25
Rijksmuseum het Catharijneconvent, 103
Rijksmuseum van Oudheden, 88
Rijksmuseum van Speelklok tot Pierement, 103
Rijksmuseum Voor Volkenkunde, 86
Rococco ✕, 127
Rose's Cantina ✕, 44
Rotterdam, 96–100
Roving parties, 64
Roxy, The (party event), 53
Royal Windsor Hotel 🏨, 137
Roze Zaterdag celebration, 33
Rubenshuis, 118

S

Saarein (club), 60
Saunas, 64
Saur ✕, 94
Schreierstoren, 23
Sex Museum, 7
Sex shops, 66–67
's Gravensteen, 123
Shiva ✕, 45–46
Sint-Baafskathedraal, 123
Sint-Niklaaskerk, 123
Sintservaas Brug, 105
Sintservaaskerk, 107
Sisters ✕, 38
Sluizer ✕, 43
Smallest house, 13
Smoeshaan Cafe and Theatre ✕, 45
Sofitel 🏨, 129
Spoorweg Museum, 103
Squats, 61
Stablemaster (club), 57
Stedelijk Museum, 26

T

Tattoo Museum, 11
't Balkje ✕, 47
Teylers Museum, 83
Theatremuseum, 13
Topolobampo ✕, 89
Torture Museum, 7
Toscana ✕, 40
Toscanini ✕, 39
Tout Court ✕, 39
't Pakhoes ✕, 108
Tropenmuseum, 23
't Schooiertje ✕, 41
't Sluisje ✕, 38
't Swarte Schaep ✕, 41–42
Tulip Inn Amsterdam 🏨, 71

U

Ulcke van Zurich ✕, 119
Ultimatum ✕, 119
Utrecht, 101–105

V

Vandenberg ✕, 41
Vertigo ✕, 48
Verzetsmuseum, 27
Vincent van Gogh Museum, 25–26

Visitor information
Belgium, 138
Netherlands, 77
Vive-la-Vie (club), 60
Vliegende Schotel ✕, 41
Vredespaleis, 93

W

Waalse Kerk, 83
Web, The (club), 57

Westerkerk, 13
Willet-Holthuysen Museum, 13

Z

Zandvoort, 83–85
Zomers ✕, 39
Zuiderkerk, 22
Zwarte Ruiter ✕, 94

NOTES

Fodor's Travel Publications

Available at bookstores everywhere, or call 1-800-533-6478, 24 hours a day.

Gold Guides

U.S.

- Alaska
- Arizona
- Boston
- California
- Cape Cod, Martha's Vineyard, Nantucket
- The Carolinas & Georgia
- Chicago
- Colorado
- Florida
- Hawai'i
- Las Vegas, Reno, Tahoe
- Los Angeles
- Maine, Vermont, New Hampshire
- Maui & Lāna'i
- Miami & the Keys
- New England
- New Orleans
- New York City
- Pacific North Coast
- Philadelphia & the Pennsylvania Dutch Country
- The Rockies
- San Diego
- San Francisco
- Santa Fe, Taos, Albuquerque
- Seattle & Vancouver
- The South
- U.S. & British Virgin Islands
- USA
- Virginia & Maryland
- Walt Disney World, Universal Studios and Orlando
- Washington, D.C.

Foreign

- Australia
- Austria
- The Bahamas
- Belize & Guatemala
- Bermuda
- Canada
- Cancún, Cozumel, Yucatán Peninsula
- Caribbean
- China
- Costa Rica
- Cuba
- The Czech Republic & Slovakia
- Eastern & Central Europe
- Europe
- Florence, Tuscany & Umbria
- France
- Germany
- Great Britain
- Greece
- Hong Kong
- India
- Ireland
- Israel
- Italy
- Japan
- London
- Madrid & Barcelona
- Mexico
- Montréal & Québec City
- Moscow, St. Petersburg, Kiev
- The Netherlands, Belgium & Luxembourg
- New Zealand
- Norway
- Nova Scotia, New Brunswick, Prince Edward Island
- Paris
- Portugal
- Provence & the Riviera
- Scandinavia
- Scotland
- Singapore
- South Africa
- South America
- Southeast Asia
- Spain
- Sweden
- Switzerland
- Thailand
- Toronto
- Turkey
- Vienna & the Danube Valley

Special-Interest Guides

- Adventures to Imagine
- Alaska Ports of Call
- Ballpark Vacations
- Caribbean Ports of Call
- The Complete Guide to America's National Parks
- Disney Like a Pro
- Europe Ports of Call
- Family Adventures
- Fodor's Gay Guide to the USA
- Fodor's How to Pack
- Great American Learning Vacations
- Great American Sports & Adventure Vacations
- Great American Vacations
- Great American Vacations for Travelers with Disabilities
- Halliday's New Orleans Food Explorer
- Healthy Escapes
- Kodak Guide to Shooting Great Travel Pictures
- National Parks and Seashores of the East
- National Parks of the West
- Nights to Imagine
- Rock & Roll Traveler Great Britain and Ireland
- Rock & Roll Traveler USA
- Sunday in San Francisco
- Walt Disney World for Adults
- Weekends in New York
- Wendy Perrin's Secrets Every Smart Traveler Should Know
- Where Should We Take the Kids? California
- Where Should We Take the Kids? Northeast
- Worldwide Cruises and Ports of Call

Fodor's Special Series

Fodor's Best Bed & Breakfasts
America
California
The Mid-Atlantic
New England
The Pacific Northwest
The South
The Southwest
The Upper Great Lakes

Compass American Guides
Alaska
Arizona
Boston
Chicago
Colorado
Hawai'i
Hollywood
Idaho
Las Vegas
Maine
Manhattan
Minnesota
Montana
New Mexico
New Orleans
Oregon
Pacific Northwest
San Francisco
Santa Fe
South Carolina
South Dakota
Southwest
Texas
Utah
Virginia
Washington
Wine Country
Wisconsin
Wyoming

Citypacks
Amsterdam
Atlanta
Berlin
Chicago
Florence
Hong Kong
London
Los Angeles
Montréal
New York City
Paris
Prague
Rome
San Francisco
Tokyo
Venice
Washington, D.C.

Exploring Guides
Australia
Boston & New England
Britain
California
Canada
Caribbean
China
Costa Rica
Egypt
Florence & Tuscany
Florida
France
Germany
Greek Islands
Hawaii
Ireland
Israel
Italy
Japan
London
Mexico
Moscow & St. Petersburg
New York City
Paris
Prague
Provence
Rome
San Francisco
Scotland
Singapore & Malaysia
South Africa
Spain
Thailand
Turkey
Venice

Flashmaps
Boston
New York
San Francisco
Washington, D.C.

Fodor's Gay Guides
Los Angeles & Southern California
New York City
Pacific Northwest
San Francisco and the Bay Area
South Florida
USA

Pocket Guides
Acapulco
Aruba
Atlanta
Barbados
Budapest
Jamaica
London
New York City
Paris
Prague
Puerto Rico
Rome
San Francisco
Washington, D.C.

Languages for Travelers (Cassette & Phrasebook)
French
German
Italian
Spanish

Mobil Travel Guides
America's Best Hotels & Restaurants
California and the West
Great Lakes
Major Cities
Mid-Atlantic
Northeast
Northwest and Great Plains
Southeast
Southwest and South Central

Rivages Guides
Bed and Breakfasts of Character and Charm in France
Hotels and Country Inns of Character and Charm in France
Hotels and Country Inns of Character and Charm in Italy
Hotels and Country Inns of Character and Charm in Paris
Hotels and Country Inns of Character and Charm in Portugal
Hotels and Country Inns of Character and Charm in Spain

Short Escapes
Britain
France
Near New York City
New England

Fodor's Sports
Golf Digest's Places to Play
Skiing USA
USA Today The Complete Four Sport Stadium Guide

WHEREVER YOU TRAVEL, HELP IS NEVER FAR AWAY.

From planning your trip to providing travel assistance along the way, American Express® Travel Service Offices are always there to help you do more.

Amsterdam

American Express Travel Service
Van Baerlestraat 39
Amsterdam
20/673 8550

American Express Travel Service
Damrak 66
1012 LM Amsterdam
Amsterdam
20/504 8777

do more AMERICAN EXPRESS
Travel

http://www.americanexpress.com/travel

Listings are valid as of October 1997.
© 1997 American Express Travel Related Services Company, Inc.